UNREAL CITY

LAS VEGAS, BLACK MESA, AND
THE FATE OF THE WEST

JUDITH NIES

NATION
BOOKS
New York

Designed by Jack Lenzo

Library of Congress Cataloging-in-Publication Data
Nies, Judith, 1941–
Las Vegas, Black Mesa, and the fate of the West / Judith Nies.
pages cm
Includes bibliographical references and index.
ISBN 978-1-56858-748-6 (hardcover : alk. paper)—ISBN 978-1-56858-487-4 (e-book)
1. Southwest, New—History—20th century. 2. Las Vegas (Nev.)—History—20th
century. 3. Coal mines and mining—Southwest, New—Political aspects. 4. Black Mesa
(Navajo County and Apache County, Ariz.)—History—20th century. 5. Indians of
North America—Arizona—Black Mesa (Navajo County and Apache County)—Social
conditions—20th century. 6. Coal mines and mining—Southwest, New—History—20th
century. I. Title.
F787.N54 2014
979.3'135—dc23
2013048336

10 9 8 7 6 5 4 3 2 1

In memory of Roberta Blackgoat (1916–2002)

This extreme reliance on federal money, so seemingly at odds

with the emphasis on unfettered individualism that constitutes

the local core belief, was a pattern set early on.

—Joan Didion, Where I Was From

In 1492 the natives discovered they were Indians;

They discovered they lived in America;

They discovered they were naked;

They discovered there was sin.

—Eduardo Galeano, Children of the Days

CONTENTS

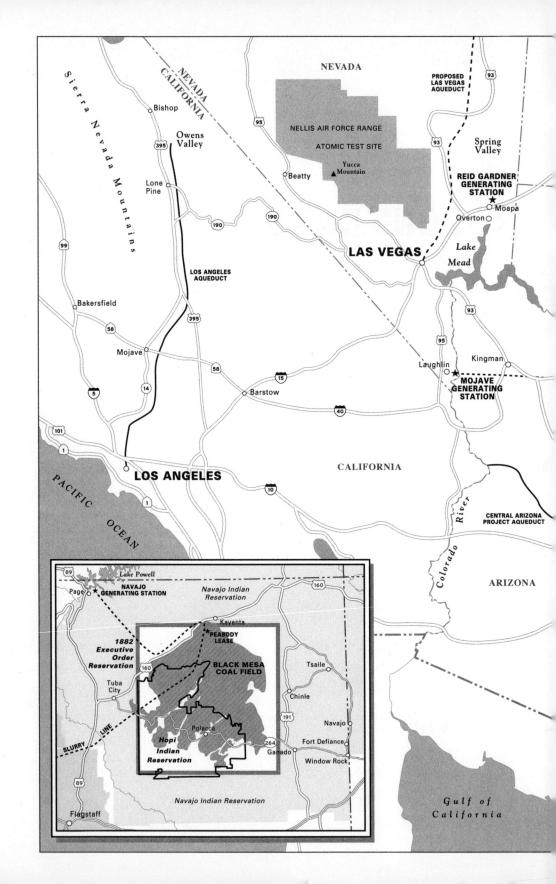

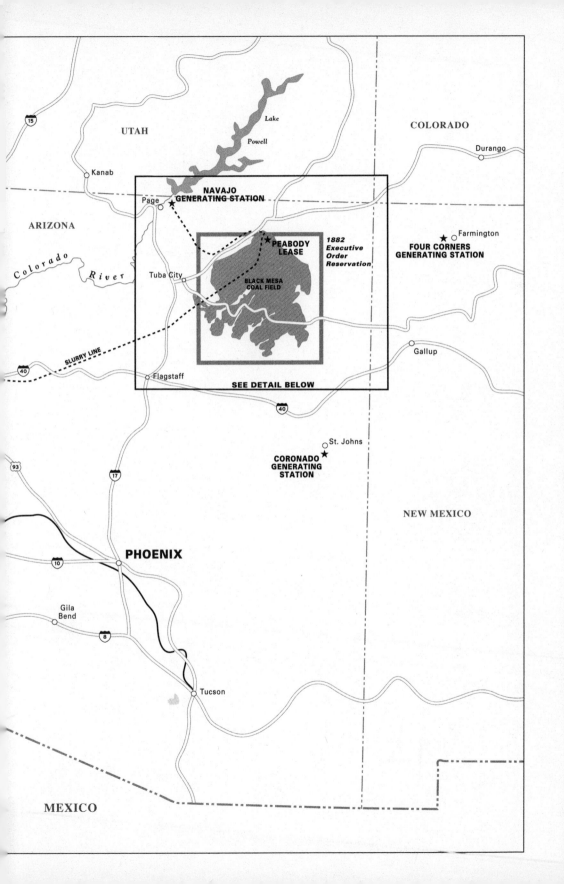

INTRODUCTION

Phoenix, 1982: A Pattern Set Early On

In 1982 Robert Redford starred in a modern cowboy western called *The Electric Horseman*. Set in Las Vegas in the early 1980s, the story was about a former national rodeo champion—and current alcoholic—who made his living pitching cereal as a "breakfast of champions" for a giant American food conglomerate. The corporation merchandised his former glory by sending him out into rodeo arenas mounted on a beautiful horse, both cowboy and horse trimmed in glowing electric lights. Often too drunk to remain upright on his horse, the electric horseman in the saddle was frequently a cowboy double substituted by the corporation.

Then, in one existential moment in a Las Vegas ballroom, the cowboy (Redford) decided he had been a commodity long enough and rode the horse off the stage, out through the endless corridors of casino slot machines, down the Las Vegas Strip, and into the magnificent wilderness of Nevada's purple mountains. The movie had all the elegiac themes of the contemporary American West: soulless corporations, feckless media in the character of Jane Fonda as a television reporter, the symbolic lone cowboy striking out on his own, and the transformative power of western spaces. The movie was a huge success.

• • •

About the same time the film was in the theaters, a man named Leon Berger—not a household name—had his own existential moment. As director of the Indian Relocation Commission located on East Birch

Street in Flagstaff, Arizona, he resigned from his job with a public statement of shocking clarity: he called the congressionally mandated relocation of ten thousand Navajo people the equivalent of "American genocide." Berger, who had once worked for Senator Barry Goldwater, was an unlikely rebel.

Thousands of Navajo families were being expelled from a 4,000-square-mile reservation that was jointly occupied by the Navajo and Hopi Indians. Located some 150 miles northeast of Flagstaff and ending some 25 miles before Monument Valley, the entire reservation was known legally as the Executive Order Reservation of 1882 and geographically as Black Mesa. In 1974 Congress passed a poorly conceived bill that divided the surface of the Executive Order Reservation on a fifty-fifty basis between the two tribes. As a practical matter, only a handful of Hopi, who lived clustered in villages at the rocky edge, were affected, but thousands of Navajo families, who lived in sheepherding camps spread out in the interior, had to be moved. Black Mesa was so isolated it was not mapped in the grid system of the US Geological Survey until late in the twentieth century.

Berger had been handpicked to direct the commission. But as the man charged with removing thousands of Navajo families from the newly delineated Hopi lands, he was no longer able to ignore the realities of an impossible job. For one thing, no one had ever accurately counted the number of Navajo to be moved; for another, no planning had been done to buy alternative land or provide social services or build housing to relocate them; and finally, the Navajo relocation marked the first time in a hundred years that a boundary issue between two tribes was being settled by removing uncounted thousands of the opposing tribe. Why hadn't the usual arrangement of alternative public lands and a financial settlement been worked out as compensation? This last was a question no one seemed able to answer, especially since that was the solution already in motion to compensate the Passamaquoddy Indians of Maine who otherwise might have requested the removal of many prominent Boston and Philadelphia families from their oceanfront property on the Maine coast.

Berger's incendiary resignation brought unwanted publicity to certain complex details that had theretofore remained invisible. As it turned out, those same disputed Navajo-Hopi lands contained the largest untouched coal deposit in the country. Black Mesa was made of coal. Mapped and measured by the Arizona Bureau of Mines, the Black Mesa Coal Field lay entirely beneath the Hopi-Navajo lands and held more than 21 billion tons of valuable low-sulfur coal. ("The Black Mesa Field," said the *Keystone Coal Industry Manual*, "is totally within the jurisdiction of the Navajo and Hopi Indian tribes.") Two huge strip-mining sites on the reservation lands were already in operation, feeding coal to two massive power plants that ran air-conditioners in Los Angeles, pumped water from the Colorado River into Phoenix, and illuminated dazzling neon signs in Las Vegas. One plant, called the Mohave, was ninety miles south of Las Vegas. Another, called the Navajo Generating Station, was one of the largest generating stations in the country and was located in Page on the Navajo reservation at the Arizona-Utah border. It had little to do with the Navajo because the tribal government had no ownership. More than half of Navajo families did not have electricity.

More nuanced interpretations of the relocation began to emerge on a daily basis. But before the details behind Berger's remarkable announcement could gain media traction, another event distracted public attention. The Electric Horseman himself was coming to Phoenix.

● ● ●

The iconic image of an astonishingly handsome Robert Redford on the party invitation for a celebration of Hopi arts and culture was from *The Electric Horseman*, a modern cowboy in a dusty denim jacket, his hand raised to the brim of his cowboy hat, squinting off to a distant horizon. The invitation seemed both wonderfully glamorous and a window into the New West. "For the good purpose we will gather," promised the invitation in both Hopi and English. The celebration, sponsored by an Indian education group called Futures for Children, included a press conference at the Valley National Bank Building; an exhibit of Native American–themed paintings, photographs, and sculpture at the Gallery Wall in Scottsdale; and a dinner at the Marriott Mountain Shadows Hotel.

My invitation came from a photographer friend, Susanne Page, whose book about the Hopi was to be launched as part of the celebration. We had been neighbors in Washington, DC, when I was working as a speechwriter in Congress, and in 1973 I got to know her more when a graduate school friend, Steve Hirst, came to Washington to lobby with the Havasupai Indians. At that point, I knew little about Indian history, but one of the congressmen I worked for was on the Interior Committee, formerly known as the Committee on Public Lands. The Havasupai lived in the bottom of the Grand Canyon in the staggeringly beautiful Havasu Canyon, but had originally lived, hunted, and grazed livestock on the plateau and farmed the side canyon only in the summer months. In 1881 the government surveyor gave their plateau lands to white settlers and confined them to a reservation at the bottom of the Grand Canyon. (There are as many terms to describe Indian lands as the Inuit have for snow—*allotment, leasehold, trust title, treaty, checkerboard*—so I am giving only the general outlines of the Havasupai claim.) They were lobbying for a bill that would redefine their reservation back to the 1881 lands. Their strongest opponent was the national Sierra Club, whose leaders distorted the Indians' position and maintained that the Havasupai reservation must be included as part of the Grand Canyon National Park. I put Steve in touch with Susanne Page, who had just published a much-praised book of photography about the Navajo and was chair of the Sierra Club's national committee on Native American issues. Susanne's committee passed a resolution supporting the Havasupai bill, opposing the national directors of the Sierra Club. I called an editor at the *Washington Post* who was sufficiently interested in the split in the Sierra Club's position that the paper ran an editorial in favor of the Havasupai and questioning the national Sierra Club.

By 1982 I had just revisited some of this story with Steve and his wife, Lois, because in August I had made a trip down into Havasu

Canyon to visit. By then they had lived on the Havasupai reservation for more than a decade, and Steve had written a book about the Havasupai, which included their remarkable perseverance over four generations in pushing for the return of their original lands. (By air the village of Supai is only 35 miles from Grand Canyon Village; by car it is roughly 128 miles, the last 8 of which are by foot or horseback down an old streambed into the canyon.) After the hike in, I understood what it had meant for their leaders to negotiate the marble halls of Congress. We laughed about the Sierra Club's fear of the tribe's commercializing the Grand Canyon because the morning I had been sitting by the natural swimming pool at the bottom of Havasu Falls, a helicopter from Las Vegas had choppered in, depositing an Australian film director and two actresses/hookers.

Thus, I saw this invitation for the Hopi celebration as being in the same spirit of restitution for past wrongs. I thought an event that recognized the value of Native Americans' voices and cultural achievements was both historically enlightened and forward thinking. Because Hollywood films have claimed such a large space in the American imagination and have long presented a pseudohistory of the American West—a simple morality tale of good (white cowboys, cavalry, settlers, homesteaders, ranchers) versus bad (dark Indians)—I thought the use of a Hollywood movie star to present a counternarrative was both interesting and newsworthy. I also thought it would be fun to meet Robert Redford.

A week before Christmas in 1982, I flew to Phoenix from Boston with a press credential from the *Atlantic Monthly*. I had proposed a short article along the lines of "New Voices from the New West," and editor Mike Curtis gave me a letter. In truth, I couldn't have been more misinformed.

On December 16, 1982, a well-tailored and glamorous Robert Redford arrived at the Phoenix Press Club to launch a three-day celebration of Hopi arts and culture. Accompanied by the chairman of the Hopi Tribal Council and a retinue of well-known Native American artists such as Hopi Dan Namingha, photographers, authors, publishing executives, and filmmakers, he told the crush of reporters on the twenty-first floor of the Valley National Bank Building how "at home" he felt on the Hopi mesas. Noting the national historical significance of the Hopi villages, he pointed out that Old Oraibi, a pueblo village on the tip of the rocky peninsula called Third Mesa on the road between Tuba City and Gallup, was the oldest continually inhabited settlement in the United States. He also said, rightly, that archaeological evidence dated back to 1140. Historical documents recorded by a priest in the conquistador Coronado's exploring party described entering a Hopi village in 1540.

The only Navajo associated with the event were a small group of protesters who clustered outside the entrance to the Valley National Bank, twenty floors below the press club, handing out flyers to anyone who would take them. The single fact sheet thrust into my hand reproduced excerpts from Leon Berger's resignation statement and described some of the anomalies that led to congressional passage of the Hopi Land Settlement Act in 1974, a bill that I actually remembered because I had been working in Congress when the bill was making its way through committee hearings.

The tone of the press conference was not oriented to probing questions because the entire press corps jumped to its collective feet in a standing ovation the minute the movie star entered the room. Only one lone reporter from a small Arizona newspaper asked Redford how he felt about supporting a relocation project that affected thousands of Navajo families and was characterized as "a tragedy of genocide and injustice." The reporter was booed before he even finished the question.

Redford was unfazed. He stepped back and gestured to Abbott Sekaquaptewa, the Hopi Tribal Council chairman, to take the microphone. Leaning on two canes, the result of severe arthritis that he had had since he was a teenager, the tribal chairman was articulate and passionate in his defense of the Hopi cause in pressing for return of lost ancestral lands, particularly the 1882 Executive Order Reservation that had been allocated to the Hopi, but invaded by the Navajo. Sekaquaptewa, who had been tribal chairman off and on since 1962, and who was known among congressional staffers for his dramatic testimony, explained that for more than a century, Hopi lands had been encircled by the Navajo reservation until the Hopi reservation had been reduced to a small island in the midst of the "mighty Navajo." He described the ten-year lawsuit between the two tribes and said the Hopi won because of steady encroachment by the Navajo on land that did not belong to them. He did not employ the dramatic style he had used during congressional hearings when a public relations firm was writing his testimony, but he was effective. "This was a centuries-old land dispute," he masterfully concluded. "This case went all the way to the Supreme Court. The Hopi won. The law is the law. The question is, do you believe in enforcing the law or not?"

After that, there were no further questions about the Navajo relocation project. Or about who wanted the coal that lay under the lands from which the Navajo were being removed. Or how the coal was being used to bring water and electricity to the parched desert cities of the Southwest. Or about where the profits from these massive strip mines were going. Anyone witnessing the scene could be excused for not delving more deeply into whether there was far more complexity to this story than a boundary issue between two fractious Indian tribes. The basic story line told in every mainstream newspaper from Boston to Los Angeles was that these two tribes were the Arabs and Israelis of the American western desert.

It was at this point that I had my first nagging doubts. I wondered how it could have been a centuries-old dispute when a century earlier, the Navajo, who then numbered around eight thousand people and had mostly lived in New Mexico, were still recovering from having been rounded up by Kit Carson and the US Army and confined in a miserable labor camp at the New Mexico–Texas border for five years. When they were finally released in 1868, their former lands had been taken over by white settlers or miners, and they were sent to a small reservation at the Arizona–New Mexico border, which even at the time was recognized as inadequate. How could a "centuries-old" dispute have developed in the intervening twelve years? Then while driving to the gallery in Scottsdale, I had another question: How could the Hopi sue the Navajo? There was no court in the American legal system authorized to hear such a case. That's why Indian peoples were always coming to Washington to petition Congress. Only Congress had authority over the status and boundaries of Indian lands. A congressional colleague, a Stockbridge Indian from Wisconsin, introduced me to the idea of legal theft when it came to Indian lands. Always ask: How did the law get to be the law? Why do anything illegal, he proposed, if you have the power to rewrite the laws?

Robert Redford, however, was a superstar supporter who was hard to refute. He made intelligent films about the modern West, owned a ski resort in Utah, had married into a Mormon family, founded the Sundance Film Festival for independent moviemakers, and was an outspoken environmentalist and board member of the Natural Resources Defense Council. His pedigree as a liberal activist included raising money for progressive Democratic candidates such as Arizona's governor Bruce Babbitt—later a presidential candidate and secretary of interior in the 1990s—and making public appearances for Mo Udall, then chair of the US House Interior Committee, and Stewart Udall, former secretary of interior. It was impossible to imagine him on the side of extraction and energy corporations. Symbolically, having Redford on the stage with Abbott Sekaquaptewa validated the Hopi version of events. And that was what the television cameras and the newspaper reporters recorded.

If, however, I had not moved on to the Scottsdale art gallery for the evening cocktail party, my doubts might have slipped away. The reporters from the afternoon press conference were explicitly not invited. But if they had been, they too might have come up with a few other queries. They might have noticed the vice president of Peabody Coal chatting with a vice president from the Bechtel Corporation, the largest engineering and construction company in the world. Peabody Coal was strip-mining those same Navajo and Hopi lands on Black Mesa, extracting close to 15 million tons of coal a year—at the time it was the largest strip mine in the country—that were feeding two Bechtel-built generating stations. Bechtel was also in the process of constructing a three-hundred-mile open-air aqueduct that would pump water from the Colorado River up over three mountain ranges into arid Phoenix and Tucson. Unimaginatively named the Central Arizona Project

(CAP), the aqueduct and its fourteen pumping stations were the most expensive federally financed civil engineering project since the Hoover Dam. Observant reporters might have identified a vice president from New York–based Equitable Life Insurance, the single largest financier of mineral exploration in the country.

If the other reporters had done a little corporate research, they might also have discovered that Equitable Life along with Bechtel were owners of Peabody Coal through a private holding company. Not only did the Peabody Holding Company not have to report profits because it was not a publicly traded company, but each of its constituent entities (Newmont Mining, Boeing Corporation, Equitable Life, Bechtel, and Fluor Engineering) had a large public relations department that issued its own press releases about the "good" Hopi and the "bad" Navajo. As Susanne Page later observed to me, "That was probably the only time these men were ever assembled together in one room." No photographs allowed.

• • •

"Barry, come out and join us," Governor Bruce Babbitt called to a white-haired man hovering on the edge of the terrace during the $500-a-person cocktail reception. Senator Barry Goldwater was Arizona's most famous politician, the man who almost single-handedly had taken the Republican Party away from eastern moderates and put it in the hands of states' rights, small-government, no-tax, individual self-reliant western conservatives who had elected Ronald Reagan in 1980. Our little group included the Arizona governor, several of his aides, and Mary Wedge, a friend of mine from Phoenix who was active in local politics. Everyone, including me, congratulated Senator Barry Goldwater on looking so healthy after being only three weeks out of Ted Dietrich's clinic for open-heart surgery. "And who is this?" Goldwater turned to me, peering curiously through his heavy black-frame glasses. Governor Babbitt repeated what he had been told, that I was a former congressional speechwriter, former environmental assistant secretary in Massachusetts, and currently on assignment for the

Atlantic Monthly. Goldwater was smiling and about to shake my hand when he registered what the governor had said. His smile vanished, his face hardened, and he turned on his heel and walked away so rapidly he left me with my arm extended in midair.

"Wow," breathed a shocked aide to the governor. Everyone was speechless, even the unflappable Governor Babbitt. But as I retrieved my dangling arm and watched Barry Goldwater's rapidly retreating back disappear into the illuminated dazzle of the gallery, I had a thought of great clarity: there is something here that Barry Goldwater doesn't want me to see.

When I looked around the room with new eyes, I saw a scene of corporate money and power. It looked like a Washington fund-raiser. The men in the room represented a significant cross-section of Wall Street, Washington, and the West. The Indians were not the major players. The real story was about energy and resources, about how coal was going to be used, and about who would make money. I had unintentionally intruded on the people whose companies were in the process of creating a new Hoover Dam, and with it the water and energy infrastructure that would fuel the next thirty years of metastasizing growth in the West. The irony was that the few people at the time who understood the implications of burning 15 million tons of unfiltered coal a year were the Indians, both Hopi and Navajo, whose traditional people had a very different point of view from the tribal council members. They saw the boundary issue as having been manipulated in order to remove the people who lived on top of the coal and therefore in the way of the strip mining. They knew that coal dust caused pollution and health problems, turned water toxic, pumped out groundwater in the desert, and caused drought. But those Indians couldn't get to the microphone.

• • •

Northern Arizona might seem remote, but it is a spot where five cultures come together—Hopi, Navajo, global energy corporations, Mormons, and assorted US government agencies. The question that I, like many others, did not ask was why were Robert Redford, Barry

Goldwater, and corporate executives from giants like the Peabody Holding Company together at a fund-raiser for the Hopi Tribe? The movie that had far greater relevance to the Phoenix gathering than *The Electric Horseman* was *Chinatown*, Roman Polanski's 1974 moody thriller about how money and power shaped the way that Los Angeles obtained its water supply in the early twentieth century. Based on true events, the story revolved around the men who set up dummy land companies to buy out the ranchers and farmers of Owens Valley, a rich valley two hundred miles to the north of Los Angeles in the Sierra Nevada foothills, with a lake and a river and constant groundwater from the mountain snowmelt. Future plans involved pumping the water from the valley into Los Angeles for municipal use and surrounding valley lands for agricultural development. Real estate development became the source of the city's great fortunes. Although the Owens Valley–Los Angeles aqueduct was built in 1913, the movie placed those events in the 1930s.

In the 1930s Phoenix and Las Vegas were just waking up. They were still tiny towns surrounded by scorching deserts. Las Vegas, in the Mohave Desert, had a population of five thousand and Phoenix, in the Sonoran Desert, forty-eight thousand. But they had seen the template for growth. It involved water, electricity, air-conditioning, and, most important, federal money. In the 1930s the federally financed, but privately built, Hoover Dam was under construction only thirty miles from Las Vegas, and most of the water and hydroelectricity would go to California, making it the wealthiest state in the country. The formula required political power in Washington. As Joan Didion wrote in *Where I Was From*, about political attitudes in California where she grew up, the local mythology of individual self-reliance was not the real engine of wealth. "The California settlement had tended to attract drifters of loosely entrepreneurial inclination, the hunter-gatherers of the frontier rather than its cultivators, and to reward most fully those who perceived most quickly that the richest claim of all lay not in the minefields, but in Washington."

By the 1960s Los Angeles needed more electricity. Phoenix needed more water for agriculture and the housing developments that Del

Webb was building. They needed to replace the groundwater that had been pumped out in such quantities that large cavities were opening up at the edges of highways. As the fastest-growing city in the country, Las Vegas doubled or tripled its population every decade. It too had subsidence as groundwater was pumped out. Although the small-government, individual-responsibility culture did not believe in bureaucracy, the casino owners knew they had to plan for water and electricity. In short, the urban Southwest was not a desert miracle, but required another new Hoover Dam to produce more inexpensive electricity and water. The key word was *inexpensive*.

Although the struggle over Black Mesa lands continues to be described as a local issue or a "centuries-old land dispute" between two tribes, it is actually an example of a global phenomenon in which giant transnational corporations have the power to separate indigenous people from their energy-rich lands with the help of host governments. What is not so well known is how it happens in America. Black Mesa is a domestic example of a global syndrome.

If a group photograph had been taken at that Phoenix reception in 1982, it would have included not only Barry Goldwater and Robert Redford, but also the executives from the five corporations of the Peabody Holding Company as well as the heads of twenty-three utilities who needed the water and energy equivalent of a new Hoover Dam.

This is a story of how they got it. And how they are losing it.

PART I

CHAPTER 1

EVERYONE COMES FOR THE MONEY

"Two years! Two years in Las Vegas!" Bette Midler was lamenting. It was January 2010, in the last week of her two-year run at the Colosseum at Caesars Palace. "Who could believe it? I'm exhausted." Then she lay down flat on the stage and called out to the wings, "Celine, come back. All is forgiven." The forty-three-hundred-seat Colosseum had been built for Celine Dion, who was the headliner there for several years before Bette.

"Donny and Marie, cross the street! Help me out!" she yelled, pointing in the direction of the Flamingo, where Donny and Marie Osmond's digitized twelve-story portrait filled the facade. She sat up and looked accusingly at the audience. "I know what you're thinking. You're probably saying to yourself, 'They couldn't PAY ME ENOUGH to play Las Vegas for two years.' Well-l-l-l . . . " She held a three-second beat before she singsonged, "YOU'D BE WRONG-NG-NG-NG-NG."

The entire audience simultaneously experienced a thunderclap of recognition and exploded with laughter. We knew what she was saying. Las Vegas is all about the money. Everyone comes for the money.

Unlike Marie Osmond, who makes her home in Las Vegas, Bette Midler is a quintessential New Yorker, famous for her public commitment to environmentalism and green space, a commitment that is of little interest in Las Vegas. For one thing, there is no green space or even much public space in the city. The best way to stop a promising conversation is to use the word *sustainability*. Environmentalism is viewed as an affectation of people from the East. Las Vegas is not a community-building kind of place. Las Vegas is a place where people come to avoid reflection, start new lives, make their fortunes, gamble on the mathematics of chance. The go-it-alone individualism of the culture, however, did not stop the Divine Miss M from bringing to the audience's attention a recent catastrophic event of nature. A week before this performance, on January 12, 2010, a massive collision of tectonic plates had occurred twenty-nine hundred miles away in the Caribbean. The island of Haiti had been devastated by the accompanying earthquake.

"The Caesar Salad Girls will be in the lobby as you leave," she trilled to the audience after her multiple curtain calls. "They will be collecting money for Haitian relief. I will personally match every dollar you contribute." Statuesque chorus girls in sequins, five-inch high heels, and full stage makeup moved majestically through the crowd as their baskets were filled with poker chips and bills of many denominations. They represented another world from the fragile island in the Caribbean where a magnitude 7.0 earthquake had toppled 280,000 buildings, killed 220,000 people, and left more than 1 million people homeless.

Las Vegas is a city divorced from nature—and proud of it. Located in the middle of the Mohave Desert, it gets four inches of rain a year and has a climate like Baghdad. As a chef at one of the better restaurants put it, "Don't talk to me about sustainability. Las Vegas is like putting a man on the moon. It has no water. Nothing grows here. And half the year, it's over a hundred degrees." It was a testament to the artistry and personality of the Divine Miss M that most in the audience reached deep into their wallets and gave to the victims of Haiti's geologic misfortune, probably thinking something like that could never happen in Las Vegas.

Las Vegas has no real downtown, no civic spaces, no historic buildings, no public parks, and no commemorative plaques—no public history. It is known for its philosophy of round-the-clock Fun and a No-Limits sensibility. City leaders—a small group of gambling oligarchs—promote the glamour and spectacle of Las Vegas as a classless neon metropolis where anyone from any economic background can live like royalty, as long as he or she has a credit card or a lot of cash. Las Vegas is designed to alter perceptions: gambling substitutes for income, night is interchangeable with day, the scale of excess refutes the idea of scarcity. As an international destination with 39 million visitors a year and fourteen of the largest hotels in the world, the city attracts more tourists than all of Great Britain. It is home to Steve Wynn, sometimes known as the Medici prince, who created an eight-acre mini Lake Como on the Strip, complete with computerized fountains that dance to Broadway show tunes. Wynn also conceived of Shadow Creek Golf Course, a 350-acre tournament-level course in North Las Vegas that was transformed into a piece of Scotland with lakes, waterfalls, and emerald-green fairways. But a curious visitor might have questions: with six months of summer temperatures over one hundred degrees and annual rainfall of four inches, where does the water come from to keep its lawns and golf courses green? Such a question confirms that the questioner comes from the Land of No Fun, or, in my case, Massachusetts.

The geologic fate of Haiti, however, was a reminder that nature is always with us and that Las Vegas is more vulnerable than it may appear. Water is a problem. As temperatures rise, more than two degrees over the past three decades, drought is an ongoing problem and air-conditioning is required for longer periods. In its own way, Las Vegas has stretched its natural resources to the limit. If a visitor starts driving around the desert bowl in which Las Vegas is located, another arrangement of nature starts to suggest itself. Behind Hoover Dam is Lake Mead, from which the townships of Las Vegas valley get 90 percent of their water supply. In January–February 2010 Lake Mead was at its lowest level since the reservoir was filled, with strange objects poking out of the water. Large peninsulas of rock and dry inlets began to appear where water used to lap the shore. At what used to be the Overton marina, cracked hardpan that used to be former lake bottom stretched as far as the eye could see, even though a sign from the long-vanished marina still announced "Boat Slips Available." And what about all that electricity that lights up the desert sky so vividly that astronauts 285 miles in space can see the Strip? (The only other man-made object that used to be visible from space was the Great Wall of China, but when I was in China my guide said air pollution from China's use of coal has occluded the Great Wall.) What fuels that electricity?

Coming up over Railroad Pass at night, 30 miles southeast of Las Vegas, a visitor sees a panorama of 100 square miles of shimmering orange lights, one of the most concentrated illuminated displays in the world. The lights appear to dance because of convection currents coming up off the desert floor. The orange color comes from high-pressure sodium lights. At Railroad Pass, desert optics make a visitor think that the illuminated city is only a few miles away and surrounded by empty desert because of the abrupt darkness at the outer edge of city limits. But a visitor couldn't be more wrong.

Las Vegas is like an atomic particle, with a bright nucleus surrounded by dense dark matter. The dark matter contains some of the most militarized real estate in the world. Nellis Air Force Base has individual parcels that are equivalent in size to Delaware, Rhode Island, and Connecticut. There is some irony that the premier city in a state famous for its no-tax, small-government, hyperconservative political culture exists within an economy that is buoyed by billions of dollars from the federal budget, spent by personnel from many government agencies. The Nevada Test Site, for example, is run by the US Department of Energy (formerly the Atomic Energy Commission), with offices in North Las Vegas. The atomic test site begins 65 miles northwest of the city limits and covers approximately 1,350 square miles. Some old-timers who were children in the 1950s still tell stories about how their families woke up in the predawn hours on test days and sat in lawn chairs in front of their trailers (no housing was being built) to watch the atomic blasts light up the sky. In an effort to make atomic tests seem more benign, the government called them "events," as in "Event Annie." Rather than watching a lethal nuclear blast of a weapon that had destroyed Hiroshima and Nagasaki, locals viewed the test as a dramatic spectacle and a tourist attraction. The Flamingo offered women guests an "atomic hairdo" for $75. The Desert Inn served an "Atomic Cocktail." Casinos like Benny Binion's took guests up to a spot on Mount Charleston that overlooked Frenchman Flat to watch the blasts. "Wear sunglasses," everyone was told. The governor redrew the state seal to include a mushroom cloud.

The curious visitor might ask about the water supply and wonder about the shrinking Lake Mead, from which Las Vegas gets 90 percent of its water. The visitor might also speculate about why more than the average number of supermarket aisles are lined with plastic gallon jugs of water. Has the fallout from underground nuclear tests reached groundwater? "Oh, no," old-timers say. "That radioactive groundwater is flowing toward Death Valley. Our drinking water comes from Lake Mead." Still, they urge you to drink bottled water. The level of Lake Mead has dropped 130 feet, so much that it has triggered laws that require the Southern Nevada Water Authority to seek new sources of water. Presently, the authority is following the Los Angeles–Owens Valley model and has bought water rights to a valley 200 miles north of Las Vegas that has a high groundwater level from mountain snowmelt. The authority has received permission for a right-of-way across federal land and plans to pump the water south to Las Vegas by pipeline.

Another section of Nellis, Area 2, is the largest aboveground weapons storage complex in the United States. This is where the bombs are stored during atomic testing at the Nevada Test Site. Other parcels have names such as the Tonopah Test Range or Area 52, run by Sandia National Laboratories; Creech Air Force Base; the Tolicha Peak Electronic Combat Range; and the now-famous top-secret Area 51, technically part of Edwards Air Force Base but run by the Central Intelligence Agency (CIA), where U-2 surveillance aircraft such as the supersecret Oxcart were tested and from which the unmanned drones currently operating in the skies over Pakistan and Afghanistan are said to be "piloted."

The US Navy SEALs who mounted the raid on Osama bin Laden's compound in Pakistan supposedly built a mock facility and practiced helicopter drills somewhere within the Nellis Air Force Range (formerly the Nevada Test and Training Range), some 5,000 square miles of land area and 12,000 square miles of restricted airspace. The men and women who work at these sites live in Las Vegas or in North Las Vegas and commute every day by air shuttle to McCarran Airport or North Las Vegas Airport. They send their children to the many private schools in Las Vegas.

The point is that Las Vegas is far more connected to world events and to Washington than it may seem. It is mistakenly characterized as an entertainment capital, a weekend getaway, a place to get married or divorced quickly, a conventioneer's paradise, or a glamorous setting for popular movies and television shows.

People think that modern Las Vegas began in 1946 when Bugsy Siegel had his epiphany in the desert and saw a vision arising out of the parched sands. He saw men in tuxedos, women in evening gowns, gorgeous bejeweled showgirls, and crowds of people partying, gambling, and throwing away money like confetti at a luxurious hotel-casino called the Flamingo. That's the Hollywood version.

Other versions point out that Las Vegas is actually the most sophisticated military border town in the world, a shadow capital for the planet's largest military power. Author and former Las Vegas resident Sally Denton describes Las Vegas's style of opulence and extravagance as having radiated out to become the dominant style of money and power in America. More than money and power, Las Vegas is where the dark markets of America intersect with the upper world markets of "free-market capitalism." As the old Mafia saying goes, "There's a million dollars' worth of groceries, and there's a million dollars' worth of influence." Influence is the Vegas style. The Las Vegas word *juice*—as in "He's got juice" or "He's a juice merchant"—embodies the combination of money, power, influence, and the nuanced ability to cultivate and wield political power.

CHAPTER 2

GOLDWATER AND THE DESERT INN

If ever a man had the right name for a western hero, it was Barry Goldwater. Gold and water are the magic elements of the West.

Although Las Vegas locals called the Desert Inn "the classiest joint on the Strip" when it opened in 1950, the Kefauver Crime Committee called it "the most elaborate gambling establishment in America." Cowboy boots mixed with alligator shoes on the casino floor. At the time, American mobsters were investing heavily in Las Vegas, and the Desert Inn was an upscale establishment in a town that was still pretty rough around the edges. Most of the old-timey gambling saloons were still making the transition from sawdust on the floor to carpets (thus the name *carpet joints* for the new places). The Desert Inn differed from Benny "Bugsy" Siegel's more notorious Flamingo, a mile down the road, because it was a multitheme resort including a casino, hotel, and nightclub. It also boasted a giant swimming pool and the first golf course in Las Vegas. Designed by noted New York architect Jac Lessman, the Desert Inn was a luxury resort with leisure features that the Flamingo and other casino-hotels were still to imitate. The real template for the Desert Inn was in Havana, where Meyer Lansky, said to be the underworld Rothschild, invested in the Hotel Nacional, operated the stately Casino Nacional, had a gambling training school at the Oriental Park Racetrack Casino, built the Havana Riviera, and was planning a huge hotel-casino real estate development on the ocean with a marina, a yacht basin, canals, and a golf course along with the usual casinos, nightclubs, restaurants, and brothels. Everyone who knew Lansky described him as a big thinker, a man who could plan years in advance. He saw Cuba as Monte Carlo in the Caribbean. Fulgencio Batista, a former army sergeant who took power in a military coup in 1933 and rose to become head of the Cuban military and president, was a longtime Lansky ally. When Batista left Cuba in 1944 to live in exile in Florida and New York (with millions deposited in American banks), he and American gangsters had grown very rich together. President Batista was described as "the muscle behind the Havana Mob." The Havana Mob was the American Mob, the same gangsters who moved to Las Vegas.

The Havana Mob's interest in Las Vegas gambling investments came about because of a California attorney general and future Supreme Court chief justice. Earl Warren had campaigned for governor on the promise to shut down the illegal gambling boats operating outside the three-mile limit off Santa Monica Pier in Los Angeles. The boats catered to a glamorous, wealthy Hollywood crowd and were staggeringly profitable. True to his word, in the 1940s Warren had shut down the boats. Nevada—remote, unscenic, sparsely populated—was the only place in the United States where gambling was legal. Would Hollywood's gambling-boat customers and high rollers drive five or six hours to a remote town in the desert simply for the opportunity to gamble?

Yes, said Billy Wilkerson, publisher of the *Hollywood Reporter*, owner of Hollywood's hottest nightclubs and restaurants, including Ciro's and Cafe Trocadero, and a man with a hard gambling habit. Wilkerson, who was Mob connected himself and knew everybody worth knowing in Hollywood, had been a gambling-boat customer. After the boats closed, he flew to Las Vegas and began spending a lot of time there at a carpet joint called El Cortez (still operating in downtown Las Vegas). Owned by Gus Greenbaum and Moe Sedway of the Cleveland Mob, El Cortez was more of a gambling saloon than a casino, but Wilkerson saw possibilities for creating a Hollywood-style nightclub and casino-hotel in Las Vegas. Although he was a great manager of restaurants and nightclubs, Wilkerson knew nothing about running a casino. So he entered into a partnership with Sedway and Greenbaum (at 48, 26, and 26 percent, respectively) for their professional management of a new gambling operation, nightclub, hotel, and casino called the Flamingo. Margaret Folsom, a sister of one of Greenbaum's dealers, had inherited from her ex-husband's family a thirty-acre parcel of ranchland that fronted the two-lane road called the Los Angeles Highway. Greenbaum proposed it to Wilkerson as a likely location. Wilkerson looked at the land and wrote a check to Folsom for $9,500 as a deposit for the future hotel-casino site. (An enlargement of his canceled check made out to Folsom is available at the Nevada State Museum and Historical Society in Las Vegas.) The land was about two miles south of downtown, outside the Las Vegas city limits, in an unincorporated township called Paradise.

Enter Ben "Bugsy" Siegel, who had grown up with Charles "Lucky" Luciano and Meyer Lansky in New York and was now working as an enforcer for Lansky in Hollywood. (All Siegel's associates called him Benny. No one called him "Bugsy" to his face. The nickname came from his early days as a young thug in New York, where people who saw his psychotic rages called him "crazy as a bedbug.") Siegel controlled a number of Hollywood unions in the movie business, ran bookmaking operations, and operated several illegal gambling enterprises, including the racing wire in Las Vegas. As a high-profile regular at Ciro's and the Trocadero, he heard about the Flamingo project in Las Vegas. Lansky told him to get participation. Greenbaum and Sedway were willing, but Wilkerson, as the majority owner with 48 percent, knew Siegel's dark reputation and refused. So Siegel, whose backing from the New York crime families trumped the Cleveland families, terrorized Wilkerson and wrested full control of the project for himself. Siegel, however, lacked crucial management skills. By the time the Flamingo opened in January 1947, it was millions of dollars over budget and two years past deadline. A meeting of the major Jewish and Italian mobsters in Havana over Christmas 1946 supposedly sealed the decision to terminate Ben Siegel as manager of the Flamingo. Siegel was famously gunned down in his girlfriend's house in Los Angeles, and the Flamingo's management immediately "changed hands" to Gus Greenbaum and Moe Sedway. The murder was never solved.

Over the next two years, the spectacular financial success of the Flamingo demonstrated that a clientele from Los Angeles loved to travel to Las Vegas to gamble and would spend a fortune to do so. New properties were purchased and construction begun, one of them by a former gambling-boat operator named Wilbur Clark. Although the big neon sign mounted over the entry gate read "Wilbur Clark's Desert Inn," Clark was a front man, a small-timer and former gambling-boat employee who had dreamed about building his own gambling empire. The real owner was Moe Dalitz.

Clark and his brother had bought land on the north end of the Strip, started construction, and soon ran out of money. For more than a year, the Desert Inn was a stalled construction site. Then the shrewd Moe Dalitz from Cleveland and a few other Cleveland and Detroit mobsters who had made a fortune during Prohibition and invested in legitimate businesses offered Wilbur Clark a deal. They would fund the completion of construction in exchange for 74 percent ownership. Wilbur Clark's name would be out front. The Desert Inn's innovations included a golf course, a huge swimming pool, and an effort to appeal to women guests by including the first luxury shopping store in Las Vegas.

The high-end women's clothing store in the Desert Inn's lobby was a branch of a chain of Arizona department stores called Goldwater & Sons, commonly known as Goldwaters. Its handsome, square-jawed, gravel-voiced forty-one-year-old president, Baron Goldwater Jr., known as Barry, was on hand for the hotel's festive opening. In fact, he would be on hand for many other evenings. Opening-night guests included Bob Goldwater, Barry's brother; Del Webb, the Phoenix contractor who built both the Flamingo and the Desert Inn; Nevada's governor, Key Pittman; and assorted Hollywood movie stars, local politicians, and big-time gamblers last seen in Havana.

Wilbur Clark personally handed out a corsage to every woman guest. The large swimming pool, cabanas, and luxury shopping were in-novations aimed at female guests, who were waiting for quickie divorces or for their gambling husbands. At the time few women took seats at the gaming tables. Old photos of the Desert Inn casino floor show an all-male clientele with a sprinkling of cocktail waitresses. Director of the Federal Bureau of Investigation J. Edgar Hoover was known to be a frequent patron of the Desert Inn casino. No photograph of Hoover at the Desert Inn was ever found, although a frequently repeated story holds that Meyer Lansky had obtained photographs of Hoover engaged in homosexual acts, after which the FBI director focused all the bureau's investigative energies on communist conspiracies. Steven Fox, in *Blood and Power: Organized Crime in Twentieth Century America*, wrote that in the early 1950s, "Hoover formed a small group within the FBI specifically instructed to 'determine and document *the nonexistence* of organized crime.'" It wasn't until the 1960s under Attorney General Robert Kennedy that the FBI began to install wiretaps and electronic surveillance of crime leaders, many at the Mob-controlled casinos in Las Vegas. (Even then, Hoover did not authorize wiretaps at the Sahara, where Hoover's friend Del Webb was the owner, or at the Thunderbird and the Flamingo, where the skim went to Meyer Lansky.)

Painted salmon pink, the Desert Inn had three hundred rooms built around a large swimming pool designed in a figure eight. The main building featured a ninety-foot bar, a ceiling dotted with twinkling electric stars, a "Doll Ranch" nursery for children (although few remember seeing any children among the guests), houses built around the golf course, and a nightclub that featured big-name Hollywood entertainers, including Frank Sinatra, a Las Vegas regular who would later own 7 percent interest in the Sands in exchange for an agreement to appear there exclusively. (He would later lose his license because of his public association with known Chicago mobster Sam Giancana, at the Cal-Neva Lodge at Lake Tahoe, but would get it back in 1980, when Harry Reid, currently majority leader in the US Senate, was head of the Nevada Gaming Commission.)

Barry Goldwater was well known in Las Vegas and not just for his boutique store in the lobby of the Desert Inn. As a pilot with his own plane, he frequently made the one-hour flight from Phoenix for a weekend of gambling, partying, and drinking. He stayed at the Desert Inn but often gambled at the Flamingo, where his Phoenix neighbor Gus Greenbaum was manager. Moe Sedway, a Greenbaum associate sometimes referred to as "the ruthless dwarf" and a former Lansky hit man, was another frequent Las Vegas companion of Goldwater's. Lansky, whose operations expanded from New York to Los Angeles,

Miami, and Havana, was characterized as "the ultimate banker" for gambling operations and the only person capable of brokering deals between Jewish and Sicilian gangsters.

The Desert Inn is gone now, imploded in 2000 by casino mogul Steve Wynn, but some of its old spirit remains on Desert Inn Road, where Steve Wynn's sleek golden-glass skyscrapers reflect the color of desert skies. The aesthetics of Wynn Las Vegas and Wynn Encore—where lobby shopping now includes a Maserati dealership—are far removed from the ranch gate and neon cactus sign that once welcomed guests to Wilbur Clark's Desert Inn, but the same spirit of unrestrained ambition and defiance of the desert lives on. ("It took Michelangelo four years to paint the Sistine Chapel," reads a brochure for the latest Wynn resort. "Your room took five years.") The pedigree of Desert Inn ownership also includes Howard Hughes—Hollywood producer, owner of Trans World Airlines and Hughes Aircraft, military contractor who once received $1.7 million a day from the CIA during one Las Vegas military test project, developer of the single largest real estate parcel in Las Vegas, now known as Summerlin—who bought it from Moe Dalitz in 1966.

Gus Greenbaum, who ran the racing wire in Arizona, also became manager of the Flamingo and later the Riviera, where he was involved in dealing drugs, womanizing, and skimming far too much money. He was murdered in his bed in Phoenix, with his throat cut ear to ear. When Goldwater attended his funeral, he answered reporters' questions about Greenbaum's Mob connections by saying, "I knew him only as a businessman."

The Senator

By the time of Greenbaum's funeral it was 1956, and Goldwater was the unlikely US senator from Arizona, an event that many maintained was not unrelated to Las Vegas Mob interests. Goldwater's political career came out of nowhere; his civic experience was limited to eighteen months on the Phoenix City Council. Goldwater's taste in Mobbed-up friends did not seem to hurt him. To have mobster friends meant you were connected, had juice. Arizona was also home to other big-time New York gangsters, including Joe Bonanno, who had a ranch outside of Tucson and investments in Las Vegas. Later, when Goldwater ran for president, his Las Vegas life was edited out of his background and his friendship with Arizona Indians emphasized instead. He was portrayed as a true son of the American West. Some might say, however, that the spirit of Las Vegas—risk, ruthlessness, guns, and greed—is the spirit that settled the West.

Goldwater's Phoenix–Las Vegas connections came through the Valley National Bank of Phoenix, where Barry's brother Bob Goldwater was a board member along with Phoenix contractor Del Webb. Although it was supposedly Teamster Pension Fund money that built Las Vegas, the Flamingo was completed with a $900,000 loan from Valley National Bank to Bugsy Siegel's builder, Del Webb. The completion of the Flamingo did not come in time, however, to save Siegel from his New York investors. Within hours after his bullet-riddled body was found in Los Angeles and long before the police publicly announced the murder, Gus Greenbaum had taken over as the "new manager" of the Flamingo.*

The complex ownership realities of the Desert Inn came to light only during the Senate committee's crime hearings in Las Vegas under the chairmanship of Senator Estes Kefauver. The US Senate Special Committee to Investigate Crime in Interstate Commerce traveled around the country in 1950 and 1951 and held hearings in fourteen cities in order to document the existence of a nationally organized crime syndicate. The committee had power of subpoena and in Las Vegas called Wilbur Clark and Moe Dalitz to testify.

---

* The bank loan was sought because Siegel could not borrow more money from the Lansky syndicate to pay the Del E. Webb Construction Company. Webb, a member of the Valley National Bank's board of directors, became a "quiet investor" in several Las Vegas casinos, including the Sahara, the Mint, and part of the Sands. His company's large planned communities, like Sun City, became a key ingredient in the population shift known as the Sunbelt Boom and the accelerating growth of Phoenix and Las Vegas. In Las Vegas suburbs, the Del Webb Corporation built the Sun City Summerlin retirement community, Henderson's Sun City Anthem, and a seniors-only development in North Las Vegas, Sun City Aliante.

When testifying Wilbur Clark was vague in his answers, forgetful about his ownership percentage, and contradictory about his title. "I'm secretary of the corporation," Clark explained at one point. He did not know how much of the Desert Inn he actually owned. The committee member questioning him said, "You have the most nebulous idea of your business I ever saw." Management of the Desert Inn Corporation was less than straightforward. Everything except the gambling was leased to outside vendors. Many unnamed investors had points. By the time Cleveland gangster Moe Dalitz testified, the Senate committee knew that Dalitz and "a few investors from Detroit" actually owned 74 percent of the Desert Inn. Up to fifty other investors had points, or partial points, of the remaining 26 percent. A year or two later and after things had quieted down, Wilbur Clark went to Havana, where Meyer Lansky hired him as entertainment director at the Hotel Nacional.

The Desert Inn Corporation was a money-generating machine and kept at least three sets of books—one for the owners, one for the state gambling commission, and another for the Internal Revenue Service (IRS). Supposedly, there was a fourth set of books that kept track of the skim that went directly into suitcases carried by the representatives of the various crime syndicates who showed up every week, walked directly to the cashier's cage, filled the suitcases with money, and left before the nightly count was made and reported. The take was enormous. "The Miami hotel men," the euphemism for Lansky's fronts, were skimming at least $3 million for every $1 million reported. Sam Giancana later admitted that his "personal" take was more than $300,000 a month, and he was only one of several dozen crime figures who had points in Las Vegas casinos. Much of the cash went first to Miami and then to numbered bank accounts in Switzerland, where it was laundered back into the United States through banks and financial institutions in the Bahamas. The money also came from heroin and opium as well as gambling. Throughout the 1950s, wrote Denton and Morris in *The Money and the Power*, "that secret, indirect, revolving traffic between the Strip and Switzerland was one of the heaviest flows of international capital of the era, making Las Vegas a center of world finance long before many knew its name." By the time the Crime Commission completed its hearings, Senator Kefauver estimated the untaxed money controlled by Mob interests at $20 billion.

Unlike Wilbur Clark, Moe Dalitz did not lose his poise before the senators. In response to Senator Kefauver's repeated questions about "the nest egg" that Dalitz built up by investing the money from his criminal enterprises into his many legitimate businesses—laundries, restaurants, insurance, health care, real estate, ranches—Moe Dalitz retained his mordant humor: "Well, I didn't inherit a trust fund Senator." Kefauver was an ambitious freshman senator from Tennessee and a Yale Law School graduate who had his eyes set on his political future. Dalitz was letting him know that he wasn't intimidated by the committee or Kefauver's position.

The Senate Special Committee to Investigate Organized Crime in Interstate Commerce went out of business in 1951 but not before Senator Kefauver, its chairman, published nineteen volumes of hearing testimony and a widely publicized summary report. The committee's hearings had been a national sensation and the subject of front-page headlines, radio news programs, and live television reports. The new medium of television entered American living rooms in the early 1950s for the first time, so Americans were fascinated to see actual gangland figures appear on live television and describe the specific details of executions, extortion, illegal gambling, murder for hire, bookmaking on sporting events, fixing dog and horse racing, and the transfer of gambling operations from Havana, Cuba, to Nevada.

This last point might not have interested the public much, but it troubled people like Meyer Lansky and other gangsters who were investing a lot of money in Las Vegas because they saw Nevada as the new Havana, the only place in the United States where gambling was legal. Las Vegas promised enormous profits. The reason Lansky ran a gambling school to train croupiers, dealers, pit bosses, and floor managers was because the cash environment and the temptation to cheat were omnipresent. Some of these men were being sent to Las Vegas. Sophisticated gambling operations had catwalks above the ceilings and two-way mirrors over the tables. Dealers were required to wear uniforms without pockets so they couldn't palm a $100 chip into a pocket. One attraction of Las Vegas and its legal gambling was that it had none of the payoffs to the police, politicians, and judges that were required costs of doing business in the rest of American cities. The highly publicized investigations of Kefauver's Crime Committee represented a real threat to investments from the kind of people who had no intention of losing money.

In his summary report of the hearings, Senator Kefauver called organized crime "a phantom government," with its own laws, its own enforcers, and its own interest in dominating politics. Kefauver cited the extraordinary amounts of money that crime families were able to leverage in local, state, and federal elections and estimated that at any given point in time organized crime controlled more than $20 billion in untaxed dollars ($280 billion in current dollars). Kefauver presented a network of links between upperworld and underworld gangsters—businessmen, organized crime syndicates, and politicians.

Kefauver wanted to continue a second round of hearings, but in 1951 the Senate majority leader, whose office held power over all special committee appointments, fell to Ernest McFarland, the powerful and highly respected Democratic senator from Arizona. Unexpectedly, McFarland, who might have supported a second round of Crime Committee hearings, lost his 1952 election. The victor was both a Republican and an inexperienced politician.

Barry Goldwater was a rich man's son and considered to be something of a lightweight. He had become president of Goldwater & Sons at the age of twenty after his father, who had built the business, died of a sudden heart attack in 1929. Barry was a freshman at the University of Arizona at the time, and his formal education ended then, a decision he called "the biggest mistake of my life." Because the Goldwater family's department stores had professional managers, Barry had plenty of time to explore his many hobbies while he learned the retail business—flying an airplane, photography, ham radios, exploration of Arizona's backcountry, and collecting Native American art.

After World War II—when, as an officer in the US Army Air Forces, he had ferried empty airplanes back and forth from the United States to England and then to Southeast Asia—he took one of the first rafting trips down the Colorado River. It was an adventure that he filmed with a handheld movie camera at a time when home movies were not common and only a few white people had seen vistas of the Grand Canyon from the river. (Commercial river rafting adventures didn't begin until the late 1960s.) The film was good enough that he toured the state, showing the film at schools, churches, and community centers, accompanying it with a lecture about the Colorado River and its canyons. Some people felt that this tour was perfect training for retail politics.

He collected Navajo rugs, Hopi pottery, and other Indian artifacts and talked about the days when he had helped his uncle Morris Goldwater of Prescott run a trading post near Navajo Mountain. Many of his photographs appeared in glossy magazines. He was a frequent speaker for chambers of commerce, rotary clubs, and any business group interested in having him. He was a Republican and became involved in politics in a state that had a tiny Republican Party. Yet he claimed to have no interest in becoming a politician himself. (As Rick Perlstein shows in his 2009 book about Goldwater's political ascent, *Before the Storm: Barry Goldwater and the Unmaking of the American Consensus,* Goldwater always described himself as a reluctant candidate who was dragged into politics by others.)

On his fortieth birthday, in 1949, his childhood friend Harry Rosenzweig, a Phoenix jeweler, asked him to run as a reform candidate for the Phoenix City Council. At the time, Phoenix had a population of forty-eight thousand people, and the "reform" had to do with the city's relationship with the military bases that were expanding outside the city.

While he was on the city council, Goldwater's speeches were legendary for their rambling syntax and non sequiturs. Even Rosenzweig, also on the council, admitted that half the time no one understood what Goldwater was saying: "He'd get wound up, and no one could understand what he was talking about." Many Arizona business leaders and politicians did not take his candidacy seriously. McFarland was highly respected, a two-term senator, and a former attorney general in a Democratic state. The much-quoted remark of Nicholas Udall, then mayor of Phoenix, was that Goldwater was "a merchant prince who liked to fly planes and get his picture in the newspaper."

Nonetheless, in 1951, after eighteen months on the city council, political neophyte Barry Goldwater became the announced Republican candidate for the US Senate against the legendary longtime Democrat, former assistant attorney general, and current Senate majority leader—Ernest McFarland. Goldwater's frequent association with Las Vegas gangsters might have proved a problem except that mass media and television were still in their infancy in 1952 and Goldwater presented a veneer of the rugged West. He was a cowboy aristocrat, a son of one of Arizona's wealthiest families, but a privileged son who could talk about the old days with his grandfather's freighting business and ownership of a saloon and brothel in Yuma. Goldwater's father, Baron Sr., had invested in land, cotton, cattle, and mining, which were the engines of the Arizona economy.

The official version of Barry Goldwater's long-shot election to the US Senate holds that he ran at a critical moment when the conservative tide was turning in Arizona and carried him to victory on Eisenhower's coattails. (President Dwight D. Eisenhower, the smart and popular Army general who had commanded the D-day invasion of World War II, carried Arizona in the 1952 presidential election.) Both of these interpretations are accurate. But Goldwater needed more to defeat an opponent like McFarland: he needed a lot of money and a new source of voters to provide a margin of victory.

Goldwater admitted to outspending McFarland three to one in the 1952 Senate campaign, and rumors of Mob money included paper bags of Las Vegas cash arriving regularly at Goldwater campaign headquarters in Phoenix. (He also got money from the Hunt brothers and other reactionary Texas energy barons.) The stories of Las Vegas cash as a factor in Goldwater's upset victory were so persistent that twenty years later, a reporter from the *New Yorker* was still asking Harry Rosenzweig, Goldwater's chief fund-raiser, about them. Rosenzweig answered, "Gus Greenbaum was running the horse-betting wire in Phoenix, and at his brother's anniversary party he handed me a package [saying] you can get this amount of money every month for the next six months." Rosenzweig claimed he took it once but never again. The article did not ask more questions about Greenbaum's role in Las Vegas at the

Flamingo or the Riviera or about his network of Mob connections or his long-term relationship with Meyer Lansky.

The second intriguing aspect of Goldwater's victory was how and where he found the margin of new voters. In 1952 Arizona was still a Democratic state. The hundreds of thousands of midwesterners who poured into the massive retirement communities that Del Webb would build were still a phenomenon of the future. Where could Goldwater's winning votes come from?

The majority of Arizona voters were still Democratic largely because miners and farmworkers outnumbered the mine owners, growers, and land developers. The entire state had a population of considerably less than 1 million. (Total Arizona population in 1950 was 749,587.) An important question for Goldwater campaign strategists was how to find enough new votes to squeak out a victory. What about the Hopi and Navajo Indians in northern Arizona who would be voting for the first time in the 1952 presidential election? Arizona Indians were prevented from voting by Arizona's constitution. This exclusion from voting rights was successfully challenged only in 1948 when Felix Cohen, the solicitor for the Interior Department, sued the state and succeeded in amending the state constitution.

"That part of Northern Arizona," Goldwater wrote to the National Republican Senatorial Election Committee in Washington, asking for funds to help secure the Navajo and Hopi Indian vote, "comprises three counties [and] is occupied by the Navajo and Hopi Indians. All that is required to vote in this state is to be able to read and sign one's name. The Indian Traders . . . will register these Indians, but it will take some money as these Indians are semi-nomadic in their living and one has to gather them in by the use of sings or barbeques as you and I would call them. Trucks and gasoline have been contributed for this effort. I feel that this might well be the margin of victory in this state." As it turned out, he was right.

Indian traders were largely white men who had political connections. They had to apply for a license from the Bureau of Indian Affairs (BIA) and submit character references, often supplied by local landowners or politicians. In the past, many were Mormons who saw the trading posts as a way of converting the Indians to Mormonism. Unlike Indian agents, who were federal employees and prohibited from commerce with the tribes, the traders controlled all commercial goods sold on the reservations. From the 1850s on, a pattern of collusion developed among the Indian agents, traders, and politicians. Known as the Indian Ring, it involved local politicians who colluded with the traders and Indian agents to defraud the Indians of payments, supplies, livestock, sheep, goats, tools, land, mineral leases, or whatever Washington had promised through treaties and agreements. The government agents tipped off the traders as to when annuities were due to be paid to the Indian tribes; the traders provided credit in advance at inflated prices; the trader kept much of the money or stole many of the supplies and gave a cut to the agent and the politician. One historian characterized the arrangement as "a more perfect recipe for corruption could not be found." Unlicensed traders set up trading posts at the edge of the reservation to sell illegal whiskey and guns. Over time the licensed trader's role was enlarged to include postmaster, banker, and creditor, especially for trade goods that Indians pawned, such as rugs, jewelry, basketry, and pottery. Although some traders, such as Lorenzo Hubbell and John Wetherill, learned Indian languages and successfully promoted economic activities that benefited the Indians, the overall pattern was one of dishonesty or lethargy about Indian economic well-being. The Indians were a captive market. (In 1969 the Southern Indian Development Institute did a study of the size of the traders' market on the Navajo reservation and found that the gross annual income of licensed traders was $17,223,338, at a time when the average Navajo family income was $1,500.)

The servant class in Arizona was Native American. Goldwater's childhood nanny, for example, came from the Indian school in Phoenix, as did Harry Rosenzweig's. Indian teenagers from Arizona's many reservations were sent, often forcibly, to high school at the Indian boarding school in Phoenix to learn English, Christianity, and skills for earning a living, including child care and domestic skills for girls and carpentry and machine maintenance for boys. It is true that unlike a lot of Arizona's new residents, Goldwater did know something about life on the Navajo and Hopi reservation, and for his own benefit he made a good case for helping to get them to vote. The Republican Senate Election Committee sent him money for organizing the "sings" and getting out the votes on the Hopi and Navajo Indian reservation.

When the votes were counted, Goldwater won by 4,600 votes out of 260,000, less than two percentage points. It was a thin margin of victory, but nonetheless it was a victory, and he was soon on his way to Washington to replace the legendary Ernest McFarland. Despite Kefauver's repeated requests, there would be no more Senate investigations into organized crime. The new majority leader, Lyndon Johnson, who had his own knowledge of Texas crime syndicates, never took the possibility seriously.

Once in Washington, Goldwater hung a Hopi kachina doll on the door of his Washington apartment and told friends about his Navajo name—Chischilly, "Man with Curly Hair." He decorated his Senate office with photographs of Arizona, many of which he took himself. He was in the Arizona Air Force Reserve and a military buff. He was a great talker, and he became a strong supporter of anticommunist Republicans such as Joe McCarthy, who was ferreting out communist infiltrators—real and imagined—in the US government, labor unions, and Hollywood. His wife and children stayed behind in Phoenix, so he was seen at many Washington watering holes and parties, often telling people that he had once run an Indian trading post on the Navajo reservation near Navajo Mountain. "When I think of the area that I had my trading post in," he later told the House Indian Affairs Committee, "the Paiute Mesa only supported about 1,500 Navajos who had their summer hogans on top of the mesa and their winter hogans in the canyons." He maintained he knew as much about American Indians as anyone in America, and since Indian policy had been omitted from American history books, most people believed him.

When Barry Goldwater came to the US Senate in 1953, it was still the most exclusive men's club in America, an all-white institution of ninety-five men and one woman. (Alaska and Hawaii were not yet states; as a widow, Margaret Chase Smith of Maine took her husband's seat in the House and ran for the Senate in 1948. The first African

American, Edward Brook of Massachusetts, wasn't elected until 1966.) Although Democrats had held the majority in the Senate for years, no civil rights bill had ever come up for a vote. All the waiters in the Senate dining room were African American, or "coloreds," as they were then called; the elevator boys were African American or Filipino or patronage appointments; and women were in support positions as secretaries. By virtue of southern senators' seniority, the bureaucratic machinery of the Senate, all the top administrative jobs as well as committee assignments were controlled by southern men who exercised power behind a scrim of elaborate protocols, overblown courtesies, and ruthless gentility.

Although Barry Goldwater was a Republican from the western state of Arizona, he felt comfortable with the conservative southern Democrats. Like them, he came from a state with a troublesome minority population that had to be managed with a minimum of federal interference. Like the southern senators, Goldwater believed in states' rights, no government intervention, anticommunism, right-to-work laws (no unions), and a strong military.

The colorful West that Goldwater merchandised when he arrived in Washington in 1953 was part of American mythology—an imaginary place of Indian warriors in feathers and war paint, Remington cowboys, flaming sunsets, exquisite Indian crafts, dusty cattle trails, and virile men of action. It is actually a vision of the West that was invented by eastern authors such as Owen Wister, Teddy Roosevelt's Harvard friend, and maintained by Hollywood writers such as Goldwater's friend Clarence Budington Kelland. In a "Dear Bud" letter to Kelland written during his campaign, Goldwater thanked him for all his help: "I don't know what the hell I'd do without you." Kelland was the prolific author of many western novels and dozens of short stories published in the *Saturday Evening Post*. His full-time job, however, was as a campaign consultant for the Republican National Committee. He became Goldwater's friend and a key adviser.

Goldwater had run an imaginative campaign against a formidable opponent and squeezed out his election victory in a Democratic state. In Washington he became the spokesperson for a new hard-right, anticommunist, conservative, small-government agenda that linked western conservative Republicans with southern Democrats. He believed and said publicly that this coalition could wrest control of the Republican Party out of the hands of the eastern moderate Republicans and energize a movement with the goal of repealing all the programs of the New Deal. He was greatly disliked by moderate Republicans and lost the support of President Eisenhower after he called the Eisenhower administration a "dime store New Deal." He was a great supporter of Joseph McCarthy's anticommunist crusade and was conspicuously absent when the vote to censure McCarthy was taken.

His overall conservative agenda was built on a platform of repealing government social welfare programs, opposition to civil rights laws, eliminating regulatory agencies, and restoring the primacy of states' rights. His reason for entering politics, he said, was to reduce the federal bureaucracy. "My aim," claimed Goldwater, "has always been to reduce the size of government. Not to pass laws but to repeal them. Not to institute new programs but to eliminate old ones."

In less than ten years, he was running for president of the United States as a leader of that same states' rights, conservative coalition. As the Republican presidential candidate, he lost big to Lyndon B. Johnson from Texas, but he succeeded in transforming the Republican Party and shifting its power center to the conservative West. The real beneficiary of his race would be a Hollywood actor turned politician named Ronald Reagan who won the presidential election of 1980. Within the party Goldwater became a national statesman, a revered figure, the architect of the new conservative revolution, and the forerunner of Fox News and the Tea Party movement. He was in demand as a fund-raiser for his fellow senators and became an elder statesman of his party. He was a member of the Armed Services and the Senate Intelligence Committees, and by the end of his career he was chairman of both committees. When someone had to tell President Richard M. Nixon that the impeachment hearings in the US House of Representatives were going forward and it would be best for the party if he resigned, party leaders chose Goldwater as their spokesperson.

As a general in the US Air Force Reserve and a member of the Senate Intelligence Committee, Goldwater frequently accompanied

Air Force generals to the various secret military installations around Las Vegas. Las Vegas reporters noted that the men in military delegations often took a short official trip, looked at a few planes at Nellis, and soon changed into civilian clothes to visit the high-end casinos. Goldwater was a welcome presence at the highest levels of government and business. During the twenty-five years of Goldwater's political career, the states of Arizona and Nevada had changed dramatically. The war in Vietnam, aerospace military contracts, enlarged military bases, and new Air Force installations accompanied by huge housing developments had brought a massive population shift to cities such as Phoenix and Las Vegas, as well as Los Angeles. Desert sprawl and uncontrolled real estate developments had built new fortunes. The five largest-growth counties in America were located in Phoenix and Las Vegas. Del Webb not only built some of the largest developments in both cities, but also owned the Sahara and the Mint and had points in other Las Vegas casinos. Housing development was as profitable as gambling. "Gaming" became a respectable occupation, and the casino complexes were publicly traded entities on the New York Stock Exchange. Goldwater's political campaigns had brought many Arizona figures to Washington, among them Richard Kleindienst, his campaign organizer who became US attorney general, and his former legal advisor William Rehnquist, who became chief justice of the Supreme Court. (Senator Ted Kennedy was among those who voted against Rehnquist's appointment to the Supreme Court because of his record in Arizona of denying voting rights to minority populations.)

● ● ●

So it should not have been a concern in July 1978 when Senator Goldwater's staff told him that two elderly Navajo women were sitting in his outer office waiting to see him. They did not have an appointment. Surprisingly, he refused to see them. And he looked concerned.

CHAPTER 3

THE LADIES FROM BLACK MESA

Black Mesa is not black and is not a mesa. It is four thousand square miles of ginger-colored high desert, an elevated tableland in northern Arizona whose distinctive dark color comes from its mass of deep piñon and juniper trees. The name proved to be particularly appropriate because Black Mesa was also found to be made up of thick beds of coal.

Until the 1990s Black Mesa was home to more than twenty-five thousand Navajo in the interior and eight thousand Hopi in cliff-top villages. The people of the two tribes intermarried, went to school together, attended each other's social dances, and traded goods (Navajo mutton for Hopi corn). The tribes' reservation boundary issue, the consequence of an ambiguously worded 1882 Executive Order Reservation, had been cleverly exploited in a series of bills sponsored or supported by Senator Barry Goldwater beginning in 1956.

The two women who entered Barry Goldwater's Washington, DC, office in July 1978 were there because of legislation he had sponsored and supported. They looked as though they had stepped out of one of his photographs of traditional Navajo sheepherders that decorated his office walls. They wore velveteen blouses, ankle-length cotton skirts with colorful tiers, and heavy silver squash-blossom necklaces around their necks. Their faces, framed by kerchiefs tied under their chins, were deeply tanned from lives spent outdoors.

The senator's receptionist asked for their names and addresses and the purpose of their visit. They looked at each other and paused.

Roberta Blackgoat, who spoke excellent English, did most of the talking. Violet Ashke made occasional comments in Navajo. The receptionist asked if they had an appointment. They did not.

Mrs. Blackgoat explained they had come all the way from Black Mesa, Arizona, to Washington to see Senator Goldwater. They were part of a multitribal demonstration called the Longest Walk, a walk and caravan of 220 automobiles that began in San Francisco in February and was joined by Native Americans from many reservations as they traveled across the country. They came to Congress to protest eleven pieces of anti-Indian legislation having to do with Indian water, land, and fishing rights, and the Navajo relocation under way on Black Mesa. It was July 1978 when they arrived, and the recent history of the civil rights movement and the Native American occupation of Alcatraz (1969–1971) had produced a new generation of Indian activists of all ages. The name, the Longest Walk, referenced the 1864 Long Walk of the Navajo, the notorious campaign beginning in 1863 during which eight thousand Navajo were rounded up by Kit Carson and the US Army and marched at gunpoint 350 miles across Arizona and New Mexico to a labor camp outside Fort Sumner at the New Mexico–Texas border, where they were imprisoned for five years. (More about the 1864 Long Walk later.)

The purpose of the women's visit was to discuss Public Law 93-531, also known as the Navajo and Hopi Land Settlement Act, a law passed in 1974 that Senator Goldwater and a freshman congressman from Utah named Wayne Owens had sponsored and supported. Roberta, like many others, believed that the legislation had been passed in order to open their lands to coal mining. When land settlements had been decided in the past—when Indians were making treaty claims to lands settled by white people—the courts and Congress always ruled in favor of money compensation and a grant of public lands to the Indians while allowing white residents to remain. The Hopi-Navajo law was the first time in memory and history that the land settlement required thousands of Indians of one tribe to move in favor of Indians of another tribe. The law had set in motion the relocation of more than twelve to fifteen thousand Navajo—no accurate count had ever been completed of the number of Navajo residents—in order to give their lands to the Hopi, who did not live there and had no plans to live there.

Even during the congressional hearings, the legislation was controversial, and as Senator James Abourezk of South Dakota asked during the Senate hearings, "[Why are we] replacing human beings with livestock. I don't like that." The two women might also have mentioned that since the coal strip mining started, their well water and watering holes for livestock were no longer drinkable for either sheep or humans.

They did not say any of these things to the receptionist except to repeat that they needed to see Senator Goldwater. They also might have mentioned that during the same congressional hearings, Congress had been told that only eight hundred families would be moved. But after the law passed in 1974, the assistant secretary of interior who made those claims left the Bureau of Land Management (BLM) to become vice president of Peabody Coal Company, and Peabody had opened a second mining site on Black Mesa. The annual tonnage made the Black Mesa strip-mining operation the largest in the country. When the relocation started, it was clear no one in Congress had any idea how many Navajo families were going to have to be moved or how much it would cost or how social services would be implemented. How could they? Goldwater had framed the issue as justice for the Hopi and a transfer of lands that were largely uninhabited.

Two years earlier the government began constructing a barbed-wire fence that looped deep into Navajo lands for more than a hundred miles. Navajo families who lived on the wrong side of the newly named Hopi side of the fence had to move. The women knew that Senator Goldwater described himself as "a friend of the Navajo," and they wanted to explain to him that land that they had lived on for generations was being fenced and given to Hopi. These were some of the reasons that they had made the long trip across the country to Washington to see Senator Goldwater.

The receptionist explained that the senator would be unable to see them unless they had an appointment because he was booked solid with committee meetings, legislative markups, and floor votes. Mrs. Blackgoat nodded. "We'll wait." They sat down on chairs in the reception area. They were patient people. They were sheepherders. They knew how to wait.

Throughout the day, many people—lobbyists, visitors from Arizona, and staff from other offices and committees—came and went. The two Navajo women left their seats in the outer office only to travel down the long marble corridors of the Russell Senate Office Building* to use the restrooms. They passed the time by gazing at his photographs of Arizona and commenting on the locations. Some of Goldwater's famous collection of Hopi kachina dolls, gifts from wealthy donors, and Navajo rugs, a few of which went back to the "eye-dazzler" period, were on display in the outer office. Both women were weavers, using yarns carded from wool taken from their own sheep. (The eye-dazzlers came from the New Mexico reservation at the turn of the century when trader Lorenzo Hubbell gave the Navajo women brightly colored commercial yarns to weave in an effort to appeal to an eastern market.)

In the afternoon, one of Goldwater's legislative assistants emerged from the inner offices, apologized for how busy the senator was, and asked if he could help them. No, we'll wait to see Senator Goldwater.

At 6:00 p.m., the office closed. They left.

The next day, Blackgoat and Ashke arrived as the office opened. They repeated the same conversations. No one could help them except Senator Goldwater. They asked for an appointment, but the receptionist repeated that she could not give them an appointment.

The receptionist asked again for their addresses. Care of the Dinnebito Trading Post. Keams Canyon, Arizona. Yes, they both had the same address.

DINNEBITO TRADING POST

The Dinnebito Trading Post is gone now, but it was one of the trading posts where Goldwater had held his first Indian voter registration back

---

* Barry Goldwater left the Senate in 1964, when he ran for president. He was out of office for four years until 1969, when he won a special election to replace the retiring Carl Hayden, and then he won again in the regular election of 1974. Although he lost the seniority that consecutive service would have earned him, by the time he retired in 1986 after five terms, he was chair of the Senate Armed Services Committee and the Senate Intelligence Committee. His replacement in 1987 was John McCain.

in 1952. Later voter turnouts on the Navajo reservation had not been so kind to Goldwater. In the 1974 election, 90 percent of the Navajo vote went against him. When asked about it, Goldwater said that the Navajo had been lured to the polls by promises of free beer. The Navajo tribal chairman at the time, Peter MacDonald, said Goldwater's remarks were "an insult to every Navajo who exercised the right of a citizen to vote."

In 1978 the Dinnebito Trading Post was a long one-story wooden structure that housed a general store, a pawn shop, display cases for Indian craft products, and a post office where Blackgoat and Ashke received their mail. The sign on Route 264 read:

BLAIRS DINNEBITO POST

RUGS CRAFTS JEWELRY

NINE MILES

The sign had no punctuation, and the dirt road leading into the reservation cut abruptly at right angles to Route 264. If you didn't know the turn, you would miss it.

The dirt road was so rough and rutted that people without a truck or a jeep with a high undercarriage had to drive much of the way on the shoulder. Two miles in, tall steel electrical transmission towers marched over the horizon, their fat cables drooping so dangerously low to the ground that it seemed a tall man could raise an arm and touch them. The steel towers and their high-voltage cables paralleled the road for about three miles, their lines forming a drooping canopy until the cables and the towers suddenly crossed the road and divided into two columns—one column heading in the direction of Las Vegas and the other toward Phoenix.

In August 1990 I was at the trading post waiting for Roberta Blackgoat's daughter. We had arranged to meet there on a Saturday because she said it would have been too difficult for me to find my way on my own to the Blackgoat sheepherding camp. An old weathered sign and a gasoline pump still stood outside. Three generations of Blairs had owned the trading post, and the latest owner, James Blair, told me that he commuted back and forth to his home in Cortez, Colorado, by means of the small plane tied down outside, anchored against the wind by four strong, taut wires. The Blair family had owned the trading-post license for years and had two other stores, one at Page, Arizona, near the Glen Canyon Dam, and another outside of Phoenix. In addition to selling dry goods and providing government services like the post office, Blair traded and sold Navajo rugs, chiefs' blankets, saddle blankets, Hopi pottery, baskets, kachina dolls, and jewelry. Hopi carvers and Navajo weavers were lined up waiting to do business with him as I slowly perused a tray of pawned silver jewelry. Roberta used to sell her rugs there, Vicki told me later, but stopped because she didn't like the price he offered. By then she was selling her rugs through a cooperative called Black Mesa Weavers for Life and Land.

I paid $75 for a turquoise cluster ring pawned by "Nonobah Hariley of Chinle," according to the tag, in order to continue to act like a tourist while reading the notices on the bulletin board outside the post office window about the relocation and the mandatory sheep reduction for all the residents of the Big Mountain area. Big Mountain was part of the stepped plateau lands of Black Mesa and, at seven thousand feet, its highest point. It was also the center for the greatest Navajo resistance where "outside agitators" were looked on with great suspicion. As a single person driving the roads of the reservation, I didn't want to be seen as an "Anglo activist," a category that Goldwater had spared no words in criticizing: "Anglo activists, most from outside Arizona, have adopted the Navajo as a social cause in recent years. These political and social engineers are still pouring kerosene on the old flames of tribal hatred and revenge. Most Indians and Arizonans have nothing but contempt for their invasion into what is totally an Indian issue. Congress became involved because of its trust or guardian responsibilities." A number of US government marshals and Hopi police in big white sport utility vehicles had passed me on the empty reservation roads.

The trading post took on the functions of a post office because it was an outpost of colonial government. The US government needed to have a legal means to officially communicate with the Navajo residents. The United States had been an internal colonial power for more than a century before the US Congress passed the Indian Reorganization Act of 1934, setting up tribal constitutions, tribal voting, and tribal councils—leadership forms that were compatible with Washington but did not necessarily reflect the cultural patterns of Indian life. The Hopi had elected their first tribal council in an election in which 70 percent of the voters stayed home. The Navajo Tribal Council had been assembled in 1922 when Standard Oil Company of California wanted oil leases on the reservation and needed a legally authorized signatory. According to Navajo tribal chairman Peter MacDonald, the BIA chose five Navajo leaders to make up the first tribal council to sign the leases. The energy companies stayed involved in the workings of the tribal councils, and the trading posts remained an important communications center for Anglo authority on the reservations.

Vicki Blackgoat had told me that the mandatory sheep reduction was executed by means of government rangers and Hopi police showing up at dawn in livestock trucks. They would open corrals, herd the sheep into the trucks, and drive away, leaving the families devastated. Sheep were like money in the bank. The sheep reduction and harassment were a means to force them to move. When used by the American military in foreign countries, this strategy is called "low-intensity conflict."

When Roberta gave her address to Goldwater's receptionist or spoke to his legislative assistant, it is doubtful that either of them could have imagined the landscape around Dinnebito Trading Post. Roberta Blackgoat's Arizona sheepherding camp was twenty miles from the trading post, deep in the interior and accessible only by a spaghetti swirl of dirt roads, many no wider than a track and some barely discernible in the scrub. I waited for hours, but Vicki never showed up. I waited outside and finally saw the plume of dust from a car coming over the horizon.

I had hoped it was Vicki, but alas, when the car pulled up, it carried two white men who were on their way to a big water conference in Phoenix. They were stopping for gas. As they filled their gas tank, they asked what I was doing there. By then it was late, and Blair would soon be closing the trading post. They suggested I follow them out to the highway, after I described the nine miles of savage ruts that awaited them on the road out to Route 264. They had come from the north on

the Peabody coal-access road, unpaved but well kept up. Arthur Jokela
and his friend Howard Wright were professors at the Southern California Institute for Natural Resources. (Weeks later, when I finally
talked to Vicki by phone, I learned she came on Sunday, a day later.
We had gotten the days mixed up.)

We set out in our little two-car caravan, but less than a mile down
the road, my vehicle started making such alarming noises I thought
I had a flat tire. I slowed down, and their car soon disappeared in a
cloud of dust. I was standing in the dust examining my tires when they
came back. We agreed that the tires had plenty of air. Soon, in order
to examine the rear tire wells, we had emptied the trunk and filled the
road with my luggage and all the groceries I had planned to bring to
the Blackgoat camp.

"You might have a bent axle," said Arthur after a test drive of a
hundred yards. "Or maybe the shock absorbers are gone. Highway cars
don't have a high-enough undercarriage for these roads. That's why the
Indians drive those pickup trucks, Indian Cadillacs they call them. But
if the axle were really broken, you wouldn't be able to move."

After an inconclusive diagnosis, Arthur offered to drive my car as
far as Second Mesa, where the Hopi had a visitors center, telephone,
motel, and restaurant. Howard would follow in their car. As we came
out on Route 264 and turned east, the car groaning and clanking, my
breath stopped at the sight of the vast desert spread out below us. We
were perched at least six hundred feet above the desert floor, at the
actual knife-edge of Black Mesa, where long peninsulas of rock cliffs
jutted out into the desert. As the road wound along the mesa edges, I
tried not to think about what an unstable axle could mean at the edge
of such cliffs.

Over dinner in the café, we discussed my car (call Phoenix and
tell the rental agency to bring another one and tell them the car hadn't
been checked out when they gave it to you), their water conference
(more than a thousand scientists, academics, and government officials
coming from all over the country were convening to discuss the ongoing drought and declining water resources of the Southwest), and
the coal-slurry pipeline. I asked them about the transmission lines and

the electricity, all the questions I didn't dare ask Blair. They asked me about the coal-slurry pipeline. Howard explained that they had driven down from Nevada because they wanted to see the Mohave plant and the coal-slurry pipeline, but they didn't see much of it. I explained that it was an eighteen-inch pipe that was not visible from the road. The Black Mesa coal-slurry pipeline was famous among water engineers for being the most egregious use of water in the water-starved West.

They left for Phoenix, and I learned I would be sleeping in my car because all the rooms in the Hopi motel were full. The members of the board of the Hopi Foundation were meeting that weekend and had occupied all the rooms. As a result, I awoke the minute the sun came up and saw the amazing sight of the desert come alive as sunlight washed over the desert floor. An hour later I was in line at the restaurant when I saw the woman in front of me sign her credit card slip with a name I recognized. "Are you Martha Blue, Roberta Blackgoat's lawyer?" I asked. From the serendipity of that meeting came a twenty-plus-year correspondence. In the parking lot, I introduced myself to former tribal chairman Abbott Sekaquaptewa, who was directing Hopi Foundation board members into vans for a trip to the destroyed Hopi village of Atawovi. Atawovi was the first Hopi town that Spanish explorers from Coronado's expedition entered and where Spanish missionaries later succeeded in building a church. Other Hopi villages were so angered by the persistent foreign presence that in 1700 they banded together, destroyed the village, killed most of the men, and distributed the women and children among the other Hopi villages. Atawovi became an archaeological ruin on Antelope Mesa, closed to visitors except by permit or special tour.

For my purposes the telephone was useless because Roberta Black-goat's camp was without electricity or telephone. I couldn't go back to the Dinnebito Trading Post because I couldn't drive my car, and it would be early evening before the Phoenix car rental agency showed up with a replacement. So I spent the rest of the day touring the Hopi villages and visiting Hopi potters on the different mesas on a tour arranged by the Hopi Cultural Center. Without that experience, however, I would not have understood the complexity of the topography and the disparate history of the different Hopi villages. Water was the determining factor. Each Hopi village had been located near a spring. The towns might look as though they sat on rock pinnacles in the sky, but each village had its own water supply.

Land and Culture

Water and the mandatory sheep reduction were among the reasons that Roberta Blackgoat and Violet Ashke went to see Senator Goldwater. The relocation orders were another. The traditional Navajo refused to move. Land was more than real estate; it was the essence of Navajo culture. Goldwater, who boasted that he had "spent more time with Arizona's Indians than any other white man," must have known that there was no word in Navajo for *relocation*. Their only word was *disappearance*.

On occasion Mrs. Blackgoat, acting as a spokesperson for the residents of the area, many of whom did not speak English, had explained to reporters how integral their connection was to the land and why they could not move: "Our great ancestors are buried here. Their spirits are still around. I had all my ancestors being buried around this area. It's where our prayers and songs and offering sites are. That's why we can't forget and can't move." She told me, "If I had to move away, I don't believe [my ancestors] would give me any prayers. I'd leave my sacred prayers back here. I'd be unknown, a strange person, and then get sick and not live long." To move *was* to disappear.

Because the land partition, the sheep reduction, and the removal of whole families into poorly built and soon foreclosed-upon tract housing in Gallop and Flagstaff had come about as a result of legislation Goldwater had introduced and supported, Mrs. Blackgoat and Mrs. Ashke were in Washington not simply to lobby or inform him but to ask him to come speak to the people at Black Mesa. They wanted him to explain the intent of his legislation. He was the only person who could give them honest answers.

On the second day, they again sat in the office all day, and again Senator Goldwater was too busy to see them. Another legislative assistant came out. They shook their heads. Only Senator Goldwater could help them, they repeated. But they told the young man a little more about their concerns.

Did Senator Goldwater want to find a peaceful means of settling the so-called land dispute, as he said, or did he mean to move thousands of Navajo off their lands? Who had given the coal company approval to pump massive amounts of water out of the ground for a coal-slurry pipeline? In the high desert, water was more valuable than coal. Their water came from an Ice Age aquifer, and after it was pumped out, annual rainfall would never replenish it. Blackgoat's well was going dry. In some areas water holes for sheep had become so toxic from sulfates released during coal strip mining that sheep died after they drank. Lambs that were born in the spring were dead by fall because of the mercury and heavy metals that leached into the groundwater. What was going to happen to the water supply of Black Mesa? These were questions the senator had never answered. No one had been able to ask him. He had counted on other senators deferring to him as the senator from Arizona, the man most knowledgeable about Indian affairs. As Congressman Sam Steiger said in introducing Goldwater to the House Subcommittee on Indian Affairs, "He is a man that not only knows the people, he knows the land. He knows it in a way that, I think, very few non-Indians know it."

What I would later come to understand is that what really separates Indians from Anglos is the idea that the universe is alive and that land is sacred. "Understanding sacred lands," explained Vine Deloria to an audience at Harvard Law School, "is not just a warm feeling you get at a waterfall. The larger society mistakes aesthetics for religious feeling."

On the third day of their visit, Goldwater agreed to see Mrs. Blackgoat and Mrs. Ashke. And after their conversation, he agreed to come out to Big Mountain and meet with the Navajo. He assured them he would come by the end of the month.

Thirteen years later, in February 1991, I asked Mrs. Blackgoat, "How did you convince him to come?" She was sitting at her loom, weaving, still on her land, having successfully resisted more than fifteen years of increasing pressures—including a government agent with papers for her to sign who had come to her hospital room after she had heart surgery—to dislodge her from it. She could not repair her buildings, two-thirds of her sheep had been taken away, but she was still there, sitting at a loom in her hogan, weaving a rug from wool that she had sheared and carded from her own sheep. She smiled at my question. I inferred that she had appealed to Goldwater's vanity by asking him to come and stay for three days and "sleep on sheepskins" like the traditional Navajo.

But she began weaving with so much determination that I asked her who the rug was for. The curve of her mouth turned up another quarter inch, and her eyes crinkled as though she was remembering a particularly satisfying moment. It was then that I remembered being told that Goldwater had a penchant for young Navajo women when he was at the trading post on Navajo Mountain. Mrs. Blackgoat smiled and said the rug she was weaving was for a "special friend" of Barry Goldwater's. Whatever she said to the senator, however, he quickly rearranged his schedule and made his way to Black Mesa in July 1978.

GOLDWATER AT BIG MOUNTAIN

A photograph taken during Goldwater's visit to the Big Mountain area of Black Mesa shows him in a striped polo shirt and khakis standing in the dappled shade of a sunlit brush arbor with his right hand raised in a fist and his left hand jammed into his pocket. He is listening to someone outside the frame of the photo, and his mouth is compressed and tense.

This was not the romantic West that Goldwater so effectively evoked in speeches and at cocktail parties. These were knowledgeable Indians who were aware of how Washington worked, how legislation worked, and how deeply corporate energy interests were involved on their reservation, as well as the massive relocation of residents under way. More than two hundred Navajo had prepared for Goldwater's visit on Black Mesa with a big spread of roasted mutton stew, fry bread, corn, and peaches, a traditional Navajo meal. (The peaches originated with the Spanish.) Accompanied by an aide and several reporters, the senator came by helicopter from Phoenix two weeks after the Navajo women's visit. A brush arbor had been erected to provide shade and a battery-powered microphone set up to ensure that everyone could hear him, even though many of the elderly Navajo did not understand English.

He opened his remarks by saying that he was happy to be back in Navajoland, that the Navajo were special friends and he would be happy to answer all of their questions. But almost immediately, he displayed total obliviousness about the consequences of the legislation that he had introduced and guided through multiple rounds of congressional hearings.

"There has been no decision that says you have to move," Goldwater insisted in answering one question about how many people would have to be relocated. He appeared unaware that the partition order of Black Mesa was already posted at the Dinnebito Trading Post and that a million-dollar barbed-wire fence looped deep into the interior, enclosing some eighteen hundred square miles. All the Navajo who lived on the wrong side of the fence were told they would have to move and had been pressured to sign relocation papers. That land would be added to the Hopi reservation. The fence, in the shape of a hitchhiker's thumb, demarcated the newly divided reservation land.

"No money has been appropriated for relocation," Goldwater insisted, answering another question, even though the Indian Relocation Commission was in operation on a side street in Flagstaff and had been receiving money for more than three years.

He said he knew of no federal orders for mandatory stock reduction. The only stock reduction he knew about, he said, was the program that had been organized by John Collier in the 1930s. So who, one woman demanded to know, had ordered the livestock trucks that showed up at dawn and kidnapped her sheep?

The English-speaking Navajo became exasperated and angry. Percy Deal, a member of the Navajo Land Dispute Commission, said, "I can tell you right now that relocation is in progress, livestock reduction is in progress, fencing is in progress, and you are here telling us that this has not come about yet. I would suggest that you go back to the Phoenix office or your D.C. office and tell your staff to get on the ball and keep you current on information going on out here."

Goldwater did not like Indians who talked to him like that. But the final confrontation came when Daniel Peaches, a Navajo member of the Arizona Legislature and a Republican, implied that they knew that Goldwater had sold them out because of the energy resources. "The people here have suffered because . . . our Republican leaders from the state of Arizona failed to understand that if the land was to be divided 50–50, it was inevitable that tragedy was going to fall on the shoulders of the Navajo people."

When it became clear that his answers were insufficient to satisfy anyone and neither the questions nor his answers were going to change, Goldwater abruptly announced that his wife was ill and that he would have to return immediately to Phoenix.

As he and his aides began walking toward the helicopter, Roberta Blackgoat came up alongside and reminded him of his promise to "stay three days and sleep on sheepskins." He didn't answer her. Instead, he turned to a reporter from the *Navajo Times* and said angrily, "I've lived here fifty years, and I probably know this land better than most of these Navajos here today do." Then he stepped into the helicopter, which rose up over the rust-red soil dotted with piñon and juniper, and he was on his way back to Phoenix, a city that was greatly benefiting from the coal mined on the Black Mesa lands because the coal was being used to run the fourteen pumping stations that rerouted a portion of the Colorado River into Phoenix. When Goldwater made his trip to Black Mesa to answer questions about the mass removal of the Navajo, ten years of strip mining had been under way at two different sites, digging out 13 million tons of coal a year, making the Black Mesa mines the largest strip-mining operation in the United States at the time. One of the strip mines was supplying coal to the Navajo Generating Station, a 2,250-megawatt coal-fired power plant. More than half of the plant's energy was supplying the energy to run pumping stations to lift the waters of the Colorado River up over three mountain ranges into Phoenix and Tucson. The other plant was a 1,580-megawatt plant in Laughlin, Nevada. From one point of view, 3,800 megawatts of electricity were being derived from the land seventeen miles from Roberta Blackgoat's home.

Sheepherding and strip mining are not compatible activities. Blasting the coal beds releases sulfates and other pollutants into the groundwater and coal dust into the air. Shallow wells for drinking become contaminated, and water holes for livestock become toxic. People living in the vicinity of the mines had unusually high rates of bronchitis, asthma, and emphysema from the particulates in the air. Additional legislation had been introduced and passed in order to implement the removal of thousands of Navajo families from these same lands. Unfortunately, no plan had been put in place to figure out where thousands of Navajo people might go, or where they should live, or how they might earn a living.

The important thing to remember, however, was that the coal was about more than money. It was about growth—the power to pump water into Phoenix, air-conditioning to Los Angeles, and the electricity to light the giant casinos and cool thousands of new homes in Las Vegas as the population doubled and then tripled every year. Las Vegas became the fastest-growing metropolitan area in the United States. Today, two-thirds of Nevada's population lives in southern Nevada, once called a "profitless locale." The magic of the Southwest Boom required the energy resources of Black Mesa.

MORE THAN MONEY

During the hearings on the Hopi-Navajo Reservation Partition, Goldwater had maintained there was no other solution except to remove the Navajo from their land. He testified: "I had hoped that this matter could have reached a mutual settlement long, long ago. But it became obvious to me back in the 1950s that this was not going to happen and I was instrumental in getting the special court set up which first heard this problem, and this court . . . ruled that the Navajo were in error, and they should get off."

The truth was that Goldwater did not have the imagination or the legal training to have a special court set up. Goldwater was not a lawyer.

His much-lauded gift for simplifying issues was often grounded in a lack of appreciation for complexity. He was notorious for becoming quickly bored with the minutiae of legislative drafting and bill mark-ups. He also, as he frequently reiterated, "didn't believe in new laws." Goldwater claimed to believe in repealing old ones.

The legal architect who designed the special court was the Hopi's lawyer John Boyden, a millionaire from Salt Lake City, a candidate for governor of Utah, and a Mormon bishop. Many people called the court and subsequent legislation that Boyden orchestrated a classic example of legal theft. Why do anything illegal when you can pass laws that make it legal? Several corporations saw opportunity and profit.

Black Mesa was home to the first coal slurry–pipeline delivery system in the world, a system that could make coal as liquid and transportable as oil and revolutionize the coal industry. Bechtel designed and built the coal-slurry pipeline with the help of a federal grant. The slurry pipeline and the plant it supplied were a template for the future. In the 1980s the Reagan administration approved the creation of Bechtel China as a joint energy venture in China; Bechtel would help the Chinese develop coal-powered generating stations, slurry pipelines, and strip-mining operations. At the time the only operating prototype in the world was the Mohave plant in Nevada.

Although tens of thousands of people go to Laughlin, Nevada, to gamble and to stay in cheap casino-hotels, very few link the little gambling town on the Colorado River with the remote section of northern Arizona called Black Mesa. I arrived in Laughlin from the opposite direction, following the slurry pipeline from Black Mesa and traveling some three hundred miles across northern Arizona to the tip of Nevada. Laughlin as a townsite didn't exist before the Mohave Generating Station. Consequently, a revised history makes the power plant a central player in the town's miracle growth.

PART II

PART II

CHAPTER 4

FOUNDING MYTHS: LAUGHLIN, NEVADA

The founding myth of Las Vegas is that it is a place for a fresh start, a place in the sun where a person is not burdened by failures in other locales. Even today, the history of Las Vegas rests on the story of an ordinary person with great gambler's luck who hits the jackpot and changes his or her life. It is mostly a man's fantasy and frequently includes "a vision in the desert," similar to the Hollywood version of Bugsy Siegel seeing the Flamingo shimmering in the desert like a religious epiphany. A lot of unexplored truths lie beneath this myth of self-reliance and individual initiative on the route to riches and empire.

Laughlin, Nevada, is a gambling enclave some ninety miles south of Las Vegas on the Colorado River. It is named for Don Laughlin, who moved to Las Vegas from Michigan in 1954 when he was twenty-one, a time when Las Vegas was still getting started as a gambling capital. Reno was the big city in Nevada. Most of the casinos—Binion's, the Flamingo, and the Desert Inn—were fronted by men without police records but owned by syndicates of known gangsters from other cities. Their histories in Detroit, Cleveland, New York, Chicago, Dallas, Los Angeles, and Havana were well known to the FBI and the Senate Committee on Organized Crime, which held hearings in Las Vegas in 1950. But as Moe Dalitz was reputed to have pointed out to the committee members, Las Vegas was attractive to Mob bosses because "Nevada was the only place in America where gambling was legal. Who else knew how to run games except gangsters?"

Don Laughlin worked as a bartender and dealer in different clubs around Vegas and managed to save enough money to buy a stake in the 101 Club, a small bar in North Las Vegas. The 101 Club enabled him to get a gambling license that was good throughout Clark County. Then in 1966, at the age of thirty-three, for reasons never really explained, he took a huge gamble on an unknown property in a nameless location in the Mohave Desert. He sold most of his stake in the 101 Club and bought a motel, bait shop, and six acres of land on an empty patch of Nevada desert, sixty miles south of Hoover Dam on the banks of the Colorado River.

It was at this bend in the river, located in the eye of the needle where the point of Nevada wedges into Arizona and California, that Don Laughlin staked his improbable future. Owned by the US government and managed by the Bureau of Land Management, the area was known mainly as a locale for the highest recorded temperatures in the entire West—a record that it still holds. Laughlin's only attractive natural topographic feature is the Colorado River, flowing flat and oily between two desert bluffs. At this point the river has turned due south, is sixty miles out of canyon country, and is following gravity down into Mexico. For the next four hundred miles, it forms the serpentine border between Arizona and California. When the river arrives at its delta in the Sea of Cortez (Gulf of California), it is so used up by multiple irrigation projects upstream that what people see as river is actually the ocean filling up tidal flats. No water is left in the Colorado River. Even when there was water, farmers in Mexico found the saline content so high that their portion of the river was unusable for agriculture. The governments of Mexico and the United States negotiated an international treaty, ensuring Mexico its share of desalinated water through construction of a dam and a desalinization plant, first signed in 1944 and amended in 2012.

Why would anyone spend $250,000 on an empty piece of desert only five hundred feet above sea level with recorded temperatures of 125 degrees? The single known economic activity took place on the Arizona side of the river at Bullhead City, where recreational fishermen came to fish for bass. The town's name came either from a rock formation called Bull Head Rock or fishermen who thought they were fishing for bullhead trout. The Nevada side remained nameless.

In 1967 the US Postal Service decided to name the place "Laughlin" after Don Laughlin himself. Laughlin was expanding his property. He put slot machines in his restaurant (his Clark County gaming license was valid), enlarged the motel, and seemingly in no time had a dependable clientele swarming in from California and Arizona. Don Laughlin became a multimillionaire and the founder of his own gambling empire. He embodied the essence of the Vegas dream. That is the official version of the story.

Another version might ask other questions. Why did this spot in the desert need a post office?

The new town of Laughlin—ninety miles by road from Las Vegas, sixty miles by river—needed a post office because a giant construction project was already under way by 1966. Even before construction began, even before Don Laughlin bought his six acres, even before the post office was looking for a name, surveyors were measuring the site where a new 1,500-megawatt electricity generating plant was to be located; construction engineers were developing the staging area where equipment would be unloaded; roads were being upgraded to transport men and equipment to the site a hundred feet above the river. This coal-fired plant, soon to be called the Mohave Generating Station, was to be the destination for the first coal-slurry pipeline in the United States, a template for a coal delivery system that could revolutionize the market. Coal was the source of air-conditioning and electricity to power the mushrooming growth of the desert cities of the Southwest. The owners of the new generating station were the utilities of Los Angeles, Las Vegas, and Phoenix. The operating utility was Southern California Edison. Like the rest of America in 1966, these cities got more than 60 percent of their electricity from coal, even though many people erroneously thought that coal had disappeared with the Industrial Revolution.

In 1950 Las Vegas had a population of 25,000 people and was mainly known for quickie divorces, brothels, bars, and gambling. Slowly and then quickly, it started to grow. By 1960 it had 65,000 people, in 1970 125,000. A visitor flying in by plane saw huge parcels of desert land bulldozed into geometric designs that would eventually become roadways and housing plots within gated communities. The land had been bought and subdivided and was awaiting the extension of city services such as water, sewer, and electrical lines. Today people will tell you when they came to Las Vegas, the city ended at Eastern Avenue on the east and Decatur on the west. Those roads are midcity today. Three of the fastest-growing cities in the country were Henderson, North Las Vegas, and Boulder City, all outside of Las Vegas. The same growth pattern was true in Phoenix, where Peoria and Chandler were booming. Real estate developer Del Webb, who operated in both cities, did not advertise his new retirement communities by saying, "Come Live in the Desert." Instead, he said, "Come Live in the Sun." The new westerners, who bought model homes in new developments of ten, twenty, and thirty thousand houses, wanted lawns and golf courses and green vegetation like they had in the East and Midwest. The huge development of Summerlin on the western side of Las Vegas, where houses backed up the slopes of the mountains, had five separate developers creating communities with preplanned hospitals and schools and swimming pools and golf courses. The developers targeted buyers in communities around Los Angeles, where the average home price had pushed people either out of the housing market entirely or into three-hour commutes to work. Where were the resources to come from to make this growth possible? The Mohave plant was the first of what some people called "the new Hoover Dam," four coal-fired plants and two nuclear that were to provide the water and electricity for the selling of the New West.

Despite the antigovernment rhetoric, millions of dollars of federal money were being fed into the payrolls of the Bechtel Corporation of San Francisco to build the new generating station as well as to design the new technology of a coal slurry–pipeline delivery system. The unique aspect of this particular generating station was that it would be the first plant in the world to be supplied by slurried coal.

Railroads are the most expensive aspect of supplying a generating station. As I learned from the film I watched at the Black Mesa Pipeline office, the new plant in Laughlin would not require construction of a dedicated railroad with hundred-car trains delivering coal twenty-four hours a day. (A 1,500-megawatt coal plant burns a freight car of coal every ten minutes.) The Black Mesa Coal Slurry Pipeline was the first in the world to demonstrate that a generating station could run from slurried coal. The great novelty of the plant in Laughlin was the technology of turning hard coal into liquid slurry and delivering it through a pipeline, making coal potentially as fluid and transportable as oil.

Although the pipeline was owned by Williams Technologies of Tulsa, Oklahoma, it had been designed and built by Bechtel with the help of a $3 billion research and development grant from the federal government, helped along by Peter Flanigan, an economics adviser in the Nixon White House. The film's narrator explained that the cost of building a 300-mile railroad was prohibitive. But a pipeline was plausible even though it would be on Indian lands. "The final decision was theirs," Morgan Greenwood, the president of Williams Technology, said portentously. "Indians too want the better things of life."

The narrator went on to explain that the slurry-pipeline water "would have no effect on the Indians' water supply" because the slurry-line water came from two-thousand-foot wells "encased in steel." The Indians dug "shallow wells." The pipeline company "paid the highest royalties the Indians ever received." "Indian applicants would get jobs." In fact, the jobs were not so plentiful because strip mining is machinery intensive. A rule of thumb is that 105 full-time miners in the field can strip-mine 2 million tons a year. (The Kayenta Mine on Black Mesa has a 430-man workforce extracting 7.8 million tons of coal a year.)

After the film I went outside to see the slurry pipeline in operation. A conveyor belt carried raw coal to the processing center, where it was crushed into egg-size pieces no larger than two inches. Then it was weighed. The coal royalty paid to the Navajo and Hopi was based on the weight of the coal. Operating on the same principle as the home garbage disposal, the coal was fed into a giant mixmaster (not its technical name), pulverized, mixed with water, and then washed through a pipe, in this case a 273-mile pipeline helped along by five pumping stations.

Lowell Hinkins, an operator at the slurry-pipeline office who described himself as an "old farm boy from Wisconsin" but who "had worked for mining companies all over the world," explained to me that the mix of water and coal had to be carefully calibrated so that the coal particles stayed suspended. If the water flow was too slow, the solids settled to the bottom of the pipe and caused the system to clog; if it went too fast, it caused abrasion to the pipe. Although the pipeline was buried, the route follows Route 40 to Flagstaff, Williams, Seligman, Kingman, and then across Davis Dam into Laughlin.

I asked Hinkins about the number of jobs. He said that "the three top people are Anglo. We have two Hopi, thirty-one Navajo. We receive about three thousand applications a year. We're trained to understand the Indian culture." He showed me the certificate from a course he had to taken in Page on "cross-cultural communications."

Once arriving in Laughlin, Nevada, the coal slurry was dewatered, dried out by means of a centrifuge, and the water sent to huge evaporation ponds. The Mohave Generating Station and the Black Mesa Pipeline were the first coal slurry–pipeline system built in the United States and the first generating station in the world to be run by dewatered coal. Desolate Laughlin was the hub for a revolutionary new coal technology that utility engineers from around the globe would come to visit. Bechtel Corporation was developing and promoting slurry-pipeline systems to countries with large coal reserves.

Similar to the industry descriptions of "clean coal" technologies today (as of 2013 no successful clean coal plant has been built), the Mohave plant and slurry pipeline promised a new era in coal economics and cheap electricity. The federal grant in process in Washington was key to funding the research and development costs of the slurry pipeline and the plant it would run, both of which were already under construction.

The Bechtel Corporation advertised its role in the project—"1500 Megawatts for the Southwest" ran the headline in its in-house magazine, *Bechtel Briefs*—over a drawing of the Mohave plant. The plant was identical to two new 750-megawatt units Bechtel was already building at the Four Corners plant in Farmington, New Mexico, making the capacity of that plant 2,250 megawatts. In other words, the activity in Laughlin was not a secret.

The plant's construction required massive equipment and hundreds of workers—drillers, explosive experts, electricians, plumbers, concrete technicians, utility engineers—going to work every day in Laughlin and getting a paycheck every week. Many of them lived across the river in Bullhead City, but as soon as construction started they moved to trailers at the site. In no time Don Laughlin's restaurant and motel and slot machines were filled with construction workers and utility engineers engaged in the billion-dollar project. It might be less colorful, but far more accurate, to say that Don Laughlin made a smart investment based on good information rather than a stroke of gambler's luck and a magical "vision in the desert."

The best place to gauge the massive size taken up by the Mohave Generating Station is in the main restaurant of the faux Mississippi steamboat known as the Colorado Belle. Designed to look like a riverboat pilot room, the restaurant is dominated by a huge backlit chart of the Colorado River that shows the Mohave power plant and its two giant holding ponds taking up more land than the town of Laughlin itself. The plant itself is at least twice the width of the river and, when combined with the holding ponds, larger than the downtown.

The Mohave was the first of four new coal-fired plants planned and built for the unpopulated interior West between 1967 and 1975. Los Angeles, Phoenix, and Las Vegas needed the electricity infrastructure to power the Sunbelt Boom. The electricity lit up the elaborate neon signs of Las Vegas, powered air conditioners in Los Angeles, and pumped water into Phoenix. Although some people called this massive infrastructure the "new Hoover Dam," it was quite unlike Hoover Dam in that it was not focused in one easy-to-understand location. The generating stations were strung out along the Colorado River and into the unpopulated interior of the Colorado Plateau. And the coal for all them was to be strip-mined on the Navajo and Hopi reservations. (The coal for the Four Corners plant was being mined on another section of the Navajo reservation by Utah International, then a subsidiary of General Electric, soon to become a subsidiary of the Australian mining giant Broken Hill Proprietary.) The two new units for the Four Corners generating station in Farmington, New Mexico, were the first to be built; the Mohave plant in Laughlin was the second; the third was the Navajo Generation Station in Page; and the Coronado Generating Station in St. Johns, Arizona, was the fourth. All were built by Bechtel. A fifth was planned for southern Utah, called the Kaiparowitz project, but Utah citizens were able to defeat the plant and the slurry pipeline on the evidence of its long-term damaging effects on groundwater in a desert climate.

By the time the Navajo Generating Station went on line in 1974, Don Laughlin's bait shop and motel had morphed into the fourteen-story Riverside hotel-casino, and he was a multimillionaire. Harrah's and Bally's and an ersatz Mississippi riverboat casino had followed him to this remote spot in the Mohave Desert. Steve Wynn, not yet known as the Medici prince of Las Vegas, bought the Nevada Club (now the Golden Nugget) in Laughlin. Three Las Vegas brand names came together when the Hilton chain opened the Laughlin Flamingo Hilton in 1990. In the wake of the big casino-hotels came the hunter-gatherers of real estate capitalism—condo developers and retirement-community entrepreneurs. To distract from the stark conditions of desert living, they promoted water taxis, new restaurants, big-name entertainment, a river walk, golf courses, retirement communities, and, of course, Laughlin's unique location at the edge of a mighty flowing river in the middle of the desert. "Tee off by the Colorado River in the Nevada desert," advertises one golf course.

Laughlin, however, is noted for four things: its stupefying heat (113 degrees when I was there in early June, and it didn't cool down at night), picture windows in the casinos (Las Vegas casinos are built without windows so a visitor loses track of time), notoriously cheap hotel rooms ($23 for my room at the Edgewater, $39 at Harrah's), and the visible failure of Nevada's real estate capitalism. A series of films on YouTube takes the viewer on a ride around deserted real estate developments in Laughlin and Las Vegas—houses built, grounds landscaped, no one there.

It is probably a safe bet to say that few Las Vegas or Laughlin visitors have ever been to Black Mesa. But if a visitor followed the coal-slurry pipeline backward from Laughlin 273 miles to its source, as I did, she would find herself at a remote spot in northern Arizona off Highway 160, some twenty miles west of Kayenta, Arizona. Travel another 10 miles down Route 41, and you pass an airfield on your left before arriving at Peabody Coal's Black Mesa office, where you are asked to watch a film on mine safety before being given a hard hat to wear on your way to the Black Mesa Coal Slurry Pipeline office. If it is winter, you will see cone-shaped piles of coal the height of a three-story building covered with a dusting of grayish snow, an overhead conveyor belt depositing coal chunks into a giant mixmaster, and a huge water tank where, somewhere out of view, pumps are sucking water out of the Navajo aquifer, the sole source of water for both the Hopi and the Navajo.

In the enthusiasm for the new coal slurry–pipeline technology, some questions often went unasked. "Where does the water come from to run the slurry pipeline?" I asked Lowell Hinkins. How much water does it take to transport five and a half million tons of coal a year?

"We take out 4,300 acre-feet a year." That is roughly a billion gallons a year, drawn from an Ice Age aquifer called the Navajo aquifer, or "N" aquifer, beneath the Hopi-Navajo lands on Black Mesa. "And we pay a good rate for the water."

He claimed not to know how much they paid, but later litigation showed that in the original leases, the Hopi got $1.67 per acre-foot and the Navajo got $5. In 1987, almost twenty years later, the Navajo renegotiated the price from $5 an acre-foot to $600 an acre-foot; the Hopi rate was reassessed to $427 an acre-foot. According to Marjane Ambler in *Breaking the Iron Bonds*, Peabody Coal was also required to pay $1,200 an acre-foot when it used more than 2,800 acre-feet in any one year. The water-table level had dropped from 10 to 70 feet in those Navajo and Hopi communities that use the same aquifer, making their wells and springs unusable. The groundwater level is projected to drop as much as 175 feet by the year 2032. During the public commentary section in the Black Mesa Environmental Impact Statement, from a hearing held in 1988, many people said the water levels were jeopardizing an entire culture. As Hopi resident Marilyn Masayevsa said, "The water is more valuable than the coal." Her cousin Vernon Masayevsa, a former Hopi Tribal Council chairman, was so concerned about long-term effects on groundwater supply that he started the Black Mesa Water Trust to educate people about what pumping more than a billion gallons a year was doing to their life and livelihood.

By 2001 an intertribal group of young adult Hopi and Navajo established the Black Mesa Water Coalition to advocate for a move away from the region's fossil-fuel economy and develop a green economy to replace it. Wahleah Johns, the coalition's solar project manager, pointed out that the promised riches from the fossil-fuel development never materialized for the larger population. Millions of dollars in royalties didn't change the 54 percent unemployment rate or alter the average income of $7,500 a year on the Navajo reservation.

The Hopi, who depended on the aquifer water for religious, cultural, and daily use, found that their springs were drying up. These are people who are in touch with climate change and have seen changes in their ecosystems and weather patterns. The Black Mesa slurry pipeline eventually came to represent some of the most profligate and indefensible water use in the world, even though the owners insist even now that the water they use comes from a totally different source than the Indians' water supply.

"The pipeline water comes from a completely different place in the aquifer than the water the Indians use," Hinkins told me. How is that? "There's a layer of rock in between. Two different basins entirely."

"Then why are the Navajo wells and Hopi springs going dry?" I was asking these questions in March 1990 after the slurry pipeline had been operating for more than twenty years, pumping out more than a billion gallons a year. Water holes on the reservation had turned to mud, Hopi springs were drying up, and the Navajo sheepherders had to drive more than twenty miles to a deep-water well at the Rocky Ridge School to haul drinking water. I went with Roberta Blackgoat to the school and watched Vicki help her seventy-four-year-old mother, using a hose and a nozzle something like a gas pump, fill a hundred-gallon barrel carried in the back of her pickup truck. The processes of desertification were already visible. Plants didn't reseed. Wells didn't recharge. Drought conditions were lasting longer. As groundwater levels lowered, rain clouds didn't form and coalesce. The winters were shorter and the summers longer.

"No effect on their water," Hinkins insisted. "We draw from a completely different section of the aquifer." This was the stock answer of the slurry-pipeline company, repeated whenever the question of water was brought up. Theoretically, an impermeable layer of rock separated the water used for the slurry operation and the shallow water sources that the Indians used. It was an answer that seemed to belie the nature of both water and rock. The environmental impact statement accompanying the permit renewal application for Black Mesa mining omitted mention of any impact on water, except for the public comments.

After we had walked around and chatted about other water resource projects and he told me that his son, who works for the Bureau of Indian Affairs, lives in Kayenta but can't get permission to build a home, Lowell Hinkins finally admitted there was some connection between the slurry-pipeline draw and the water levels. "In 1985 there was an accident at the power plant in Laughlin. The pipeline and the plant had to shut down for six months.* After that the groundwater level did start to come up again."

I asked if many visitors come to Black Mesa to see the pipeline and if there were any other operations like it. "People come from all over the world to see it," he answered. "There's nothing like it." Alvin Jack, another worker at the pipeline office, added, "They might have built some others in Russia. And maybe in China." In the twenty years since the Mohave plant and the slurry pipeline began operation in 1970, the

---

* The 1985 accident in Laughlin was so serious that six people died and another ten were seriously burned when a reheat pipe at the Laughlin plant exploded, releasing high-pressure superheated water into the plant's control room with such force that it knocked down a wall and sealed the exit door shut. Later investigation showed that the plant was heating water at higher than recommended levels.

Bechtel Corporation had sold the same coal technology to Russia and China, both countries with a lot of groundwater and a lot of coal. Black Mesa was the template. Bechtel needed the slurry line and the plant in Laughlin to show to new customers. During the Reagan administration of the 1980s, both Bechtel and Peabody Coal had former employees in important energy regulatory positions in Washington.

When I asked about the pipeline terminus in Laughlin, both Hinkins and his colleague corrected me, saying it was Bullhead City, Arizona, rather than Laughlin, Nevada. Supposedly, it is illegal to pump water out of Arizona. But the eighteen-inch coal-slurry pipeline carrying 1.2 billion gallons of water mixed with coal originated in Arizona and ended almost three hundred miles later in Nevada. It disgorged its cargo into huge ponds after the coal was "dewatered" in what would soon become famous as the most polluting coal plant in the country.

While the Black Mesa Coal Slurry Pipeline gained a reputation for being the most profligate use of water in the West, the Mohave Generating Station gained distinction as being the most polluting coal-fired plant in the United States. Built before the Clean Air Act without antipollution devices, on some days during its thirty-five-year life, visitors at Hoover Dam and at Grand Canyon Park, hundreds of miles upstream, would get a soot-filled wind blowing in their faces. The polluting winds moved in a northeasterly direction, eventually obscuring views of the Grand Canyon with a scrim of white haze for more than two hundred days a year. (Kit Owens, the public relations director at the Four Corners plant in Farmington, told me in all seriousness that the pollution came from Los Angeles smog drifting over the mountains.)

SMOG IN THE GRAND CANYON

During one of my trips to visit the infrastructure of the West, I hiked down to the bottom of the Grand Canyon and back up, an eighteen-mile round-trip. I was with several friends, two of whom were experienced hikers and quickly left me behind. I had planned to go only partway, but the views and the geology were so exhilarating I kept going until I was at the bottom. "Vishnu Schist," I was explaining to Anne Spraker about the basement rock formations of the canyon, almost a billion years old. Anne is a quiet and unassuming librarian, but she is also a cyclist who had once biked over the Rockies facing a headwind. In quiet but unmistakably urgent tones, she told me to take my feet out of the cool Colorado River, put on my sneakers, and turn myself around. "The nine miles up are the hard part," she warned, "and we don't want to be climbing out in the dark." In the following seven hours of what I remember as torturous climbing, I took frequent rests, and as I gazed out over the astonishing multicolored canyons that the river had cut, revealing hundreds of millions of years of time, a question finally became larger than my fatigue: Why is there a white haze over everything?

I expected the remarkable layers of the canyon to be crystal clear. After all, it was a sunny day in March. And it was cold. There had even been a light dusting of snow on the trail when we started at dawn. I remembered seeing deer hoof prints in the snow. We were hundreds of miles from the nearest city. How could there be something that looked like smog hovering over the Grand Canyon?

Less than a year later a coalition of environmental groups confirmed that indeed the Grand Canyon—America's single greatest visitor attraction—was covered in smog for more than two hundred days a year. They sued Southern California Edison, Los Angeles Water and Power, Nevada Power, and the Phoenix utility called the Salt River Project—all owners of the Mohave Generating Station near Las Vegas. It had been built in 1969, before passage of the Clean Air Act, and had no scrubbers or antipollution devices of any kind. The prevailing winds blew the particulate matter and gases from burning coal—ash, carbon, mercury, selenium—in a northwesterly direction and put the Grand Canyon directly in the path of its pollution plume. The coal the Mohave plant was burning came from Black Mesa.

Designed and built before information about acid rain, or mercury, or arsenic released in burning coal, or the climatic effects of carbon gas in the atmosphere, the Mohave plant sent millions of tons of carbon and sulfur dioxide into the pristine air of the Southwest. Most people never saw the equally damaging environmental effects that came from extracting coal from lands that could not be reclaimed and groundwater that could not recharge from rainfall. In a desert climate there is not enough rainfall for seeds to germinate to reclaim the strip-mined land. Eight to ten inches of annual rain is not enough water to recharge the aquifer. A study done by the Ford Foundation for the National Academy of Sciences suggested that these lands be considered a National Sacrifice Area. The question remained: Whose sacrifice and for what reasons?

Today the Mohave plant no longer operates. It closed in 2006 after thirty-six years of operation. Las Vegas no longer gets any electricity from the plant, nor does Phoenix or Los Angeles. The operating utility owner, Southern California Edison, determined it was too costly to bring it up to current environmental standards. A visitor to Laughlin today sees the Mohave Generating Station behind a chain-link fence, wrapped in scaffolding and ready for demolition. By virtue of the Internet anyone can see a video of the demolition of its five-hundred-foot smokestack. The power plant, however, was on a bluff outside of Laughlin, so the gambling town is undisturbed by the closed power plant.

The Mohave plant should be seen as the cautionary story for Peabody Energy's current extravagant claims for "clean coal" technologies. Many experts consider clean coal an oxymoron, and the insistence on its viability raises ongoing questions about the true costs of sustaining unsustainable cities within the global phenomenon of climate change.

Although Peabody says it has reclaimed thousands of acres of strip-mined land, this is not the scene from an airplane. The replanted acres are near roads, and they are replanted with oat grass, not an indigenous plant. The contours of the land have taken on unnatural forms. When seen from plateau overlooks, acres and acres of gray land stripped of topsoil and vegetation stretch to the horizon. Whole valleys and canyons have disappeared into the dragline buckets. Thousands of Anasazi archaeological ruins also disappeared into the slag piles.

Laughlin, like Las Vegas, is disconnected from the source of its growth. It is still considered one of those western miracles, brought into existence by individual ingenuity and sheer gambler's luck. Another version holds that it is a by-product of the new cowboy and Indian wars, resource wars where the cowboys are now lawyers in expensive suits.

There is no better example of the cowboy lawyers than John Boyden. He had a background in Indian law before becoming the Hopi's tribal lawyer in 1951. He understood that when it came to Indians, the law was plastic and could be shaped according to new needs and new industries. The water use for the slurry pipeline represented the first sale and marketing of Indian water rights. The removal of the Navajo from what were renamed Hopi lands marked the largest Indian removal of Indians since the 1880s. It was all done legally in what many called legal theft. Boyden was one of the few people who had the time, ambition, legal background, and corporate backing to go back into the tangled history of Indians and white settlers in northern Arizona and New Mexico to figure out how to finally separate the Hopi and Navajo from the mineral resources that lay beneath their lands.

According to legal definition, "An Indian reservation consists of land validly set apart for the use of Indians, under the superintendence of the government, *which retains title to the lands.*" In other words, the best place to determine use of resources beneath Indian lands is not with the Indians themselves, but in Washington, DC.

CHAPTER 5

GILDED AGE LAND GRABS

In the 1880s the great opportunities for great wealth in America lay in land development, mining, and opening public lands in the West to Anglo settlement. The conditions for success required political corruption, Wall Street speculation, and many wild moneymaking schemes, not so different from our own era, which some journalists have called the New Gilded Age.

Chester Arthur, the twenty-first president of the United States, was an accidental president, but he was no stranger to turning public service into private wealth. One of the least studied of American presidents, his résumé included training as a lawyer; a rise to political prominence as a protégé of Senator Roscoe Conkling, the powerful Republican machine boss in New York; and his appointment as supervisor of the Port of New York, a patronage job that transformed him into a wealthy man. He became a vice presidential candidate only because the fractious Republican convention of 1880 could not come to agreement among the reformer delegates who wanted a government civil service and the patronage bosses. "To the victor belongs the spoils" was the motto of Conkling's machine.

Though reformer John Garfield of Ohio was selected as the presidential candidate, Conkling won out on the choice of vice president. Chester Arthur, Chet to his friends, became the vice presidential candidate. Garfield quickly moved Arthur to the sidelines, where he intended to keep him. But destiny revealed another unfortunate outcome for Garfield. Four months after his presidential inauguration, Garfield was shot in a Washington, DC, railroad station, en route to give a speech in Massachusetts. (Conkling was accused of being implicated.) After lingering for two and a half months—the fatal blow was that his doctors did not wash their hands and he got a postwound infection— he died in September 1881. "So Chet Arthur is president," marveled one senator at the improbability of Chester Arthur in the Oval Office.

In fact, Arthur did not rush to inhabit the Oval Office. He took over the presidency but refused to occupy the White House because it was lacking in elegance and not up to his Gilded Age standards of conspicuous wealth. He rented an opulent mansion at taxpayer expense and called in his New York decorator, Louis Tiffany, to remove all the furniture and undertake a thorough redecoration of the White House. The preexisting furnishings—some of which dated back to John Adams—were loaded into twenty-four wagons and sold at auction. (Jackie Kennedy retrieved some of them during her restoration project in the 1960s.) He ordered new china and glassware. He brought a French chef from Delmonico's, one of New York's famous restaurants, to supervise the kitchen, and he stocked the wine cellar with imported French wines. He entertained lavishly and often. The guests at his fourteen-course dinners were political bosses, wealthy industrialists, military men, lobbyists, and representatives of European royalty, one of whom was the American representative for King Leopold of Belgium.

Always a fastidious dresser, he had eighty-two suits hanging in his White House closet. After a luxurious vacation paid for by the king of Belgium, President Arthur gave the United States the dubious distinction of becoming the first sovereign nation to give diplomatic recognition to the Congo Free State, King Leopold's spurious claim to a huge chunk of Africa that was later renamed the Belgian Congo. Only decades later did the world learn that the Belgian Congo was Leopold's private real estate deal from which he extracted millions in rubber and gold and enslaved or killed an estimated 6 million African laborers. As Adam Hochschild points out in *King Leopold's Ghost*, the money did not go to the Belgium treasury, but went instead to the king's personal bank accounts. The Belgian Congo was a fictitious country imposed on Africa by the king in order to extract a personal fortune.

In America a similar fever for land and mineral wealth gripped speculators as well as the compulsion to contain nomadic Natives onto fixed reservation lands and to remove them from lands that could be valuable for farming, ranching, or mining. Among Arthur's dinner guests were investors who were willing to pay for access to public lands in the western territories. Oklahoma's Indian Territory, for example, was especially prized. Arthur authorized the opening of five hundred thousand acres of Creek and Winnebago lands in Oklahoma to speculators, homesteaders, and ranchers. Although his act was declared illegal after Arthur was out of office, the displaced Winnebago and Creek Indians, removed to Oklahoma by treaty and guaranteed their lands "in perpetuity," were overwhelmed by a flood of white settlers. They had no redress.

Farther west, in the territories of New Mexico and Arizona, said to be especially rich in minerals, America had its own version of Leopold's Congo. The first historical documents that refer to Black Mesa are in Spanish, one of them written by a Spanish priest who entered a Hopi village in 1540 as part of an exploratory party from Coronado's expedition to discover gold for the Spanish crown. Three centuries later, the documents in English are maps of the huge area the United States extracted from Mexico after its victory in the war of 1848. By 1879 two specific government maps referred to Black Mesa. One is called *Territory of Arizona*, published by the General Land Office, and refers to a "Proposed Reservation for the Moqui [Hopi] and Other Indians." The other is a map called *Navajo Country* and marks all the mineral resources of the area.*

---

* The *Territory of Arizona* map includes a carefully drawn rectangle for the Navajo Indian reservation as determined by the Treaty of June 1868 after the Navajo had been removed from their lands in New Mexico and imprisoned for four years at a labor camp called Bosque Redondo. The *Navajo Country* map, dated 1879, is a detailed topographic map of the northeastern corner of Arizona, part of a report organized by US Indian inspector Howard that identified the location of all the mineral resources of the area. Navajo Country is delineated by rivers—by the San

In the 1880s public lands in the western territories were the equivalent of start-up technology companies today. It was during this period that the Black Hills of South Dakota were claimed for gold miners and the Sioux Indians chased north to reservations. The gold mountain in Ledeville, which is still producing gold (and was the model for the television series *Deadwood*), was the source of the Hearst family fortune. (The Hearst newspapers came later.) Millions of acres of Indian treaty lands were lost. Half of the entire Navajo Tribe, for example, which had been prosperous and living in northern New Mexico, had been rounded up by Kit Carson and his battalion of soldiers, marched 350 miles to the New Mexico border at Bosque Redondo, and imprisoned in a desolate labor camp near Fort Sumner. Their lands were believed to be rich in gold.

The White House Solution

In 1882 the superintendent of Indian affairs came to President Arthur with a problem in that same corner of Arizona Territory. It was about establishing a reservation for the Hopi Indians. For a variety of reasons, they had never had a reservation boundary that enclosed their lands. The superintendent also showed him the several maps along with correspondence from his Indian agent in Keams Canyon. The current agent, J. R. Fleming, was facing complaints from the Hopi because of white men believed to be Mormon missionaries who were coming into their villages, harassing them about religion, and claiming lands the Hopi had farmed. "The lands most desirable for the Moquis," wrote Agent Fleming, "and which were cultivated by them 8 or 10 years

---

Juan and Colorado Rivers to the north and the Little Colorado River and the Rio Puerco to the south. The mineral and coal deposits of the region were well known and well marked, even in 1879. Howard labeled the exact locations of the coal, copper, and timber. Both maps indicate a region at the Utah border labeled *diamond fields*. The diamonds were never found, but the coal lay so close to the surface that it could be seen squeezing out through the layers of canyon walls. Even then both the Hopi and Navajo Indians used coal for fires, as did the Indian boarding schools on the reservation.

ago, have been taken up by the Mormons and others." The agent was powerless to do anything because without a federal reservation boundary, he was without authority. The agent had threatened to resign.

In addition, the Indian trader in Keams Canyon, Thomas Keams, reported problems with Navajo Indians stealing the Hopi corn and crops from their fields in the dry washes. A previous Indian agent, who was impatient with the amount of time the Hopi spent on their religious ceremonies and dances in their plazas calling for rain, had recommended resettling all the Hopi on an entirely new reservation down on the Little Colorado River, where they would have plenty of water and wouldn't need to spend so much time in ceremonies. That solution was considered impractical because the Hopi had lived there for centuries and would never agree to move.

The new Hopi reservation that the superintendent proposed, however, was approximately thirty-six square miles and enclosed all the Hopi villages and some of the dry washes where they grew crops. The Hopi used a system of dry farming that drew on the water from spring rains that sank beneath the soil in dry washes but could be tapped by corn plants with long roots. (This system is still in use.) A much larger reservation area had been proposed by the current agent. Although no record exists of the conversation between President Arthur and his Indian superintendent, other correspondence and maps show that there had been lively discussion about the possible mineral resources of the area and that the Interior Department had a series of maps showing where the mineral resources were located. The hand-drawn map called *Navajo Country*, which extended from northwestern Arizona all the way to Monument Valley, identified all the valuable mineral resources—copper and coal and timber as well as "diamond fields." The other government map referring to Black Mesa, called *Territory of Arizona*, included a carefully drawn rectangle for the Navajo Indian Reservation. The great difference in the two maps was that the "Navajoe [sic] Indian Reservation of 1868" had no minerals within it.

A letter accompanying the 1879 map *Navajo Country* from government surveyor A. M. Stephen noted, "The only minerals discovered in this region are coal and copper." He informed his superior, Indian inspector Howard, also a general in the US Army, that "the coal deposit lies between Oraibi and Moenkopi." He continued to describe the inhabitants. "There are 1000 Hopi, 300 Navajos and some Paiutes. The only white people . . . are about twenty families of Mormons at Moenkopi and Tuba City."

Chester Arthur immediately grasped what his superintendent did not, namely, that if those twenty Mormon families were allowed to continue to settle and improve their lands—as Brigham Young and the Mormon leaders had directed them to do—they would be legally entitled to the mineral wealth beneath those lands. If those twenty Mormon families remained, they could, according to the provisions of the Homestead Act of 1863, file a claim for 160 acres for free; if they planted trees, they could file for another 160 acres; and if they irrigated and improved desert land, as the Desert Land Act of 1877 allowed, they could file claim to an additional 640 acres. In total they would thereby gain title to whatever mineral resources lay beneath the surface. Multiply those claims by twenty families, and a potential fortune in valuable mineral resources would be lost. But if those same lands were designated as federal reservation lands, they would be removed from the public domain and closed to white settlement.

No stranger to the alchemy of transforming government land into personal wealth, Chester Arthur had the Executive Order drawn up that created a 3,900-square-mile federal reservation known as the 1882 Executive Order Reservation. The order described the 2,508,800 acres of the reservation boundaries and proclaimed that the "tract of country in the territory of Arizona . . . is hereby withdrawn from settlement and sale and set apart for the use and occupancy of the Moqui (Hopi) and other such Indians as the Secretary of the Interior may see fit to settle thereon." The Executive Order is dated December 16, 1882, and signed by Chester A. Arthur.

The same year that Chester Arthur signed the Executive Order Reservation for northern Arizona, Thomas Edison electrified J. P. Morgan's mansion in New York. One square mile of Manhattan was lit up by tungsten lightbulbs, replacing gaslights. The energy source came from the coal-fired Pearl Street Generating Station. With Morgan's financial backing for Edison's coal-fired generating stations, electricity systems spread to cities throughout the country. Coal lit up America.

Chester Arthur had kept control of the coal resources of the region for another day. The question was, when would that day arrive? And who would be able to access the mineral wealth?

CHAPTER 6

THE INDIAN LAWYER AND A BRIEF HISTORY OF COAL

Coal is a portable climate. It can make Canada as warm as Calcutta.

—*Ralph Waldo Emerson*

That day of reconnecting Black Mesa with the White House began to dawn in 1950, some sixty-eight years later, when John Boyden arrived on the Hopi mesas. Boyden was part of a new generation of Mormons—a millionaire attorney, a Mormon bishop from Salt Lake City, and one of the most knowledgeable lawyers in the country about Indian law. Having been born and brought up in Coalville, Utah, whose coal mines sustained Salt Lake City, he also had a special affinity with coal. In the years between President Chester A. Arthur and President Harry S. Truman, the United States had been transformed. The country had 150 million people instead of 50 million. It had fought two world wars, and it was the world's leading industrialized nation. Coal had been the fuel that drove industrialization.

Many people mistakenly think coal use has faded away or died out since the Industrial Revolution. In *The Quest*, Daniel Yergin's exhaustive and influential book on energy sources, he points out that this is faulty thinking: "Since 2000, though not recognized, the biggest increase in global energy output has come from coal—double that from oil and triple that from natural gas." In 2012 the US Geological Survey published a graph of America's coal use with an upward arc that was almost a ninety-degree right angle. In 2013 British Petroleum (BP) published its annual *Statistical Report of World Energy Use*, showing that coal use not only equaled oil in volume, but had increased more than any other fuel.

The United States is second only to China in its consumption of coal. The BP report points out that the United States and North America have the largest coal reserves in the world. It also estimates that America has 104 years of energy from recoverable coal. This is good news for our energy expectations, bad news for the atmospheric carbon that is surrounding the planet and pushing global temperatures into the danger zone.

The major impetus in coal use has come from increasing electricity demand by a growing population that uses ever more electrical devices. Unlike oil, natural gas, coal, uranium, or the sun, electricity is not an energy source. It is a commodity, produced only by converting other resources into electrical energy. One hundred and thirty years after Thomas Edison electrified Manhattan, computers, smartphones, tablets, the Internet, and the wired world of the twenty-first century require ever more electricity, its energy source from coal-fired power plants largely invisible.

In reality, America still gets more than 40 percent of its electricity from coal. In the arid cities of the West, electricity is doing more than running air conditioners and computers. It is also pumping water. Coal-fired energy is running the pumps that suck water from distant rivers and deliver it to the urban centers of the Southwest. Without electricity to pump water from water sources hundreds of miles away, Las Vegas, Phoenix, and metropolitan Los Angeles wouldn't exist as the population centers they are today.

Earlier in my career I had been an assistant secretary of environmental affairs for the state of Massachusetts, and I spent a lot of time dealing with issues that fall under the heading of "energy infrastructure." It was the 1970s and the peak of the debate over nuclear power. (The last American nuclear power plant was licensed in 1976.) I remember the head of Boston Edison furiously telling me that my boss, the governor, was a Luddite for refusing to approve more nuclear power plants. "How any sane man can't recognize the need for nuclear power I don't understand." Actually, the governor was ahead of his time in recognizing that nuclear power was too expensive, was politically problematic, and had not solved the key issue of how to dispose of spent nuclear fuel. It was the first time, however, I realized how much of our electricity came from coal. As President Jimmy Carter rightly said, "America is the Saudi Arabia of coal."

A Brief History of Coal

If you watched the opening ceremonies of the 2012 London Summer Olympics, you saw a remarkable reenactment of the power of coal in transforming rural England into the central locale of the Industrial Revolution. The ceremonies at the Olympic Stadium opened with pastoral green fields filled with thatched cottages, hedgerows, farm fences, grazing sheep, and all the elements of the rural English countryside of romantic memory. In minutes the green fields were rolled up and replaced with high smokestacks belching smoke and flames. Out of a huge oak tree emerged hundreds of soot-covered coal miners smeared with coal dust. The center of the stadium magically filled with the machinery of the industrial age—beam engines, iron smelters, a blacksmith's forge, textile looms, and a waterwheel. In fifteen minutes producer Danny Boyle (director of *Slumdog Millionaire*) had compressed four centuries of English history into a human story, a history that we are still living. He showed how the genie of coal raised up Anglo-Saxon civilization and made possible all the forces that came later—the empire, the navy, the many different peoples of the Commonwealth, "the civilizing force" of Britain through education, law, and English literature. As Barbara Freese writes in *Coal: A Human History*, "Coal was no mere fuel, and no mere article of commerce. It represented humanity's triumph over nature—the foundation of civilization itself."

Although the year 1530 is best known for Henry the Eighth's successful effort to divorce his wife Catherine of Aragon, marry Anne Boleyn, throw off the Catholic Church of Rome, and establish the Anglican Church of England of which he was the head, it was also a year when there were *6.5 billion fewer people* on the planet than there are today. And it was the year that England began using coal in a more systematic way as heating and cooking fuel. At the time, England had a total population of 3 million and was cold, rainy, and poor. The pope in Rome owned more than a third of England's real estate and derived an income three times that of the Crown. One of the church's income-producing properties was a series of small-scale coal mines near Newcastle, in northern England, at the mouth of the river Tyne.

The local bishop had his serfs—both the nobility and the Roman Catholic bishops still had serfs—digging out surface coal from the riverbanks to sell as a heating fuel. The coal was smoky and had a rank odor from its high sulfur content, but was in demand when firewood was scarce. The Catholic clergy, corrupt and lazy, were not interested in mining technologies or in improving the lot of the coal merchants, former serfs who had purchased their freedom and a coal lease.

After Henry appropriated most of the Catholic Church's property for the Church of England, his administrators, looking for new sources of revenue, rewrote the terms of the leases to the advantage of the Newcastle merchants so that the more coal they produced, the higher their "royalty fees." More money motivated the coal merchants to innovate. Soon coal was being loaded onto barges, floated down the river Tyne to the port, where it was loaded onto coal transport boats, colliers, and shipped to London to be delivered to the surrounding manor estates of the nobility. The nobility had fireplaces, so the coal smoke and the sulfurous gases dispersed up the chimney. Coal was a reliable heating source for their drafty manor houses. But common people, who lived in thatched-roof houses with an open fire pit and no chimney, had no protection from the smoke or the unpleasant smell from the sulfur. Common people disliked coal and refused to use it.

Other external forces, however, soon changed their minds. First was the increasing scarcity and expense of firewood. England's great forests were being cut down at an alarming rate. Firewood for heating, cooking, building, and charcoal for smelting became scarce and expensive. (The designation of "the king's wood" was an effort to save some of the great trees of the old forests.) The second was a change in climate.

CLIMATE CHANGE

By the time Henry died and his daughter Elizabeth I took the throne in 1558, Europe had entered into a little Ice Age that would last until the 1700s. The Thames froze, as did canals in the Netherlands. Caused by an increase in the Atlantic ice pack and a change in ocean currents, the drop in temperature created a great demand for heating fuel. Ordinary people began to install stoves or chimneys in their homes and got used to burning coal. As the amount of coal burning increased, the air quality in London began to deteriorate. The air over London often had a yellow tinge from sulfur, and its famous fog was formed by coal particulates suspended in moist air. The fog was so dense that people walked into the Thames and horse-drawn carriages ran over pedestrians. At the same time, while the demand for coal was increasing, the ability to supply coal was diminishing.

As the surface coal was used up, the miners had to tunnel deeper to follow the coal seam. Once they were tunneling below the water table, they were in constant danger of drowning from flooded tunnels. At first they used buckets to remove the water, but the volume of water in the deeper tunnels was too great for a manual bucket brigade. Collapsing tunnels became the greatest single hazard. The coal merchants adapted a waterwheel used for milling. The horse-drawn waterwheel was used to sluice water out of the treacherous tunnels. The cold temperatures meant that the demand for coal kept increasing. The life span for miners was brief; children were used inside the tunnels to manually shut doors if there were water leaks.

Then in 1712 Thomas Newcomen, a commoner, had a brilliant inspiration. Why not use coal itself to fire a steam engine that would replace the horses to keep the waterwheel running? Such an engine could run twenty-four hours a day and never stop. Like oil pumped from the

Saudi Arabian sands to provide air-conditioning for the magnificently impractical glass skyscrapers in a scorching desert, coal was so plentiful in northern England it didn't matter how much coal Newcomen's steam engines used. Coal was both the problem and the solution.

Newcomen's engine did the work of fifty horses, could run for twenty-four hours at a time, and could pump from much deeper tunnels. By the 1760s Newcomen's steam engines were pumping water out of coal mines all over England and Scotland. (Alas, Newcomen was not given the credit he deserves for his invention, largely because of his class. His portrait was never painted and his grave has been lost because the institutional scientific body of the era, members of the Royal Society of London, didn't believe that a commoner could be "the most inventive intellect of the era.") The increased transport of coal made Newcastle (Tynemouth) a major port and shipbuilding center and stimulated both the growth of the navy to protect the coal transport boats and the development of maritime technologies.

The Newcomen pumping engine, however, had limitations. It was inefficient and used huge amounts of coal. Because of the quantities of coal required, the engine was limited to use at the mines themselves. Then in 1776, a year better known in America for the Declaration of Independence and the colonies' split from England, the steam engine took a qualitative leap forward. It was improved to such a degree that it left the mines and became, in coal historian Barbara Freese's words, "an all-purpose industrial workhorse." The new engine was called "the Watt."

James Watt, a Scot with some wealthy backers, stood on Newcomen's metaphorical shoulders and devised a steam engine that was four times as efficient as the Newcomen engine. With its fuel efficiency, it liberated the engine from the mines and allowed the Watt steam engine to become an all-purpose power source—for iron smelters, for wagons on rails (railroads), and for factories. Textile mills, which, of necessity, had been located on rivers because they were dependent on water-power, moved to new locations and became huge factories in new cities. Manchester, for example, whose textile trade began with a guild of Flemish weavers who moved there in the fourteenth century, became a city of factories unlike any in the world, the world's first industrialized city, employing thousands of people under one roof, producing textiles of cotton and linen. Manchester was the template for Lowell, Massachusetts, America's first industrial city (1820–1821), and cotton textiles were the foundation of America's Industrial Revolution.

One German factory owner sent his son to Manchester to learn the textile business. Young Frederick Engels wanted to be a professor of political philosophy, but he did as his father requested and went to England to learn the textile manufacturing business. At the same time, he was appalled by the conditions of the laborers in Manchester and the economics of capitalism. He wrote articles about the bleak living conditions, the environmental degradation, and the political economy of how the profits of the merchants were never shared with the workers who produced the wealth. In 1844 he published *The Condition of the Working Class in England* in a German publication whose editor was Karl Marx. After Marx moved to London, Engels continued working at the Manchester mill to earn an income that could support them both in their research and writing about industrial England.

Although other European countries rushed to copy England's industrial system, England had a fifty-year head start and didn't stop innovating. Its government ignored the smog, the deaths from inhaling coal dust, asthma and respiratory ailments, diseases like rickets that came from lack of exposure to sun, and the polluted air that enveloped London and other industrial cities. Thousands died from asthma attacks, emphysema, bronchitis, and secondary heart conditions that arose from breathing problems. Daylight was often so dark because of smog, it required gaslights to be burned all day. One observer sent from India to England to study their industrial system described the smog-covered cities and wrote back, "The sun may never set on the English empire, but it never shines in England."

England's culture enforced the values that powered the industrial way of life:

- The desire to conquer nature,
- a faith in technology,
- a belief in private enterprise,

+ tolerance for the misery of the working class,
+ and a conviction that their nation had a larger destiny as a
  world power.

These values, needless to say, had crossed the Atlantic, where Anglo-Americans were rapidly industrializing. Equally important, America had astonishing amounts of coal, even more than Britain.

In the United States huge coal beds ran the length of the Appalachian mountain chain, from Pennsylvania to Alabama, with an especially hard coal called anthracite at either end that was used for smelting steel. Consequently, America's steel industry grew up in Pittsburgh and Birmingham. Another massive coal deposit of bituminous coal that was 85 percent carbon ran from Illinois through Indiana and deep into Kentucky. Known collectively as the Illinois Basin, it was in Illinois that Peabody Coal Company got its start. (The enormous coalfields in the western states that parallel the Rockies weren't mined until after World War II.)

PEABODY COAL COMPANY

Francis Peabody started the Peabody Coal Company in 1883, the year after Chester Arthur signed the Executive Order. A Yale graduate, the son of a prominent Chicago lawyer, he began his career as a banker.* From a financial vantage point he saw coal as an investment of the future, particularly the bituminous coal of the Illinois Basin. He started the Peabody Coal Company with two partners and bought them out by 1890. Peabody was a coal retailer, buying coal from the mines in Carbondale and transporting it by rail to sell to Chicago home owners and businesses for heat. In addition to coal as a heating fuel, coal was the power source for America's ever-expanding railroads.

At the turn of the century, a major new market for coal appeared: electricity generating stations. Thomas Edison's innovation had spread

---

* Francis Peabody of Boston, who was one of the founders of Kidder Peabody & Co., an investment bank, was not a relative.

to other cities. Light was what attracted people to cities. Chicago's World Exposition of 1892 was called the "White City" because the exhibition buildings covered in white stucco were illuminated at night by electric streetlamps. By 1913 Francis Peabody's Peabody Coal Company owned several mines and had won a long-term contract to supply Chicago Edison, a major electric utility, with coal. As the century unfolded, the demand for electricity was unstoppable.

Peabody's business evolved into the production of electricity as well as the mining of coal. Rate setting, plant siting, distribution systems, peak loads, use projections—all were factors in Peabody's contract negotiations and coal pricing. From a small Illinois operation to a dominant force in the industry, Peabody Coal became the owner of more than thirteen mines and supplied the major electricity utilities in the country. Francis Peabody was in the business of power—generation, transmission, distribution.

The marketing innovation that Francis Peabody brought to the coal industry was to precontract the coal supply to the utilities at a fixed price. The benefit to the utilities was that they were protected from changes in price and spot market fluctuations; the benefit to Peabody was that his company had a known amount of coal it needed to produce every year. With new contracts, the company bought more mines. These long-term, high-volume contracts put Peabody Coal ahead of most other coal companies. By the time of Francis Peabody's death in 1922, his company had contracts with major utilities throughout the country and owned the largest mines in the Great Basin states. He had a personal fortune of $35 million ($487 million today) and a business fortune of $75 million ($1 billion). The coal industry's relationship with its workers, however, was among the worst of any in the country—hostile labor relations, harsh working conditions, lax mine safety, health issues, and frequent strikes. Like Britain, America's coal industry had a high tolerance for the treacherous working conditions and poor pay for its miners. Peabody Coal was no different.

By the 1950s Peabody Coal was the eighth-largest coal producer in the country and had added many more mines and more utilities to its portfolio. Led by Merl Kelce, a former coal miner who had held many jobs for Peabody, its headquarters had moved from Illinois to Henderson, Kentucky, where it had some of its largest mining operations. But in 1966 Peabody began a global growth spurt that led it to become the largest coal company in the world. Kelce was able to buy the leases on Black Mesa, Arizona, at the time considered the largest untouched coal reserve in the country. (Powder River, Wyoming, and the Montana mines were still in the future.) Kelce had purchased the leases from a Salt Lake City exploration company called Sentry Royalty Company, now a subsidiary of Peabody Coal. Industry journalists thought he had paid too much because the coal deposit lay beneath Hopi and Navajo Indian reservation lands, and many thought the leases could not be exercised. The business journalists did not know about John Boyden.

John Boyden and the Black Mesa Leases

John Boyden had arrived on Black Mesa to recruit the Hopi tribe as a client for his legal services. As one of the lawyers who had just successfully helped the Ute Indians of Utah and Colorado receive the largest financial judgment ever entered against the US government, he was seeking to find another Indian client with a good case to take before the Indian Land Claims Commission. Later some people mistakenly thought Boyden and his partner, Ernest Wilkinson, did the Ute work pro bono, for free. In fact, the two lawyers shared a fee of $2,794,606 ($25.4 million in current dollars), at a time when $1 million really meant something.

With the Ute case settled and his $1.4 million safely in the bank ($12.5 million today), John Boyden knew that Indian land-claims cases could be highly profitable work. The Claims Commission was a quasi-judicial body whose legislated five-year existence was due to expire in December 1951, so Boyden had no time to waste. (Congress subsequently extended the commission's existence until 1978, when all remaining cases were transferred to the US Court of Claims.)

He went first to the Navajo Tribal Council in Window Rock because he had spent time on the Navajo reservation in the 1940s as an observer for the FBI and knew their legal system. But someone on the Navajo Tribal Council remembered Boyden's earlier role as a US attorney in enforcing the disastrous and devastating livestock reduction of the 1930s ordered by John Collier in Utah's San Juan River section of the Navajo reservation. Theoretically, the livestock reduction was a policy instituted to prevent overgrazing and to encourage land conservation. It had, however, a more immediate rationale: to prevent silt buildup behind the newly opened Hoover Dam. In its precipitous descent from the Colorado Rockies, the Colorado River carried so much sediment that the dam engineers were afraid the dam would silt up before they could build the already planned second dam upstream, at Glen Canyon. During the depths of the Depression, in what seemed incomprehensible to the Navajo families, tens of thousands of Navajo sheep and goats were shot and burned, devastating the families who owned them. "Bought, shot and left to rot," said former Navajo tribal chairman Peter MacDonald, who was a child in that section of the reservation in the 1930s and whose family was one of those deeply affected. The hundreds of once prosperous, but now impoverished, Navajo families never recovered. The Navajo Tribal Council told Boyden, "No thanks."

Undeterred, Boyden left Window Rock and continued west on Route 264, heading toward Keams Canyon and the Hopi Indian Agency, where the Hopi lived in eleven separate pueblo villages at the southern tip of Black Mesa. There, long peninsulas of sandstone cliffs jut out into the flat desert floor like the ocean headlands they once were. The layers that compose Black Mesa slope at such an angle that water from the aquifer flows out in springs at the edge of the cliffs. Each Hopi village was located with a spring for water, and each village—Walpi, Hano, Mishnognovi, Shipaulaove, Shungopovi, Oraibi, Hotevilla, Bakabi, and Moenkopi—also developed with separate leadership traditions, priests, and political cultures. Although the Bureau of Indian Affairs continued to deal with the Hopi as a tribe, their history was more like the separate pueblo villages of New Mexico.

"It is well to remember," wrote Harold Colton, the director of the Museum of Northern Arizona, in a 1939 land-use report,

that the Hopi Tribe exists only in the eyes of the Indian
Bureau and the general public. The Hopi themselves do not
think of themselves in terms of a tribe. They owe allegiance
only to the village in which they live and, with a couple of
exceptions, the villages are as independent of one another
as certain Rio Grand pueblos like Santo Domingo, Sia,
Cochiti and Acoma, which are bound together by culture
and language. There is no political unity. It is, therefore,
necessary to deal with each village separately. The Indian
Bureau after sixty years of struggle is just learning this fact.

Unfortunately, the BIA had not learned. In Keams Canyon the
Hopi Indian agent, H. E. O'Harra, was still hoping for a centralized
Hopi tribal council. He gave Boyden the bad news and good news.
The good news was that the Hopi certainly had a good land-claims
case. The bad news was that they had no functional tribal council with
authority to hire him. Even though Hopi voters had voted in 1936 to
adopt a constitution and elect a Hopi tribal council, 70 percent of the
voters had stayed home. Consequently, the council that had been recognized by the BIA was ignored by the majority of Hopi and had not
met for more than a decade.

Agent O'Harra suggested that Boyden visit several of the Hopi
villages, like Hotevilla, where some of the more "progressive" Hopi
lived. Perhaps Boyden could interest them in a land-claims case.*
Soon Boyden was traveling through the villages, meeting with some
of the progressive, Christianized Hopi, who had a history of cooper-
ating with the Bureau of Indian Affairs. Among the most prominent
was Emory Sekaquaptewa, who had been educated in Indian boarding

---

* The federal government set up tribal councils in the 1930s and '40s as a way of
organizing Indian tribal structures to fit into the American legal system. John
Collier sent author Oliver LaFarge to the Hopi to help them write a constitution.
In 1936 the Hopi held a referendum on adopting a constitution and an electoral
system, but only a third of eligible voters participated. Consequently, even though
the BIA counted the small majority vote as approval, the tribal council was out of
sync with cultural forces of clan and village.

schools, spoke excellent English, and was in favor of a modern tribal government. As his son, and future Hopi tribal chairman, Abbott Sekaquaptewa said, "My father was a driving force to get the tribe back to functioning in the 1940s. . . . The BIA people told him that what [he] really needed to do was organize the Tribal Council. They said that is the only entity that the federal government would listen to."

Abbott's father gathered together some members of the disbanded tribal council to hear Boyden's explanation about the special commission set up in Washington to hear Indian land claims. Boyden told them about his success with the Ute Indians and how it paved the way for other Indian tribes to make a claim for lost land. He warned that the deadline to file a case was only months away and they would have to act quickly. Abbott Sekaquaptewa said, "Boyden went through the villages, holding meetings and talking to people about the Indian Land Claims Commission. He explained that the filing deadline was pretty close and if they wanted to file a claim they needed to act now. He got the support of some village leaders in addition to the disbanded tribal council . . . and an oral contract was entered into with the tribe."

A letter signed by the Hopi traditional priests that appeared in a local Gallup newspaper and was forwarded to Senator Goldwater said that Boyden simply wrote up a contract and had the assembled people agree to it by voice vote. "We have explained plainly," wrote Dan Katchongva for the traditional priests, "how the so-called tribal council approved the resolution which attorney John S. Boyden drew up on the spot. . . . This was done without consulting the Hopi people. The majority of the Hopis are against him as a lawyer." Another letter written by Hopi Caleb Johnson added that there were only four legitimate members of the tribal council: "On top of all this the chairman of the tribal council is a man who does not have a good record and has been convicted of a felony in a federal court."

Boyden himself knew his oral contract would not hold up for long if there was a legal challenge, so he moved quickly to transform the contract into an official written document and the tribal council members into an official council. Because all the new tribal council members were unelected, he arranged for all sixteen Hopi men to travel to Salt Lake City to be officially sworn in by a federal judge. A famous photograph taken in a Salt Lake City courtroom shows half the Hopi members in sunlight and half in shadow, half in traditional dress, half in white shirts and ties. Boyden is sitting on the dark side, his face half in shadow. The calendar on the wall reads July 12, 1951.

Land claims were not a straightforward issue among the Hopi villages. As Harold Colton wrote in his land-use report, "Several recent efforts to settle the boundary, such as the meeting at Washington, failed because the Hopi made the boundary a religious question and demanded all of northeast Arizona from the Little Colorado to the Four Corners." In other words, the Hopi had a different view of the land they were entitled to because they included all their religious shrines rather than settlements. (Some of these shrines extend into Mexico.)

John Boyden would change that. The boundary issue with the Navajo had been a subject since the government had relocated (by military force) the Navajo from northern New Mexico onto a reservation in eastern New Mexico, almost at the Texas border. After the Civil War, in 1868, the US Army and the Navajo signed a treaty that released the Navajo to a small reservation that straddled the Arizona–New Mexico border and was too small for the number of people to be supported. Some extended families spread out into the interior of Black Mesa in sheepherding camps composed of multigenerational families. The Hopi lived in the cliff-top villages but dry farmed and grazed livestock in the dry washes many miles distant. The Hopi traded corn and vegetables for Navajo mutton. But conflicts arose when Navajo goats and sheep trampled Hopi crops or Navajo families spread out onto lands that the Hopi had farmed. A reservation boundary between the Hopi and the Navajo had never been settled, although many efforts had been made.

Among the many things that John Boyden did not tell his Hopi clients about the Ute case was that no actual land was ever returned. The $32 million settlement granted to the Ute Indians (of both Utah and Colorado) was for 1.5 million acres of lands taken by signed treaty but never paid for. Reimbursement was based on the price of land at the time it was taken in the 1880s, not on present market value, and the government placed many strings on how the Indians' money was disbursed—the Ute needed a business plan to explain how they were going to use the settlement money, while the lawyers got their fees immediately.

THE HOPI LAND CLAIMS CASE

Boyden did file a land claim for the Hopi and a few years later won a $5 million settlement for the tribe and another large fee for himself. Although he worked on a contingency basis, he was eventually well paid. (A Freedom of Information suit filed by the Native American Rights Fund revealed that Boyden received $2.7 million in total fees from the Hopi, equivalent to $16 million today.) Former Hopi chairman Abbott Sekaquaptewa said that Boyden expected to be paid. "We were a poor tribe," he told Anita Parlow. "We had no significant income. . . . So we were in a great need of money. For tribal operations—to build up the tribal organizations and to continue to have legal counsel." The Indian Claims Commission awards, however, had significant limitations about which Boyden had not advised his new clients. First, the Claims Commission law stipulated that *no return of actual land* was possible, a fact that the Hopi did not understand when they hired Boyden to file a "land claim" for them.* Second, the financial settlement was to be based on the *value of the land when it was taken in the nineteenth century*, not its market value in the middle of the twentieth century. Third, the law provided for attorneys' expenses and additional fees that were "not to exceed ten percent" of the monetary award. Finally, and most important, in accepting the financial settlement, the Indian tribes *relinquished forever* any title to aboriginal land.

---

* The Bureau of Indian Affairs had to approve the Claims Commission attorneys the tribes selected. The BIA generally recommended those lawyers they knew to be sensitive to the needs of the US government and energy companies. Before the Indian Claims Commission went out of business in 1978, it had facilitated many tribal mineral leases with large mining corporations by serving as a vehicle for inserting BIA-appointed lawyers into already weak tribal structures. Twenty-five tribes in the western states became known as the "energy tribes" because they held *30 percent of America's untapped mineral resources*, large deposits of oil, coal, uranium, and natural gas.

Where was the land? the Hopi council members asked. They thought they were going to get land, real land. Why else would people in their villages agree to hire a lawyer to file a suit? Why call it the Indian Land Claims Court if it can't give back land? (Actually, the Indian Land Claims Commission was its popular name, not its legal name.) The claims were all about lost land. Even though the Hopi Tribal Council was often called Boyden's puppet council, they didn't budge on this point. They wanted real land.

So Boyden was obliged to explain that once the Hopi cashed the government's check, they would relinquish all rights to any claim on aboriginal lands. So the Hopi refused to cash the check. Rather than return the check to the commission, Boyden worked out an agreement whereby the money would be put in a trust account in Salt Lake City in case a future tribal council saw things differently. The Hopi's check sat for years, earning interest, and by 1990 it was supposedly worth $11 million. Meanwhile, there was the question of how the Hopi, a people with a subsistence economy, could keep earning enough money to build tribal offices, pay salaries for tribal government, and pay Boyden's legal fees. By this time Boyden was also appointed as tribal attorney, a separate designation from claims attorney. In this role he was authorized by the BIA to give general legal advice and opinions on various possibilities for business development. He could draw up contracts for mineral leasing. The extent of the Black Mesa coal reserves had been confirmed since 1911. Mining was the most promising avenue for economic development, and it was this possibility that eventually took Boyden to the Department of the Interior to clarify the Hopi's right to issue mineral leases on the 1882 Executive Order Reservation. Coal mining had been an integral part of his life and the town where he grew up. As a Mormon it was also part of his religious belief that if there were minerals under the ground, you had to get them out and make the earth productive.

COALVILLE, UTAH

Although photographs of Boyden make him look like a small-town lawyer or a bank title attorney, he was an extremely ambitious man, politically, economically, and in terms of the Mormon Church. In fact, the word *ambitious* was the single adjective most often used to describe John Boyden, beginning when he was a teenager growing up in Coalville, Utah.

> When it comes to AMBITION, we will all have to take our hats off to this boy. . . . After being graduated from North Summit High School in June, he went to work on the section [railroad], a real day's work for most men, but not for John. Each night he comes home, gets on his wheel [bicycle] and takes care of his paper route. Not being satisfied with the day, he goes into the dark room and develops film for people about town. . . . [H]ere's hoping his fondest ambition will be realized, that of finishing the university course and thence to an eastern law school.

> *Summit County Bee,* Spring 1924

Coalville was a small, rural Mormon town in the Wasatch foothills that was noteworthy for an outcropping of coal that would prove to be a small tail on the monster coal deposit just over the border in Wyoming, later known as Powder River Basin. Boyden grew up understanding how coal could make a family and a town wealthy and prominent. He believed in coal.

When I visited Coalville in 2010, I found a semideserted town with empty storefronts on Main Street dotted by "For Lease" signs in the windows. The view from Boyden's old house included speeding trailer trucks winding through mountain passes, heading for Salt Lake City. I imagined that when Boyden was a boy, it was still an expansive green valley with rich agricultural fields and snow-topped mountains, punctuated by the train whistle of the Park City Railroad as it wound through mountain passes, carrying freight cars of gleaming coal. Today most automobiles are more likely to exit ten miles down the highway at Park City, a former silver-mining town that is now an overbuilt ski resort.

Boyden's family held prominent positions in the town. His grandfather, father, and uncles all held posts of importance in the town, the county, and the church: bishop of the Latter-day Saints (LDS) church, Coalville mayor, secretary for the Park City Railroad Company, Summit County tax assessor, clerk for the Utah Territorial Legislature, superintendent of schools, pharmacist and owner of the Boyden & Son Drug Store. The drugstore was such an important institution, it is now replicated in the city hall museum. It was in the drugstore that I found copies of John Boyden's stationery after he had moved his law offices to the Kennecott Building in Salt Lake City. By then Kennecott Copper had bought Peabody Coal and was one of the owners of the Black Mesa leases.

His grandparents were among the many land-hungry immigrants recruited in England who arrived in Utah during the pioneer era of the 1860s. They were sent to an agricultural settlement in the Wasatch foothills called Grass Creek. Salt Lake City, forty-five miles away, was largely treeless, bitterly cold in the winter, and desperate for heating fuel. Brigham Young, the Mormon president in Salt Lake City, offered a large reward to anyone who could find coal in the nearby Wasatch Mountains. Within a year some resourceful prospector located a rich coal seam in the foothills near Grass Creek, and soon hundreds of tons of coal were being extracted. With no railroad, the coal was loaded onto ox-drawn wagons, transported to Salt Lake, and sold for an extravagant $35 to $40 a ton. Coal became so profitable that in many families, the men worked as miners in the winter and farmed in the summer. Boyden's grandfather worked for the Park City Railroad, and the town became so wealthy from coal that Grass Creek was renamed Coalville and became the site of a Mormon temple. The memory of its early history with coal is still commemorated with a rail wagon filled with coal that sits outside city hall.

John Boyden grew up in his grandfather's house with an aunt, his parents, and several uncles. According to family lore, one day in the 1880s forty Shoshone Indians descended from the hills and did a "war dance" in front of Grandfather Boyden and the Mormon bishop. The two men, clearly outnumbered and wanting to negotiate the Indians' quick departure, gave them several head of cattle and sacks of flour. The official history of Summit County records this incident, but without the participation of Grandfather Boyden. (The Indians were probably starving because by then the sixty thousand Mormon settlers had shot all the game.) Boyden's daughter reports that from an early age, Boyden was interested in Indians and collected arrowheads and pieces of pottery he found in the mountains and in the property around the house. Coalville was on the migration route of Ute and Shoshone into Wyoming. (*Wasatch* means "pass" or "passage" in the Ute language.)

Boyden went to the University of Utah Law School, worked as a US attorney for sixteen years in Salt Lake City, and then in 1946 partnered with Washington, DC, attorney Ernest Wilkinson in the successful Ute claims case. After that he understood how a fortune could be made in representing Indians.

· · ·

Although Chester Arthur's 1882 Executive Order specified that the 3,900-square-mile reservation was for the Hopi (Moqui), it also included "for other Indians" as a general category. At the time an accompanying report estimated the number of Hopi to be eleven hundred, the Navajo at three hundred, and an uncounted number of Paiute—some fifteen hundred people in an area three-quarters the size of Connecticut.

The thousands of Navajo families who had settled within the interior of Black Mesa naturally claimed they were those "other Indians." Consequently, neither tribe had clear title to mineral leasing on the 1882 Executive Order Reservation land. And without clear title, no mining company would take a chance on signing a lease with one tribe that could be challenged by the other. Mining required so much capital investment, no energy company would buy leases that could not be exercised. Seven years before Boyden, Standard Oil of California had asked the BIA in 1944 which tribe owned—and therefore had authority to lease—the mineral deposits of the Executive Order Reservation.

In a letter of exceptional clarity, the BIA's legal counsel, Felix Cohen, had written an opinion for the secretary of interior. With the title "Ownership of the Mineral Estate in the Hopi Executive Order Reservation," Cohen set out the issues in a single-spaced seven-page report and concluded, "I therefore hold that the rights of the Navajos within the area who settled in good faith prior to October 24, 1936 are coextensive with those of the Hopis with respect to the natural resources of the reservation." In short, both the Hopi and the Navajo had equal rights to the subsurface minerals.

Boyden repeatedly petitioned the secretary of interior to revise Cohen's opinion so as to clarify the boundaries of Hopi and Navajo lands. Each time, the interior secretary and his legal counsel told Boyden that the determination of all Indian reservation boundaries lay solely with Congress. With typical thoroughness, Boyden studied the problem and came up with a bold, but ingenious, solution. At the time he knew as much as any lawyer in the country—except for his partner, Ernest Wilkinson, and Felix Cohen—about how the Indian Claims Commission had been set up and worked. Wilkinson had helped write the law that created it. Why not use the precedent of the Indian Claims Commission, with which he was uniquely familiar, to set up a special three-judge court to hear a "friendly" suit between the Hopi and Navajo? The court could hear the case, decide the boundaries that each tribe was entitled to, and go out of business. Boyden assumed he would win and the Hopi would be free to lease. All it would take was an act of Congress. This was not as difficult as it might appear.

Senator Goldwater's Office

John Boyden arrived in Barry Goldwater's office in 1956. Despite Goldwater's conservative Republican politics and Boyden's Democratic credentials—Boyden was a second-time Democratic candidate for governor of Utah—the two men got along. They were both westerners from the same class, prominent sons of prominent families, and about the same age. Boyden was a man with impressive legal credentials, an insider in the making of Indian law, and a man who craved the big stage. In addition, it was a period in the mid-1950s when another Utah senator and prominent Mormon, Arthur Watkins—the Republican chair of the Senate Indian Affairs Subcommittee—had succeeded in making termination of Indian tribes official government policy. Later viewed as an utterly shameful period in American Indian history, it was eventually repealed and the terminated tribes restored to federally recognized status, although many had lost their lands in the interim.*

Boyden presented his idea for introducing a bill that would create a special three-judge court to decide the boundaries within the 1882 Executive Order Reservation. What might have impressed Goldwater most about Boyden's idea for the special court was his success in the Ute case. He also would have been aware of Boyden's connections with Senator Watkins, the Mormon Church, Kennecott Copper, and Ernest Wilkinson's law firm. Wilkinson, Cragun, and Barker was a center for one of the important Mormon networks in Washington, and the firm's clients included the Mormon Church (before they had in-house counsel), Standard Oil of New Jersey, and Kennecott Utah Copper. Goldwater knew Kennecott well because he was supported by the mining interests in Arizona, and Kennecott, known for its intransigence in regard to labor issues, had a number of large copper mines and many labor troubles in Arizona. Wilkinson himself was well known in Washington because his firm specialized in land issues and hired former Interior Department attorneys (all Mormons) as staff. After success in the Ute case, Wilkinson's firm went on to represent more Indian tribes than any other law firm.

As Wilkinson's partner, Boyden and his associates in Salt Lake City had traveled to the Ute reservations, taken depositions, discovered old maps, found interpreters, researched correspondence between the Ute and Indian agents, dug around in the BIA archives, and managed the negotiations with three separate bands of the Ute Tribe. The

---

* During the official period of termination, 1953 to 1962, thirteen tribes and more than a hundred bands, communities, and California Mission Indians were terminated or lost many federal protections and services. In practice, termination meant that the tribes lost trust status and had to start paying taxes, often selling off land to meet tax obligations, and providing their own educational and health services. In 1961 the National Congress of American Indians met in Chicago and declared termination to be "the greatest threat to Indian survival since the military campaigns of the 1800s." Termination was officially ended in 1962 by the Kennedy administration.

presentation of research and historical correspondence was so detailed and extensive that one of the Justice Department attorneys on the losing side of the case said, "The amount of service and research performed by Wilkinson and his associates almost staggers our imagination. . . . I never saw anything like this in my life. I never expect to again." Interestingly, Wilkinson, who recorded this quote in his nine-hundred-page autobiography, did not share any praise or credit. He never mentions Boyden's firm, nor does he mention Felix Cohen's role in drafting the Claims Commission legislation. By 1956 Wilkinson himself was back in Utah as president of Brigham Young University but still listed "of counsel" on the firm's letterhead.

Boyden brought all this unique experience and a network of connections with him when he arrived in Goldwater's office. Goldwater might have also been impressed that Boyden was able to pull together a tribal council among the notoriously fractious Hopi. To outsiders the Hopi are the "people of peace." Among themselves they are known for many feuds and long-standing resentments and grievances.

THE MORMON CONNECTION

Although Senator Goldwater and attorney Boyden maintained that their bill was solely for "justice for the Hopi" and adamantly denied that the bill had anything to do with mineral leasing, the real intent was inadvertently made clear by freshman congressman Stewart Udall, their cosponsor in the House. Udall, who had just been elected to Congress from Tucson, where he and his brother Mo had been in law practice together, added an "interim leasing clause" that provided for royalty moneys from mining or oil drilling to be put "in trust accounts" for the Hopi and Navajo while the special three-judge court was deciding the case. The vice president of the Valley National Bank of Phoenix wrote Udall to request three copies of his version of the bill and congratulate him for his initiative. "A number of us have wondered for some time why it would not be possible for the . . . Bureau of Indian Affairs to lease the Hopi Navajo disputed lands while the oil boom is [under way]."

"Dear Tom," responded Udall, "I am enclosing a copy of my interim leasing amendment which is now pending before the committee. (Incidentally, Senator Goldwater's bill passed the Senate last week in its original form without an interim leasing provision.)" Although the bill for the three-judge court passed the Senate, it did not pass the House. For one thing, US Attorney General William P. Rogers (later secretary of state) opposed the bill, saying there was no legal issue to be decided, all reservation boundaries were the responsibility of Congress, and that it was an improper use of a three-judge court. For another, individual Hopi argued against it and tried to enlist Senator Carl Hayden of Arizona on their behalf. Caleb Johnson, a graduate of the University of California who was on his way to Princeton Seminary, asked Senator Hayden to open an investigation about how John Boyden and the tribal council came to power. "We have two problems out here," he wrote to the senator on March 5, 1957. "One is the Navajo and Hopi boundary issue. The other is the internal Hopi government problem. These are closely related."

Dan Katchongva sent another letter to Senator Goldwater, protesting his bill for a "court test of the so-called conflicting claims of the Navajo and Hopi. . . . If this bill becomes law it will destroy our Hopi way of life, religion and land. It will surely destroy the land and life of the Navajo."

The bill did not pass the first time around. But Goldwater and Udall introduced it again in 1958 without any mention of mineral leasing, and the second time it passed. Like a boat throwing off cargo to float free from a sand bar, the subsurface mineral wealth of Black Mesa was on its way to becoming electricity for Las Vegas, Phoenix, and Los Angeles. In 1959 Boyden and the Navajo counsel filed papers, the case was heard in 1961 (with the US Attorney's Office appearing in opposition), and in 1962 the decision was handed down.

If the conflict had really been about establishing a boundary, it could have been settled. But because it was about mining, it forced other issues, such as water rights and access to the coal seam and the growing populations of Phoenix and Tucson. It turned out that John Boyden was representing the Hopi at the same time he was representing Peabody Coal and soon Kennecott Copper. In any other state but Utah, he would have been a candidate for disbarment. (The canon of legal ethics prohibits a lawyer from representing two sides in the same legal issue as a clear conflict of interest.) But from the point of view of the Mormon religion, Boyden was fulfilling his religious duty at the highest level. As a devout Mormon, John Boyden saw Indians through the prism of the Mormon faith.

When a reporter asked Boyden what he felt his greatest life accomplishment was, he answered, "Being a true friend of the Lamanites." In this case, both friendship and Lamanite require definition in the context of the Mormon West.

CHAPTER 7

THE MORMON WEST

"Polygamy? Yes. Fundamentalists in the Mormon Church still practice polygamy, although the church doesn't condone it," the wife and manager of the motel was telling me. I was in Utah in a town called Big Water, somewhere north of Page, Arizona.

I had gone to see the Navajo Generating Station outside of Page and then stopped to take a tour of the Glen Canyon Dam. Glen Canyon was the second-biggest dam on the Colorado River, after Hoover Dam. Designed to provide water and hydroelectricity for the Upper Basin states (Utah, Wyoming, Colorado, and New Mexico), the reservoir behind Glen Canyon Dam was the second-largest man-made lake in the world after Lake Mead. Deciding that I should balance two days of looking at concrete, smokestacks, and turbines with some natural landscape, I drove north into Utah on my way to red-rock country and Bryce Canyon. But it got late and I was tired, so I stopped at a rather odd-looking motel made up of double-wide trailers that, I learned later, had once housed the construction workers building the Glen Canyon Dam.

The motel manager was young, fair, and pretty. She had three beautiful blonde daughters, ages somewhere between nine and thirteen, who had knocked on my door to return my credit card and then stood in the doorway silently staring. Is anything wrong? I asked. "We've never seen a woman traveling alone before," said the oldest. The three girls, all blue eyed and long-haired with perfect complexions, looked as though they could be waiting to go on set for an Ingmar Bergman movie.

I described this incident to their mother as I was getting ready to leave the next morning. She allowed that not many women traveled alone in Utah, at least not to Big Water. She acted as though I should have heard of the town, but I shook my head.

Big Water, I repeated. How big is this town? "Two hundred," she answered, adding, "and at least eighty are children under seven. Mayor Joseph believes in polygamy."

That's when I said, "Polygamy?" in a high voice. "This town is a center for fundamentalist Mormons," she continued in a matter-of-fact tone. "Like my father-in-law. He believed in polygamy. When he died, he had eleven wives and sixty-four children at his funeral."

I'm sure my eyes grew wide. "The family must have filled up the entire church," I said, trying to come up with some mild conversational response to this rather remarkable fact. I was having troubling keeping up my end of this conversation. I thought polygamy had died out in the 1890s when the Mormon Church outlawed it in order for Utah to become a state. One Mormon woman I knew in Boston told me that as a child, she used to visit the Navajo reservation with her mother in order to visit her grandmother. Her grandfather had returned his Navajo wives to the reservation and kept his Anglo wife and children in Salt Lake City.

The motel owner's wife expanded on the fundamentalist beliefs of her father-in-law and concluded with an interesting explanation of the Mormon diaspora. "It took forever to probate my father-in-law's will because he had property all over Utah and Arizona and Nevada. There are lots of Mormons in Arizona and Nevada. Idaho has the most Mormons after Utah and California. Pioneers went everywhere. With all those mouths to feed, they had to keep moving." She didn't believe in everything the Mormon Church did, she continued, but added approvingly, "It is a culture that supports its people."

She appeared remarkably curious and open, quite different from other Mormon women I had met in Utah and Nevada. They were careful and cautious in speaking with an outsider. She told me that she and her husband owned the motel but he had another job, so she pretty much ran it herself. She also seemed in no hurry to get back to work and interested in pursuing a conversation, so I asked where her daughters went to school. "The kids used to go to a school in Page. But when there were too many kids, Big Water built a school."

Did I have any children? she asked. One daughter. How many children did she and her husband have? "Ten, seven from his previous marriages. The three girls are ours." Then she offered, unprompted, that she and her husband had a monogamous marriage. I asked what a Jack Mormon was. I had recently read an interview about Stewart Udall, and he described himself as a Jack Mormon. "They believe in the culture, but they don't tithe. If a man doesn't tithe, he can't be part of the church."

"Where are you from?" I finally asked, deciding that she couldn't have been brought up in Utah. "My husband's from Utah, but I'm from Washington State. I find the desert a hard environment. I have to hug a tree every so often. But my kids all have alkali in their veins."

The Alkali Kingdom

Alkali is a soluble salt found in arid soils, a common ingredient in the lands of Utah and Nevada and the arid territory that make up what is still called the Great American Desert. It was the alkali soil along with lack of reliable water that made agriculture difficult in what otherwise should have been the Mormons' promised land. It is also what sent so many Mormons from these arid states into working for the Bureau of Reclamation, building dams, flood-control barriers, and irrigation systems throughout the West.* Reclamation meant reclaiming land from flood and irrigating desert into farmland. When Mormons lost their rich farm- and grazing lands in Missouri, Joseph Smith had asked the US government to reimburse the twelve thousand Mormons more than $1 million for farms and ranches taken from them illegally by the State

---

* The Bureau of Reclamation, still largely unknown in the East, was founded in 1902 to build and operate water projects in the western states. It should not be confused with the Office of Surface Mining Reclamation, which deals with land restoration from mining.

of Missouri. (The federal government said it had no jurisdiction. They would have to work it out with the state government.) Alkali soils were not what they expected when they moved west, crossing the Wasatch Mountains to the uninhabited lands beyond the Rockies where they planned to found their own Zion in the desert.

It is important to know that in 1847, when the Mormon pioneers began their legendary fifteen-hundred-mile journey from Illinois across the plains and over the Rocky Mountains to settle Salt Lake City, they were not going to Utah. There was no Utah.

They were going to Alta California, a vast, arid, mountainous region that belonged to Mexico and filled the map between the Rockies and the Sierra Nevada at the edge of California. This alkali kingdom was originally part of Spain and then part of Mexico after the Mexican War of Independence, lightly inhabited by Europeans and barely administered by Mexico. In the East, Alta California was known mainly for the cattle ranches that exported leather to the shoe factories of New England.

From the Mormon point of view, Alta California's status outside the boundaries and legal system of the United States was its main attraction. The Mormon leaders believed that once on the other side of the Rockies, they would be outside the US laws and free to set up a theocratic government, enjoy plural marriage, create their own laws, and live as they believed the Book of Mormon instructed them to live.

Their tormented experiences in the previous seventeen years—as they moved west from New York to Ohio, then to Missouri, and finally to Illinois—led them to believe they would be safe only after they were beyond the reach of the United States' legal system. When they first began planning the move in the 1840s, the territory of the United States ended at the Missouri border. After that, there were no roads, only tracks and trails—the Oregon Trail, the Santa Fe Trail. The Plains Indians were still dominant on the plains because the US Army under President Andrew Jackson was still occupied in clearing the Five Civilized Tribes from southeastern states in order to open up their lands for cotton production. Jackson, whose supporters included the richest men in the southern states, ordered the federal troops to join with state militias to forcibly move the Cherokee out of Georgia and the Choctaw, Creeks, Chickasaw, and Seminoles out of Mississippi, Alabama, and Florida. Their fertile lands became cotton plantations. After passage of the Indian Removal Act, the Natives were removed "legally" and forcibly marched to Indian Territory, in what are now Oklahoma, Arkansas, and Kansas. It wasn't until the 1860s, and the construction of transcontinental railroads, that the US Army began building forts along the routes of the Oregon Trail and negotiating treaties with the Plains Indians before confining them to reservations.

The second element to consider was that many of the Saints', as Mormons called themselves, troubles in Missouri and Illinois arose from apostate Mormons, that is, disaffected Mormons who became disillusioned but refused to leave the church quietly. When former Mormon believers left the church, they often sued in state courts to recover the titles to properties that they had signed over to the Mormon leadership. Called the United Order, the Mormons' system of communal ownership meant private property became church property. During the relatively short life of the early Mormon Church—founded and led by Joseph Smith from 1830 to 1844—the new converts pledged their wealth to the church. If they died, the church, not their children, inherited. When someone wanted to leave the church—and they did for many reasons—or if their children tried to retrieve their inheritance, the only recourse was to sue through the state legal system. In the process of making their case to state attorneys, the apostate Mormons revealed Joseph Smith's proclivity for marrying multiple young, attractive female converts (many of them with money), the widespread practice of plural marriage among the leadership, illegal land speculation, and the practice of doing business only with "their own kind."

Evidence of polygamy came out in court documents when disaffected Mormons testified that they had personally seen or read about Smith's revelation granting every man the privilege of "marrying ten virgins." They described the different kinds of marriage among the leaders, some sanctified in the temple, some for eternity, some in name only. They told about Smith's sermons in which he included reference to polygamy mentioned in the Koran (permission for a man to have four wives), and he frequently preached on the polygamous marriages of Jacob in the Old Testament. He is believed to have begun his first polygamous marriage in 1835 and disclosed this fact as a revelation to his closest followers sometime in 1839, when he encouraged them to take additional wives as well. At first cautiously, then enthusiastically, most of the top leadership had followed his lead into the institution of plural marriage. (Plural marriage was only for the men; women couldn't have multiple husbands.)

The issue of polygamy engaged the opposition of disaffected Mormons as well as disapproving Gentiles. The difference was that the disaffected Mormons, unlike the Gentiles, didn't want to bring about the downfall of the church. They wanted to reform Joseph Smith and the church. To that end, they started a reform movement.

The Mormons' closed economic system and other aspects of what historians have described as "evangelical socialism" enflamed hostility among their neighbors and created confrontations so violent—in Missouri their land was confiscated and outlying farms were torched, killing thirteen people—that the Mormon leaders believed they had no choice but to leave the United States. Like the seventeenth-century Pilgrim separatists who left England to found a theocracy in Plymouth, Massachusetts, the nineteenth-century Mormons wanted to found a theocratic community "beyond the Rocky Mountains." Their vision was to create a Christian church in the form that they believed it to have been in the days of Jesus Christ, thus the naming of their church as the Church of Jesus Christ of Latter-day Saints.

In their quest for a theocratic state, Mormons violated the separation of church and state embedded in the US Constitution. Their private armed militias and their elaborate system of plural marriage, which Joseph Smith denied in public but expounded in private as a divine revelation, seemed to be legal evidence that the Mormon leaders saw themselves bound by religious revelation rather than the US Constitution.

At the time of his death on June 27, 1844, Joseph Smith was a candidate for president of the United States, a lieutenant general commanding a private army of four thousand armed men (the Nauvoo Legion), the president of the Council of Fifty (a political arm of the church), the secret husband of perhaps fifty wives, and the best-known man west of the Mississippi. The *New York Herald* predicted, wrongly, in its obituary, "The death of the modern Mahomet will seal the fate of Mormonism. They cannot get another Joe Smith. The holy city must tumble into ruins and the 'latter day saints' have indeed come to the latter day."

Beyond the Rockies—Deseret

One of the first references to the planned settlement "beyond the Rockies" came from Lucy Walker, one of Joseph Smith's wives. (Smith had forty-seven recorded wives.) In 1842, five years before the actual migration to Utah, seventeen-year-old Lucy Walker later reported that Joseph Smith told her, "I have been commanded of God to take another wife, and you are the woman." He assured her that eventually, after they left Illinois and went to Alta California, she would be acknowledged as his legal wife: "Although I cannot under existing circumstances, acknowledge you as my wife, the time is near when we will go beyond the Rocky Mountains and then you will be acknowledged and honored as my wife." "Existing circumstances" meant that public admission of his multiple marriages was impossible outside the small circle of privileged Mormon leaders.

Lucy Walker was seventeen years old and a ward in his home when Joseph, age thirty-six, told her God had commanded him to take her as a wife. She had come from Vermont, Joseph's home state, to live in the prophet's home following the death of her mother. She was shocked at Joseph's revelation. "My astonishment knew no bounds," she recalled. Atypically—women's voices are not an integral part of Mormon history—she recorded their conversation. "It is a command of God to you," he told her. "I will give you until tomorrow to decide this matter. If you reject this message the gate will be closed forever against you." Lucy became Joseph's twenty-fifth wife. Following his murder two years later, she became the plural wife of Heber Kimball, second in the leadership after Brigham Young. (Kimball had a recorded forty-three wives and sixty-five children by seventeen wives.)

Joseph Smith was young, only thirty-eight years old, when he died, and his religious martyrdom obscured the power of his charisma and personal magnetism. He did not look like the stern, bewhiskered men who came to dominate the Mormon Church in Salt Lake City. He was clean-shaven, more than six feet tall, robust, and by many accounts handsome, charismatic, and with prodigious charm. He was known to drink wine and whiskey, loved to wrestle, and could speak poetically and compellingly to men and women alike. Surrounded by people who hungered for the transformative experience of the spiritual realm and believed in the power of his revelations, Smith's Mormon Church attracted thousands of converts who signed over their property and wealth for the opportunity to live in an ecstatic religious community. Smith was said to have developed a gift for liturgy—much of it based on the secret Masonic rituals—and during church services the congregants were said to be so transported that they spoke in tongues and other languages of the biblical-era Mediterranean. When he and Brigham Young met for the first time, for example, the two men spoke in tongues. Smith's power was not in doctrine but in his imagination and his powerful use of symbols. As Fawn Brodie wrote in her biography of Joseph Smith, "He was a mythmaker of prodigious talent."

Few ministers in the nineteenth-century West had ever seen the inside of a seminary. Many were self-invented. Some were insane. Many of their converts could not read the Bible even if they owned one. In the Book of Mormon, people learned a theological doctrine that persuasively described North America in biblical times. Its stories gave wholeness and unity to the actual experience of their lives. The Book of Mormon provided a story for many things they had seen, like the impressive Indian ruins that dotted the landscape, for which neither they nor anyone else had an explanation. As a modern-day prophet, Joseph Smith was both approachable and personable. He had four handsome brothers, and the vigorous, masculine family that surrounded him was an important element of his charisma and his power. His parents and siblings had all been with him since the beginning in upstate New York, and the faithful had followed him, first to Ohio, then to Missouri, and then back over the border into Illinois.

Mormonism is America's only homegrown religion, and much of its power came from its ability to speak to the nineteenth-century mind, its belief that prosperity was evidence of God's favor, its unique explanation of North America during biblical times, and its exceptional ability to organize people into cohesive communities. The Book of Mormon explained the reality of vast cultures that had previously existed in the United States. (Estimates of the pre-European population of North America at the time of Columbus, excluding Mexico, range from sixteen million to forty million. In 1491 Mexico alone had twenty-five million people.)

THE GREAT MOUNDS

The American West in the 1820s began in western New York and flowed into Ohio, particularly the rich farmland of the Ohio River valleys. Settlers moving into the Ohio Valley, still called the Western Reserve, as Joseph Smith and his family did, saw countless impressive, but unexplained, remnants of former residents—large earthworks in precise and geometrical forms. Henry Brackenridge, a Pennsylvanian who had invested in Ohio real estate, was one of the first to write and publish about the Indian antiquities of his day. He wrote about the extensive mound complex at Newark, the great site at Chillicothe, and other sites at Cincinnati. He noted in one of his letters that "all of these vestiges invariably occupy the most eligible situations for towns or settlements."

That America had a large population of previous inhabitants was evident in the thousands of archaeological ruins that dotted the Ohio and Mississippi River valleys. Some of the grave goods the settlers discovered in the mounds were so sophisticated and so well made that many believed the makers had to be ancient Egyptians or people from the lost tribe of Israel. The lost tribe of Israel was the most popular and widely held theory of the time to explain the origin of all the ubiquitous Indian mounds and impressive ruins. Joseph Smith borrowed from both theories. The original documents for the Book of Mormon were written in "reform Egyptian"; the stories in the Book of Mormon were about the lost tribe of Israel, the Lamanites and the Nephites, who had come to America in 600 BC.

Some white settlers called the mounds "Spanish forts" because they couldn't credit such immense structures to a non-European source. Only a few unusually well-placed Americans—among them Albert Gallatin, Henry M. Brackenridge, and Thomas Jefferson— were able to invest the indigenous earthworks with historical meaning and understood that this "virgin land" contained a vast history of previous inhabitants. Albert Gallatin, Jefferson's secretary of the treasury, correctly theorized that the builders of the great mounds had migrated from Mexico, bringing corn and horticultural techniques with them as they migrated up the Mississippi and its tributaries. Gallatin personally traveled through the Old Northwest Territory (Ohio, Indiana, Illinois, and the Great Lakes region), studying Native American tribes of his day, their extraordinary artifacts, and their extensive trade routes. (Turquoise jewelry, for example, was unearthed in Michigan.) Treasury Secretary Gallatin sponsored the first major study of the Indian archaeological mounds, at first privately published, then years later issued as *Ancient Monuments of the Mississippi Valley* by the newly established Smithsonian Institution.

Henry M. Brackenridge was an attorney from Pennsylvania who had invested in Ohio land and explored the profusion of Indian mounds he found along the Ohio and Scioto Rivers as he looked for town sites. Later appointed as a federal judge in St. Louis and subsequently sent to New Orleans as assistant attorney general, he made the correct connection between the similarities of the great mounds he had seen at Cahokia on the Mississippi River, opposite St. Louis, and the similar ruins of geometric settlements he saw around the tributaries of the lower Mississippi River near New Orleans. Cahokia was the center of what is now called the Mississippian civilization, and similar sites were found throughout the tributary river system flowing into the Mississippi.*

---

* A chronicler from de Soto's 1539 expedition across the southeastern states described the lush and extensive agricultural fields of the Coosa kingdom, spread across Georgia, Alabama, and Tennessee. They saw hundreds of settlements with temples and houses and fields laid out in identical geometrical designs. They told

In what is today Illinois, some fifteen miles from East St. Louis, the enormous pyramid mounds of Cahokia rose on the banks of the Mississippi River. Archaeologists have since determined that a city existed there from AD 750 to 1250 and held a population estimated at between fifteen and forty thousand people, far larger than Paris or London at the time. The original massed pyramid structures of Cahokia are the largest pyramids outside of Egypt. The pyramids were arranged in mathematical measurements having to do with the seasons and planting times. (The pyramidal shapes gave rise to the belief that ancient Egyptians had lived in North America.)

Today most of those ancient ruins have been bulldozed into shopping malls or housing developments, but a few remain to give testimony to a mysterious population with considerable engineering skill and artistic finesse. The Great Serpent mound in the Ohio Valley, for example, is four football fields in length, ranges from three to twenty feet high, and holds a globe or a comet in its mouth. It was saved from destruction only in the 1890s when a former director of the Peabody Museum of Ethnology purchased sixty acres surrounding it.*

---

of the Great Sun of the Coosas being carried out on a stretcher to meet de Soto, accompanied by a thousand men in "great feathered headdresses." Almost two hundred years later, around 1719, a French architect named Antoine Le Page du Pratz spent four years among the Natchez Indians, near present-day Natchez, Mississippi. A trained architect and engineer, he drew a site plan of their grand village, including the central ceremonial site for nine surrounding villages, with two temples at the south end flanking the temple of the Great Sun, also known as the Tattooed Serpent. He also drew and described the rectangular dwellings of ordinary people, the class structure organized around sun worship, and the floodplains in which individual families tended gardens of corn, beans, and pumpkins. Within two years of Le Page's final visit in 1725, the Natchez, including the Great Sun, were conquered by the French and sold into slavery in the Caribbean. A few survivors went to live with the Cherokee and took on mystical stature as the last descendants of the Mississippian civilization.

* The Serpent Mound was saved from destruction in the 1890s by Frederick Putnam of the Peabody Museum in Cambridge, who raised the money to save it. Supposedly, it was the women of Boston who collected the needed funds. Cahokia was not seriously studied by archaeologists until the 1960s. Today it is a United Nations World Heritage Site.

The majority of settlers in the 1800s were not interested in archaeology; they were interested in land. The impulse for land was a sacred
hunger. The settlers knew that it was important that the mounds and
artistic objects not be related to the Indians of their day because they
needed to take their lands. It was equally important that the Indians
be perceived as wild, uncivilized savages of the forest, and in this con-
ceit the Book of Mormon obliged them.

THE LAMANITES

The Book of Mormon holds that an original tribe from Israel came to
North America sometime around 600 BC and divided into two fac-
tions—the Lamanites and the Nephites. Much of the description of
the Lamanites, as predecessors of the Native American tribes, is found
in the Book of Enos, where Enos describes the depravity of the Lamanites: "Their hatred was fixed, and they were led by their evil nature that they became wild and ferocious; feeding upon beasts of prey;
dwelling in tents and wandering about in the wilderness with a short
skin girdle about their loins and their heads shaven; and their skill was
in the bow, and in the cimeter [scimitar] and the ax. And many of them
did eat nothing save it was raw meat; and they were continually seeking
to destroy us."

The Nephites, on the other hand, were a thrifty, hardworking people, "a pure and delightsome people." They "did till the land and raise
all manner of grain, and of fruit, and flocks of herds, and flocks of all
manner of cattle of every kind, and goats, and wildgoats, and also many
horses." They were white-skinned, lived industriously, were devoted to
their large families, and prospered. The Indians were descendants of
the Lamanites; the Mormons were descendants of the Nephites.

As the personification of the fallen, the Lamanites' skin turned
dark, and they became "a blood-thirsty people, full of idolatry and
filthiness." Enos, himself a former Lamanite, tells of constant wars between the Nephites and Lamanites, and much of the Book of Mormon
is devoted to describing these savage battles between the two branches
of the Israelites.

The Book of Mormon was a holy script mystically transmitted to Joseph Smith, at the age of twenty-one, by the angel Moroni, who directed him to discover ancient golden tablets buried in a hill near his home in Palmyra, New York. Palmyra was near Rochester, a region visited by so many evangelical, spiritualist, Shaker, and fire-and-brimstone itinerant preachers that it was said to be "burned over." (The hill at Palmyra is now a holy site, and when I visited, I saw tour buses of Mormons coming to visit, although I was too early for the annual pageant of Cumorah, enacting the story of the ancient American inhabitants of biblical times.) Written in a form of Egyptian hieroglyphics, the translation was accomplished by Smith through divine intervention and a gift of tongues. He dictated the contents to a local schoolteacher, Oliver Cowdray. No one ever saw the tablets because the angel Moroni asked for the tablets to be returned, and Smith obliged.

The resulting text was the story of North America in biblical times, which combined many of the stories of the Bible with the archaeology of the frontier. The *Book of Mormon: Another Testament of Jesus Christ* proved to be hugely persuasive to many disoriented European settlers, as they tried to make sense of the foreign environment in which they found themselves. Instead of a "virgin continent," they encountered Native Americans of many different tribes, customs, and languages. They also saw many mysterious and unexplained ancient ruins of previous inhabitants.

Published in 1830, and underwritten by a neighbor of Smith's who mortgaged his farm, the Book of Mormon became the foundation for the church that Joseph Smith named the Church of Jesus Christ of Latter-day Saints. Converts to Mormonism established a utopian agricultural community and a church as it supposedly existed during the historical time of Jesus. Many were called and many were true believers. But not everyone.

THE DEATH OF JOSEPH SMITH

By the 1840s a critical mass of disaffected Mormons had publicly charged Smith with being a false prophet. Even one of his brothers,

William, left the church, charging him with "false prophecy," but he later returned. His brother's defection, however, was an injury that—combined with a dozen lawsuits, a failed bank, undocumented land titles, anger at taking other men's wives as a "commandment from God," irregular business dealings, and an armed militia of four thousand men—signaled internal institutional unraveling.

The final chapter of Joseph Smith's life came about not from anti-Mormon Gentiles, but from disaffected Mormons who set in motion the events that led to his imprisonment and murder. The apostates sued him in court. Most dangerously, they started a newspaper criticizing his behavior and that of other church leaders. His death was not an "American Crucifixion," as some writers have suggested. There is considerable irony in the fact that Joseph Smith's ultimate downfall was set in motion by a man whose last name was Law.

William Law was a wealthy Canadian who joined the Mormon Church in Nauvoo, Illinois, with his wife, Jane. Law was a good businessman and invested in real estate, land development, and steam mills. More than anyone else, Law helped to guide the economic development of the settlement, and Joseph Smith depended on his financial acumen. Their break came after Joseph Smith told the attractive Jane Law—while her husband was away on a business trip—that God had commanded him to take her as one of his wives. Jane Law told her husband, and soon the Laws joined the camp of disgruntled Mormons, filing suit in Illinois courts, charging Smith with adultery, polygamy, and slander. Most dangerous to Joseph Smith, Law became editor of the *Nauvoo Expositor*, a newspaper that exposed some of Joseph's financial maneuverings, polygamy, land speculation, and misuse of state charters. Smith responded by ordering his Nauvoo militia to wreck the press, destroy the type, and burn every issue of the paper. This took place in early June 1844.

Governor Thomas Ford of Illinois could not afford to turn a blind eye to the destruction of the press and violation of the federal statute of "freedom of the press." After first trying to escape, Joseph Smith gave himself up and landed in the Carthage, Illinois, jail. Although the Illinois governor was determined to hold a legal trial—or perhaps follow the example of the Missouri authorities, who had arranged for

Joseph to "escape" from the state—the governor was weak, and units of his state militia were out of his control. As soon as he departed from Carthage, some of his troops stormed the jail and shot Joseph Smith and his brother Hyram.

Alta California

The second phase of Mormonism "beyond the Rocky Mountains" began under the leadership of Brigham Young and the removal of the church to the alkali kingdom of Alta California, called the Empire of Deseret by Brigham Young and his apostles and Utah Territory by the US government.* The map of the Mormon state of Deseret included much of Alta California, including some or all of nine future states— slices of Oregon, Idaho, Wyoming, all of Southern California, all of Nevada and Utah, half of Colorado, much of northern Arizona, and a wedge of New Mexico.

The great success of the Mormon settlement in the Far West was due to both Young's leadership and changes by the leadership in religious practice and governance. The former United Order of communal property ownership, for example, was abolished and the practice of tithing substituted. A tithe was calculated at 10 percent of a man's income. Material prosperity was identified as God's favor. Polygamy was openly practiced and the number of wives seen as testimony to a man's faith. In Utah there were no apostates, no tolerance for disaffected Mormons. If someone wanted to leave the church, they slipped away quietly in the dead of night. Rumors surfaced that certain disaffected members were murdered. (The Mountain Meadows massacre of a wagon train of white settlers illustrated that Brigham Young was not squeamish about killing.)

Young was an organizational genius who had both a vision and a plan. Equally important, the new Mormon leadership recognized the practical failures of Smith's governance and corrected them. They no

---

* Not everyone followed Brigham Young. The reform Mormons voted to follow another leader to St. Louis. Some went to Texas. The reorganized church under Joseph's son went to Independence, Missouri.

longer ruled by prophetic revelation. Historian Bernard DeVoto called Young "one of the foremost intelligences of the time" and "the first American who learned how to colonize the desert." Although Joseph Smith's martyrdom gave the migrating Mormon pioneers a sense of divine mission that fueled the incredible stamina required to undertake a journey of more than fifteen hundred miles over the Rocky Mountains, it was Brigham Young's command of logistics that successfully delivered some ten thousand Mormons into Salt Lake City.

It is possible that without Young's leadership to execute the stages of the long migration—setting up colonies at planned intervals along the route to grow food and provide supplies for successive waves of thousands of Mormon pioneers—Mormonism might have remained a small sect that disappeared in the nineteenth century like the Shakers of Annie Lee or the utopian colony of Robert Owen in New Harmony, Indiana. Instead, Brigham Young and his Quorum of the Twelve Apostles and his Council of Fifty designed an empire. They drew a map of their new lands in the West and called them Deseret. Deseret was short-lived because the year after the Saints arrived in Salt Lake Valley, the United States won the Mexican-American War and Alta California became part of the United States, the country the Mormons had tried to leave behind. The Mormon leaders were not deterred. Within the first ten years of arriving in Salt Lake, Brigham Young sent out explorers and missions to establish more than one hundred colonies in the nine states within the original boundaries of Deseret. Two of those missions are important to this story. One was in Tuba City, Arizona, which contained the Mormons who caused the Indian agent of Chester Arthur's era such annoyance that he threatened to resign unless the Indian Bureau created a reservation boundary for the Hopi; the other was a small outpost and fort in Las Vegas that lasted for only two years but remained a location for future Mormon settlers.

To successfully colonize these lands required significant planning. Unlike the individual pioneers who claimed lands under the Homestead Act and frequently lost them for lack of water, the Mormons scouted water sources ahead of time and sent parties of twenty or thirty families at a time to establish a settlement. They were equipped with the layout for a town plan and tools for farming, irrigation, or mining. The church also provided them with information about how to file mining claims and claim public domain lands through the Homestead Act, the Desert Lands Act, and the Timber Act.

The Mormons claim they settled the West, and to a significant degree they are right. The geographical location of their colonies was always based on sites with water, minerals, or timber. Successful settlement required locating water sources for irrigation, iron ore to produce tools and machinery, and timber for charcoal and construction. By the time Brigham Young died in 1877, he had plans for the establishment of more than 350 colonies throughout the West. By 1869 there were as many as sixty thousand Mormons in Utah, many of them recruited in England, former rural farmers who were eager to escape the factory life of England's industrial cities. Land was the key enticement to emigrate.

In Washington government mapmakers were rearranging lines on their maps, reducing the state of Deseret into Utah Territory, which included present-day Nevada and Utah (land of the Ute). Brigham Young was appointed territorial governor, with the provision that the Utah legal system include non-Mormon judges. The Mormon leadership, however, implemented their original vision. Brigham Young openly advocated the practice of polygamy, a policy enthusiastically adopted by the male population of the church, not just the leadership. Among the male Mormons, patriarchal polygamy and multiple wives were seen as a testament of their religious zeal as well as witness to their economic prosperity.* (Young himself took fifty-five wives and

---

* When Mormon bishop Mitt Romney ran for US president in 2012, he told the press that his father was born in Mexico. He didn't follow up by explaining that after the first federal antibigamy law of 1862 and enforcement of a stronger act of 1880, Mormon men who had multiple wives avoided the law by moving to Mexico. His great-grandfather Miles Romney, a man of great prominence in the Mormon Church and a member of the Quorum of Twelve Apostles, had a total of five wives and thirty-three children. One of his grandsons was George W. Romney, Mitt's father. Another Romney grandson became a law partner of John Boyden. Before leaving for Mexico, Miles Romney lived in St. George and served as chief of police, attorney at law, newspaper editor, and architect. His name is on the brass plaque outside the St. George tabernacle, where he is listed as superintendent of construction.

had fifty-seven children by sixteen women.) Deseret existed with its own government, courts, and judicial system for only three years, from 1849 to 1851. A map in the Library of Congress shows the successive lands taken from Utah Territory and transferred to the states of Wyoming, Colorado, Idaho, and Arizona.

But the original map of Deseret remained permanently imprinted in the minds of Mormon leaders. Unlike the settlement pattern of individual homesteaders who claimed free land under the Homestead Act and established individual farms and grazing lands, the Mormons thought in terms of town sites and supplied the colonies (called missions) with a town plan, instructions for irrigation, and a design for agricultural lands spread out around a town center.

From the very beginning, the Mormon leadership realized that success in the alkali kingdom required colonizing locations with significant resources. Tuba City, Arizona, was one of those missionary settlements, containing both water for irrigation and coal for heating. And it had a direct connection to John Boyden, the Hopi legal suit, and the coal-fired electricity that eventually powered the Sunbelt Boom of the urban Southwest.

CHAPTER 8

LEGAL THEFT

Tuba City began as a Mormon settlement in the 1870s. Although it is on the Navajo reservation, it is near the Hopi town of Moencopi and named for a Hopi headman called Chief Toova. At some point in 1880, the Mormon leader, Jacob Hamblin, who spoke six Indian languages including Hopi, took Toova and his wife, Talasnimka, to visit Salt Lake City.

Seventy years later Talasnimka's great-niece Helen Sekaquaptewa recalled the first cast-iron stove on the Hopi mesas that arrived after their journey as well as her family's long connection with Mormon missionaries and Anglo institutions. "The first full-time missionaries . . . to come to our house," wrote Helen Sekaquaptewa, "were Brother Virgil Bushman and his wife Ruth." Like John Boyden, they were from Salt Lake City, and they were visiting the Sekaquaptewa family because their eldest son, Emory Sekaquaptewa Jr., was having a personal crisis. Emory Jr. was the first Arizona Indian ever to get an appointment to West Point. But at some point during his stay at the military academy, he became seriously ill and was given a medical discharge. Back in the village of Hotevilla on Third Mesa, he was at loose ends about what to do next. He was twenty-two years old, filled with disappointment about his failed military career, and uncertain about what his future might hold.

The missionary Bushmans suggested that Emory Jr. might want to attend Brigham Young University (BYU), where the new president, Ernest Wilkinson—John Boyden's former law partner—had just launched a special program for Native Americans. Brigham Young

University is openly supported by the Mormon Church and has a curriculum that includes mandatory religious instruction for all students. Wilkinson was an ardent believer in Mormon education and in educating the Lamanites into the Mormon religion. "The Book of Mormon," Wilkinson wrote, "holds that some of the ancestors of the American Indian once constituted a *great Christian civilization* and predicts that in modern times the Book of Mormon will speak to them as a 'voice from the dust' to remind them of their identity and help them rise to greatness once again."

Soon Emory Jr. was on his way to Provo, Utah, and a degree in anthropology from BYU.* Even after Emory Jr. had departed, the Bushmans continued to visit the Sekaquaptewa household once a week, "teaching Emory [Sr.], Abbott, and me the Gospel in a systematic way. I read the Book of Mormon. It sounded exactly like the Hopi tradition."

In 1951 John Boyden and the Mormon missionaries were able to offer the Sekaquaptewa family something quite valuable: the opportunity for their children to succeed in the white world. For parents who saw too much of the economic hardship of reservation life, the purposefulness and material success of the Mormon world seemed a compelling alternative.

Illness had also overtaken their third son, Abbott, while he was at the Indian boarding school in Phoenix. A year earlier he was struck down with an attack of arthritis so severe that he was in the hospital for a year. Helen reported that he wrote to her and told her about

---

* When Emory Sekaquaptewa Jr. died in 2007 at the age of seventy-nine, the *New York Times* obituary (December 16, 2007) described him as a university professor, anthropologist, judge, artist, compiler of the first Hopi dictionary, co-owner of a silversmith shop, and political activist in leadership positions in the village of Kykotsmovi. He also became executive director of the Hopi Tribal Council, associate judge on the Hopi Tribal Court, and member of the Hopi Land Negotiating Committee, charged with negotiating the physical division of Hopi and Navajo lands. These roles in Hopi governance—the tribal court, the tribal council, the negotiating committee—were all important aspects of providing institutions in Hopi life that met Washington's needs, a fact that did not escape the traditional members of the Hopi villages.

the kindness of the Mormon elders who had come to visit him in the hospital and introduced him to the Book of Mormon. According to Helen, Abbott said, "Here is a religion we should get interested in, and try to learn more about." Helen herself was receptive because, as she put it in her memoir, *Me and Mine,* she came from a family that "had always been progressive towards Christianity."

Although the many letters and documents discussing the boundaries for a Hopi reservation in the 1870s and '80s do not name the "white men" who were harassing the Hopi villagers, they may well have been Mormon missionaries from Tuba City and Hamblin's men delivering alien objects like the cast-iron cookstove. The intensely traditional Hopis would have strongly objected to the delivery of foreign implements from the Anglo world.

Although the Hopi live clustered in eleven villages at the top of six-hundred-foot cliffs at the western edge of Black Mesa, for centuries they lived by growing corn and other vegetables in distant dry washes that retained belowground water from spring and summer rains. The runoff collected in porous formations. Many of these agricultural fields were located many miles away from the villages. In 1882 Indian agent J. H. Fleming confirmed that "the lands most desirable for the Moquis, & which were cultivated by them 8 or 10 years ago, have been taken up by the Mormons." Two years earlier, in 1880, Galen Eastman, the Hopi Indian agent, reporting to Inspector Howard, urgently requested reservation boundaries: "Believing that the Mormons are about to settle on land that ought to be embraced in a Moquis Pueblo Indian Reservation, I cannot await the tardy appearance of the expected new Agent."

Helen reported that when Toova and her great-aunt returned from their travels to Salt Lake City, they were "like Marco Polo," telling of large cities and clever "new things" never seen on the Hopi mesas, like "yeast, a coffeepot, a dishpan, and a Dutch oven." Hamblin arranged for the delivery of the first cast-iron oven to their village, and she remembered from her own childhood how she had been "fascinated with the tiny door that had a slide in it to make a draft." She also remembered that Talasnimka adopted Mormon clothing and writes that she was "wearing a cotton dress and a bonnet."

In the 1950s while her children attended high school at the Phoenix Indian School, Helen lived in Phoenix. On Sundays she attended the meetings of the Mormon Relief Society—the Mormon women's organization whose purpose is to "build faith and personal righteousness, strengthen families and homes, and help those in need"—on the Maricopa reservation, outside of Phoenix. By then she was a baptized Mormon, and she frequently got a ride out with Louise Udall, who came from a particularly well-connected Mormon family.

Louise Udall was the wife of the chief justice of the Arizona Supreme Court, Levi Udall. A Udall cousin was the mayor of Phoenix; another was married to the president of the Mormon Church. Two of her sons were en route to impressive careers in Washington, DC. One son, Stewart, was a congressman, and during the years his mother attended the Women's Relief Society meetings with Helen Sekaquaptewa, he rose in the world to become secretary of interior. Another son, Morris, took his brother's congressional seat and was working his way up to become chairman of the House Interior Committee, the powerful congressional committee that oversees all national legislation pertaining to mining, mineral rights, water, energy, and Indian lands. (Until 1951 the House Interior Committee was called the Committee on Public Lands, renamed in 1993 as the Committee on Natural Resources.)

By the 1960s the two women became so close that they decided to collaborate on a book together. *Me and Mine: The Life Story of Helen Sekaquaptewa* (as told to Louise Udall) was published in 1969. Described as "a little classic" and "must reading for its portrayal of life among a proud people," the book was a portrait in which the inevitable conversion to Mormonism was a triumph of a life journey well lived. The book contained not one mention of the great coal deposits that had been discovered beneath the Hopi Navajo lands or that the Udall sons had a major role in extracting the coal for energy for the urban centers of the Southwest, particularly Phoenix and Tucson. There was no mention of Abbott Sekaquaptewa's negotiating the coal leases that Secretary of Interior Stewart Udall approved, no mention of the complex history that these lands contained. As Brian Morton, a scholar of the Hopi and Navajo coal leases, pointed out, "Coal mining on Black Mesa happened because of a demand for electricity in Sunbelt cities."

"New jobs, large tax benefits, and tremendous economic advantages—not only for the two Indian tribes—but for the entire southwest," proclaimed Interior Secretary Stewart Udall in announcing the leases in 1966. The leases ran for thirty-five years and were renewable for another thirty-five. They violated every guideline that the Department of the Interior had set up for leasing on public lands: no competitive bidding, no automatic renegotiation clauses, a fixed rate rather than a percentage royalty rate. The Hopi got $1.67 per acre-foot for water rights that in 1987 were renegotiated at $427 per acre-foot. The Navajo got $5 per acre-foot. The royalty rate on public lands for coal mining was $1.50 per ton. The Hopi and Navajo split a rate of 37 cents per ton.

Author and photographer Alvin Josephy, who was working in the Interior Department at the time and who took the photographs for Secretary Udall's environmental book, *The Quiet Crisis*, later wrote in *Audubon* magazine that the Black Mesa leases were "a textbook example of the lack of accountability by government agencies working hand-in-glove with industry in the United States today."

SECRETARY STEWART UDALL

Even in the glamorous, style-conscious Kennedy administration, Stewart Udall was a glittering figure. A man of great personal charm, he also had great instincts for power. Obeying the first law of the news camera, he stayed in motion. Images of the interior secretary were always appearing in magazines or on television: Stu Udall rafting rivers, Stu Udall climbing Mount McKinley (Denali) in Alaska, Stu Udall with environmentalists trekking through one of the national parks. He gave the colorless bureaucracy of Interior a new image, and in the process gave environmentalism a new platform. Like President Kennedy, he was photogenic and energetic.

He saw himself in the tradition of Harold Ickes and described himself as a New Deal Democrat, even a radical. "I was always involved . . . on behalf of minority groups and their causes. I had the kind of New Deal feelings about labor unions, economic justice, social justice. Therefore, I was pretty much, I think, in the 1950s, as a young

politician, what we'd think of as a New Deal liberal. That didn't necessarily fit my state because Arizona was growing more conservative."

He launched his political career in 1956 as a congressman from
Tucson. From the beginning he understood the key power centers in
Arizona, one of which was the Valley National Bank in Phoenix. Five
months into his first term, he cosponsored a bill with Arizona senator Barry Goldwater regarding the coal-rich lands on Black Mesa and
received a congratulatory letter from a high official of the Valley National Bank of Phoenix. Thomas Shia was actively interested in Udall's
addition of an "interim mineral leasing" arrangement while the court
case was in progress. He requested six copies of the bill, including a
copy for Walter Bimson, president of the bank.

Stewart Udall was then thirty-five years old, young, handsome,
personable, and in his first term of national office. Although he described himself as a small-town boy and the product of modest circumstances and small-town politics, the reality was different. His
father, Levi Udall, was at that time chief justice of the Arizona Supreme Court, a post his uncle would take over after his father died. "I
came out of a political family," he told an oral history interviewer. "My
father was a career judge, and judges were elected in Arizona. Therefore, living in a small town with a county courthouse, I grew up with
elections."

He learned about political campaigning after he came back from
service in World War II, where he was in the Army Air Corps in the
Italian campaign. "In the summer of 1946, my father made his big
move. He was a small county judge in one of the smallest counties in
the state, and he decided to run for the state Supreme Court, which
had been his great ambition. . . . I was sort of his campaign aide and
campaigned with him. I got my first indoctrination in politics there."

After his father's successful election to the Arizona Supreme
Court, Udall returned to the University of Arizona, got his law degree,
and in 1948 opened a law practice in Tucson with his brother Morris,
known as Mo. Although the Udall brothers described themselves as
lapsed Mormons, or Jack Mormons, they were known to be well connected at the highest levels of the Mormon Church. One uncle had

married the sister of Spencer Kimball, twelfth president of the Mormon Church. Another uncle served in the Arizona Legislature. Their cousin Nicholas Udall was the mayor of Phoenix (from 1948 to 1952) and served with City Councilman Barry Goldwater before he became US senator. Stewart's father was a Mormon bishop and a missionary president in the Mormon Church. Most of their male relatives had offices within the Mormon hierarchy.

The idea of male generational succession to political power is an important teaching of the Mormon Church, and in this regard the male members of the Udall family followed that expectation. After Stewart's nomination to a cabinet post, his brother Morris took over his congressional seat, attaining the powerful chairmanship of the House Interior Committee. In 1976 he ran for US president. For more than a hundred years, four generations of Udalls have succeeded to political power in the Southwest. In 2009 New Mexico and Colorado elected the sons of Stewart and Morris to the US Senate.

Stewart Udall's unexpected appointment to interior secretary in 1961 was crucial to the fate of the Hopi and Navajo reservation issue. In 1960 he was still an unknown second-term congressman from a minor state when he stepped into the national spotlight as head of the Arizona delegation to the Democratic National Convention. Everyone expected the western states to give their votes to Lyndon B. Johnson—a westerner, a man who understood the needs of the Southwest, and a man who referred to John F. Kennedy as "the boy." "I understand you have to give your first vote to 'the boy,'" he told Tip O'Neill. Massachusetts congressman O'Neill explained to him that with the Kennedy machine, there would be no second vote.

Stewart Udall was also subjected to pressure to vote for LBJ, but he stood firm for Kennedy. "Sam Rayburn called me into the well of the House," Udall recalled, "and said he'd hate to see anyone from the West go against his friend Lyndon." Arizona's support for Kennedy was viewed as symbolically important in order to demonstrate that Kennedy could run well in the West. (In fact, Kennedy lost the West, carrying only three small states—New Mexico, Nevada, and Hawaii.) Udall, however, delivered the Arizona delegation to Kennedy at the convention, and his support in the face of Sam Rayburn's pressure, as well as his own political skills, earned him the cabinet appointment. As secretary of interior, he was the kind of young, fresh face that the Kennedys were looking for. His appointment was hailed by conservationists as a brilliant choice, the finest appointment for Interior since Harold Ickes in the 1930s. In the West the interior secretary is considered a more important appointment than secretary of state.

In building a political base for his new vision for Interior's activist mission, he copied his president, appealing to intellectuals. His book *The Quiet Crisis* was similar in format to Kennedy's *Profiles in Courage*. With a foreword by President Kennedy, it contained a series of biographies of the white, all-male leaders of the conservation tradition—John Muir, Joseph Wood Krutch, John Wesley Powell, Teddy Roosevelt, and John D. Rockefeller. The profiles had a few surprises. (There was no mention of Rachel Carson or Marjorie Stoneman Douglas.)

Stewart Udall did not see the contradictions, nor did he see himself as part of the eastern establishment. "I would characterize myself as a bit of an idealist I guess. I'm someone who had very strong ideas about what kind of society I wanted to see us develop in this country."

The Udall-Sekaquaptewa Connection

Had Helen Sekaquaptewa converted to another institutional form of Christianity, the impact on her family would have been less profound. Had she become Baptist or Episcopalian, her religious affiliation would not have fed so directly into the political and economic structure of the American West. In joining the Mormon Church, the Sekaquaptewas' religious affiliation merged with a much larger and more powerful governing reality. And by the 1960s, with Helen's direct connection with the Udall family, she was directly involved with John Boyden's role in shaping the new Hopi Tribal Council. Her son Abbott served on the tribal council during the 1950s and as chairman from 1961 to 1964 and then again from 1971 to 1981. In the decade from 1966 to 1976, he also served as chair of the Hopi Negotiating Committee, charged with working out a land-sharing arrangement with the Navajo. Another son, Wayne, owned the English-language newspaper and a construction firm and was president of the Mormon stake on the reservation. Emory Jr. worked as executive director of the tribal council.

After the Goldwater-Boyden-Udall bill passed in 1958, setting up the special court, Boyden filed the necessary papers, the case was heard in 1960, and the decision was handed down on September 28, 1962. The Navajo appealed to the Supreme Court, but the Court declined to hear the case, supposedly after some influential input from Secretary Udall. Discussions were already under way about mineral leasing on the 1882 reservation.

The Hopi traditional leaders were horrified that sacred land was going to be leased for strip mining. Assisted by the Native American Rights Fund, traditional Hopi elders went to court to sue to stop the strip-mining leases, claiming that the leases had been obtained illegally at a time when the Hopi Tribal Council did not have a legal quorum as required by their constitution. They also called Secretary Udall's approval of the coal leases "arbitrary, capricious, an abuse of discretion."

> We the Hopi leaders have watched as the white man has destroyed his land, his water and his air. The white man has made it harder for us to maintain our traditional ways and religious life. Now for the first time we have decided to intervene in the white man's court to prevent the final devastation. We should not have had to go this far. Our words have not been heeded. We can no longer watch as our sacred lands are wrested from our control and as our spiritual center disintegrates. We cannot allow our spiritual homelands to be taken from us. The hour is already late.

Their case was filed but not heard. The Court ruled that the Hopi traditional priests had no "standing" before the Court. Only the Hopi Tribal Council had legal standing and could sue in the name of the Hopi people.

The book by Helen Sekaquaptewa and Louise Udall was published in 1969, the same year that the Mohave Generating Station opened in

Laughlin, Nevada, powered by Black Mesa coal and with water piped from the Hopi-Navajo aquifer beneath the 1882 reservation. Even though the book authored by Louse Udall and Helen Sekaquaptewa contains no mention of coal or the leases that their sons had negotiated, it tells a poignant story of how American national policies successfully alienated Indians from their own culture. When viewed as a window into America's colonial system, it both is instructive and explains how the family became John Boyden's willing ally. Anthropologist Richard Clemmer believes that the Sekaquaptewas, like other Christian Hopi, were outside the traditional Hopi world. As Mormons, they were not followers of the Hopi way; they were ranchers, not farmers; and the sons followed professions not common to most Native people. Consequently, they needed to prove themselves through the institutions that were open to them. The tribal government became an outlet for their beliefs and a stage on which to engage issues they believed were important.

The Mormons believe in the religious instructions in Genesis. Go forth and dominate: "Be fruitful and multiply; fill the earth and subdue it; have dominion over the fish of the sea, over the birds of the heavens and over every creeping thing." Productivity means extracting whatever mineral resources lie beneath the land.

Kill the Indian, Save the Man

Helen Sekaquaptewa's childhood was traumatic. At the age of six she was kidnapped by federal agents and transported to the boarding school in Keams Canyon to learn English and "be educated." She did not return to her village until she was eleven. "The first English I learned was 'get in line' 'get in line,'" Helen wrote. Until the official end of the Indian wars, in the 1880s, US policy had been active extermination of the Indians, coupled with a passive expectation that they would simply disappear. Indian peoples were uniformly described as "a vanishing race."* But when it became clear that the Indians were

---

* The government also did its part in trying to make them vanish. In 1890 Sitting Bull, his son, and six bodyguards were killed at the Standing Rock Sioux agency. Hearing

not vanishing, new policies were put in place to deal with "the Indian problem." Reformers in the East like Senator Henry Dawes decided it was important to break up Native landholdings and passed the Allotment Acts in which individual tribal members were to receive a 160-acre parcel of land and the remainder of the reservation would be sold as "surplus." Indian nations lost two-thirds of their land base while the allotment policy was in force. A corollary policy was the introduction of Civilization and Assimilation, by which Indians were to be Christianized and assimilated into the American mainstream. By 1885 the government had established 106 Indian boarding schools, many of them on abandoned military installations, with the motto "Kill the Indian and save the man." The commonly understood subtext was that in order to "civilize the savages," it was first necessary to destroy Native American culture.

As Rayna Green has written in *To Lead and to Serve* about the Indian boarding school system that executed the new policy, "It was ironic, indeed, that a society that declared the education of blacks and slaves illegal insisted on teaching Indians to read and write, often sending military units to separate them from their parents and homes."

One of the boarding schools opened in Keams Canyon, and it was for Hopi and Navajo children, although there were many more Hopi children than Navajo. The Navajo children were difficult to round up because they lived in such dispersed sheepherding camps. But the Hopi children lived in houses in compact villages located on the edge of Black Mesa. The ancient village of Oraibi was one of the first places

---

of Sitting Bull's death, Chief Big Foot decided to move his band to a more protected area of the Pine Ridge Reservation in South Dakota. He was ill with pneumonia and riding in a wagon that flew the white flag of truce when the US Seventh Cavalry sent troops to disarm his warriors before allowing them to travel farther to the Indian agency. As the troops disarmed the Indian warriors, a gun went off. The 500 troops opened fire, killing the warriors, and chased down some 250 women and children. They killed 146 men, women, and children and wounded 51, leaving a trail of bloodied Sioux bodies that stretched for miles in what is known as the Wounded Knee Massacre. Photographer George Trager made a series of photographs of the frozen bodies in the snow that were widely distributed and reproduced.

targeted by the Office of Indian Affairs to implement the new policy and place Hopi children in school. Emory Sekaquaptewa Sr., for example, was five years old in 1906 when government officers raided the Hopi village of Oraibi before dawn, plucked up sleeping children out of their beds, tossed them in horse-drawn wagons, and took them to Keams Canyon. Once at the boarding school, they could not go home until their parents signed an agreement promising they would return their children for future instruction. The next year Helen, who was six, was snatched from her family.

Government actions in the Hopi villages made the signing of a parental consent form extremely difficult. More than seventy Hopi fathers from the families who had resisted "educating their children" were taken off to jail, leaving the remaining family members in confusion and despair. Some fathers went to jail for ninety days, others for years. Emory Sr.'s father was sent to the Indian prison in Carlisle, Pennsylvania. Helen's father was given a sentence of a year in prison at Fort Huachuca, in southern Arizona. "The posts that sent out men to kill their fathers to solve 'the Indian problem' became the place where Indian children were taken to be dressed in military uniforms and absorbed into the American mainstream." Although the government policy was to keep the children for nine months and send them home for the summer, if the parents didn't sign the form, the children didn't get to go home. Helen and Emory Sr. didn't get to see their parents or their village again for another five years. In the meantime, the boarding school staff became their surrogate parents. They adapted to institutional life.

Once in boarding school, they were given Anglo names—Helen and Emory—forbidden from speaking the Hopi language, and punished if they sang any of their traditional songs or did any dances. The school matrons cut their hair, gave them military uniforms to wear, and housed them in a long military-style dormitory with cots in long rows. For the next twelve years, home was a succession of boarding schools—first in Keams Canyon, then the Indian school in Phoenix—all regimented by military bugle and drill and Christian instruction. "We marched to the dining room three times a day to band music,"

Helen wrote. "Corporal punishment was given as a matter of course [with] a harness strap."

The Indian children were expected to be part of the servant class and were taught skills they were expected to use in the Anglo world. The girls learned laundry and sewing; the boys learned carpentry and construction. In military pedagogy, discipline and obedience were key educational values. Helen Sekaquaptewa said she spent years learning how to organize in parade lines, march to military music, wash and iron vast piles of laundry, clean toilets, prepare meals, and scrub floors. "It was a military school. . . . We arose to a bell and had a given time for making our beds, cleaning our rooms, and being ready for breakfast. Everything was done on schedule, and there was no time for idleness. Our clothing was furnished by the government. We had long black stockings and heavy black shoes, but the dresses were of good material."

Roberta Blackgoat also went to the same boarding school and hated the uniforms because they were made of wool and were very itchy. She was ten years old when her family sent her to the Keams Canyon school, but it was during the 1920s and there wasn't enough to eat on the reservation. She was one of the children who resisted and ran away. She told me this as we drove through Keams Canyon, waving to a spot where the school used to be. Even before the school was built, Indian agent E. S. Merrit tried to dissuade the Indian Office from putting a school in Keams Canyon. The canyon "is very unhealthy, the air at night particularly heavy & cold. . . . [T]he Pueblo Indians of Arizona and New Mexico want day schools, that is all."

Many students tried to run away. Others feigned acceptance, never losing their Indian ways of thinking and being. But for others the uniforms and the strict discipline came to be their way of life. By the time Emory Sr. got to high school in Phoenix, the school authorities considered him so trustworthy that they sent him after the Indian runaways. "Emory would go to town," wrote Helen, "on the streetcar and look around the streets, but sometimes they would get as far away as Glendale or Peoria. Then Emory would have to go by train, and when he found them bring them back and deliver the boys to their disciplinarian and the girls to the matron." It was not taken lightly, these

Indians who resisted becoming civilized. "Boys were put in the school jail. . . . Repeaters had their heads shaved and had to wear a dress to school." Girls were given punishments like "cutting the grass with scissors while wearing a card that said, 'I ran away.'" Corporal punishment "was given as a matter of course; whipping with a harness strap was administered in an upstairs room to the most unruly. One held the culprit while another administered the strap."

The better they adapted to boarding school life, the worse they fit in when they went back to the reservation. They had new Anglo names, spoke English better than Hopi, dressed in Anglo clothes, and expected to do the same jobs they had learned in boarding school. The rift between the Hopi parents and their boarding school children was wide. Helen and Emory were good examples. They had been raised on military pedagogy: drill, discipline, the Bible.

In 1919 Emory Sekaquaptewa Sr. returned to the Hopi reservation and went to work for the BIA Agency in Hotevilla, in charge of maintaining the buildings and the power plant. Hotevilla was the new "friendly" village that had been founded in 1906 after the schism in Oraibi between the "hostiles" and the "friendlies" over education. The issue of educating their children in Anglo schools caused such turmoil in Oraibi that the village split in two between the traditional "hostile" chief and the progressive "friendly" chief, and the new village of Hotevilla was formed. Half the families of Old Oraibi resisted Anglo education and stayed put; the other half left and started a new town four miles away on the other side of Third Mesa, near the Hotevilla spring. The younger chief of Old Oraibi wanted to cooperate with the government; the old chief Yokeoma, called the Hostile Chief, resisted. In 1912 the BIA sent Yokeoma to Washington for a meeting with President Taft to force him to promise to send the Hopi children to Keams Canyon boarding school. He resisted to the very end.

When Emory and Helen married, they had a Christian ceremony as well as a Hopi ceremony. The Christian ceremony, performed by a Mennonite minister, did not sit well with their Hopi neighbors, nor did the fact that they welcomed white teachers and government workers into their home. Their third son, Abbott, was named after Helen's good friend Miss Abbott, an Anglo teacher on the reservation. When things with her neighbors became difficult, she confessed, she used to visit Miss Abbott to "talk things over."

While the Sekaquaptewas had strained relations with their neighbors, they were invaluable to the Bureau of Indian Affairs. They were Christian, progressive in attitude, spoke excellent English, and had adopted Anglo ways. They encouraged their children to get an education and become Christians. Consequently, not one of the five Sekaquaptewa sons was initiated into the Hopi priesthood. The Sekaquaptewas were known as "friendlies" as opposed to "hostiles." By the 1950s those terms had changed to "progressives" and "traditionals," but the underlying attitudes remained the same. During a crucial period the Sekaquaptewa sons all occupied pivotal positions in Hopi government.

The Invented Range War

The court case between the Hopi and Navajo established three things: the Hopi's exclusive right to a land area called District 6, the principle that the Hopi would share equally in any mineral-leasing royalties on the 1882 reservation, and that only Congress had the right to draw boundary lines. Then began ten years of maneuvering and negotiations.

The actual coal-mining leases were signed with a Salt Lake City company called Sentry Royalty Company between 1964 and 1966. Sentry was a subsidiary of Peabody Coal. Immediately, Kennecott Copper bought Peabody Coal and the Sentry leases. Later some of the Hopi Tribal Council members would say they never knew they were actually negotiating with a multinational mining company. Nor did they know they were selling water rights. Time sheets and billing correspondence later confirmed that John Boyden was working for Peabody Coal and Kennecott Copper at the same time he was working for the Hopi. "Dear Mr. Phelps," began his letters to Edward R. Phelps, vice president of Peabody Coal, when he was writing in his role as the Hopi tribal attorney. "Dear Ed," he began when he was writing as Peabody's attorney. He did far better in meeting the needs of the coal company than his Hopi clients. The discovery of his Peabody Coal file in the archives at the University of Utah confirmed his billing records and his correspondence for both Peabody and Kennecott. In addition, his law firm in Salt Lake City had listed Peabody Coal as one of their named clients in *Martindale-Hubbell*, the national index of law firms.

• • •

By 1971 circumstances had changed in relation to construction of the Central Arizona Water Project, a project of enormous importance to the people of central and southern Arizona and the politicians who had worked on it for thirty years. It appeared that it would be impossible to put another dam on the Colorado River to provide the hydroelectricity to pump 1.9 million acre-feet of water from the Colorado River into Phoenix and Tucson. Instead, the Bureau of Reclamation would have to buy a fourth of the electricity from the still-to-be-constructed Navajo Generating Station. The coal supply to run that plant would require a second mining site on Black Mesa.

In 1971 John Boyden and Barry Goldwater introduced another bill before Congress, the Hopi Land Settlement Act, a bill that would actually physically divide the Executive Order Reservation, giving approximately 2 million acres to the Hopi, and removing the still-uncounted Navajo who lived in the way.

It is a maxim of public relations that to influence opinion, events need to be organized into a story, preferably a story line that the public has heard before. A theme of many Hollywood western movies was the range war, a basic conflict between homesteaders who wanted to farm and ranchers who wanted open range to graze livestock. It made for a dramatic story that people believed represented real western history. Well coached by John Boyden and the public relations firm of Evans and Associates, Abbott Sekaquaptewa appeared before a congressional hearing in 1973 and raised the issue of an oncoming range war and open warfare between the Navajo aggressors and the peaceful Hopi.

> The Navajo tribe has systematically by use of force, threat, coercion, and intimidation excluded the Hopi people from the lands secured to them by the federal court in *Healing*

v. Jones. We cannot understand how this state of affairs
can be condoned by the federal government in the face of
a court order to the contrary. Violence and destruction are
as common today as they have been historically in this conflict. It is not beyond imagination that open warfare will
once again become the order of the day.

For two years national newspapers were running photos of burned
corrals, shot-up stock tanks, and roadside signs riddled with bullet
holes. Sunday magazine features focused on the smoldering "range
war" between the two tribes, calling them the Arabs and the Israelis
of the American Southwest. Abbott Sekaquaptewa appeared on *Sixty
Minutes*. "Marauding Navajo tribesmen [have] always been a time of
trial and tribulation for my people. Particularly during my own lifetime, the relentless Navajo dominance and forcible occupation of Hopi
land has become a creature of the night, a living nightmare."

Most of Abbott Sekaquaptewa's testimony had been written
by Evans and Associates. As it happened, Evans and Associates was
also the same public relations firm for the trade association known as
WEST (Western Supply and Transmission), the twenty-three utility companies that were building the power plants and paying for the
strip-mined coal from Black Mesa that would run them.

People on the reservation said that it was white men from out of
town who were shooting up the signs. The only national newspaper to
run an alternative version of events was the *Washington Post*. "The locus of Hopi policy seems to be in Salt Lake City," wrote Mark Panitch,
"where the Hopi's energetic and effective lawyer, John Boyden, and the
public relations counsel are headquartered. Much of the Hopi success
can be attributed to their Mormon allies." The Mormons had excellent
media and communications channels so that the Hopi side of the story
dominated in the national press. Coal, the power plants, and the coal-
slurry line and the importance of energy for the Sunbelt Boom often
went unmentioned.

By 1973 the bill to partition the Executive Order Reservation had
been revised several times, and Abbott Sekaquaptewa's public remarks
reached an operatic crescendo:

> I need not remind this committee of the constant protesta-
> tions and objections of the Hopi people for over 100 years
> to the onslaught of Navajo trespasses and other excesses
> in the destruction of life and property that have become
> a way of life with them since their arrival on this land. . . .
> Because of our long history of nonaggression we are penal-
> ized and forced to endure intolerable conditions under the
> heel of the mighty Navajo tribe which could be avoided if
> Congress would promptly take action. . . . No other mi-
> nority people on the face of this land have been required to
> negotiate for the implementation of their rights as decreed
> to them by the federal courts.

The Hopi, through their links with the media, had the best story line. The rule of public relations is that once a narrative has been established in the national media, it is almost impossible to turn it around. The story was of implacable hatred between the two tribes in which the peaceful Hopi were victimized by the aggressive Navajo. National newspapers carried constant stories about the trouble in the American Southwest.

The failure to incorporate Native American history into mainstream history greatly helped this version of events to prevail. In American culture Indians have been largely relegated to the anthropologists, not the historians. So the range war and the "centuries-old Hopi-Navajo struggle" went unquestioned. Had anyone taken the time to look at Navajo history, they might have found a different and equally fascinating story.

THE NAVAJO AND BOSQUE REDONDO

The Navajo also had a story to tell, but they couldn't get to the microphone. Before the 1850s the Navajo were prosperous and wealthy and living in northern New Mexico. Their struggles were mainly with the Spanish who kidnapped Navajo for slaves. Then after the United States won the war with Mexico in 1848, their new enemies were the

Anglo-Europeans who believed that Navajo lands were filled with gold. Anglo miners started to come into their lands, looking for gold and silver. The Navajo retaliated by raiding the mining settlements with skill and determination. The miners complained bitterly to the governor of New Mexico Territory. Governor Connelly told the territorial legislature, "The Navajo occupy the finest grazing districts within our limits [and] *infest* a mining region extending two hundred miles. [We are] excluded from its occupation and the treasures of mineral wealth that are known to exist." He went on the describe the Navajo as having "too long roamed as lords of the soil over this extensive tract of country." But it took the Civil War to provide the occasion to forcibly clear the land of the troublesome Navajo, so that mineral prospecting could go forward.

In 1862 a Texas general named Henry Hopkins Sibley crossed the Rio Grande with a regiment of Texas cowboys and claimed Santa Fe and the New Mexico Territory for the Confederate South. (A plaque in the old square in Albuquerque commemorates the Confederate campaign.) While the US Army troops were diverted in fighting Sibley, the Navajo seized the moment to retaliate against the invading miners. They raided the mining settlements with ferocity, killing miners and carrying off horses, equipment, and supplies. The mine owners screamed for protection.

The government in Washington heard them. On September 16, 1862, General James Carleton arrived in Santa Fe from California as the new commanding general of New Mexico Territory. The Santa Fe newspaper called him "the deliverer of the Southwest." The nature of his mission was to expel Sibley and quiet the hostile Navajo. Carleton also believed in the stories of mineral wealth in the lands that the Navajo inhabited. "There is evidence," Carleton wrote to General Henry Halleck, "that a country as rich if not richer in mineral wealth than California, extends from the Rio Grande, northwestwardly all the way across to Washoe [Nevada]." Carleton at first organized companies of "irregular soldiers," many of them slave raiders, to fight the Navajo. Then he enlisted Kit Carson, the famed frontiersman, explorer, and Indian fighter, to be the field commander of the regular Navajo Campaign. Carleton's war policy toward the Navajo was that of total war—killing the men, taking women and children prisoners, destroying their food base, removing them from their lands, and colonizing them as farmers in eastern New Mexico at Bosque Redondo, almost at the Texas border, where many of them died.

Using Mexican and Ute scouts, Carson discovered the Navajo settlements and sent in troops to kill or drive off the inhabitants. He captured stored grain, burned all the crops, destroyed the Navajo fruit orchards, and slaughtered the livestock. Thousands of sheep, the basis of the Navajo economy, were killed. Carson knew the Navajo could find more food sources, but not if he kept them continually on the move.

The Navajo kept moving west, crossing into Arizona Territory, and many fled into the depths of Canyon de Chelly, a mystical and beautiful canyon until then unexplored by white men and protected by quicksand at the canyon entrance. Carson set up a blockade at the canyon entrance and waited out the winter. In the spring of 1864 Carson sent a detachment of men into the canyon and rounded up fifteen hundred Navajo, by then half starved, frozen, and at the end of endurance.

Thus began the infamous Long Walk to Fort Sumner, three hundred miles away. During the march through spring blizzards, the soldiers shot anyone moving too slowly, raped women and girls, and physically mutilated their prisoners. Hundreds died. Many froze to death. "Three hundred miles at fifteen miles day!" wrote Ruth Roessel. "If a woman went into labor, she was shot. Navajos remember, 'There was absolutely no mercy.'"

> No wonder the Navajos felt they were marching to the ends of the earth. The way led gradually out of the fierce, red rocks and high plateaus of their own country, past Bear Springs, their old stamping ground, where Fort Wingate now stood menacingly ready to push them on their way, and then past the long flow of lava which is the life blood of *Yeitso*, the monster slain by the war gods. Beyond rose the long slopes of Mount Taylor, the southern sacred mountain [of the four sacred mountains]. When they left it behind, they were out of Navajoland, entering unhallowed

ground where no ceremonies would be effective. The Navajo say they held no ceremonies at Fort Sumner except the War Dance which nullifies the evil effects of contact with strangers and enemies.

General Carleton considered it a great victory. Kit Carson became an American hero, although details of the Navajo Campaign later challenged that reputation. The march, however, was merely a preview of what was awaiting the Navajo at Fort Sumner. There, other Navajo who had either turned themselves in or been picked up in other raids were brought together in a prison camp inadequate for seven thousand Navajo. (In 1864 the camp census said the number of Navajo was 8,354; in 1865 it was 9,022.) The camp, which had no economy or continuity with preexisting settlement, became known by its Spanish place-name, Bosque Redondo, for the cottonwoods that marked the area. Carleton saw it as a permanent solution for the Navajo problem and directed that a forty-square-mile area be set aside as an internment zone. He ordered the digging of irrigation trenches and the planting of fifteen hundred acres of corn, beans, melons, and pumpkins. Unhappily, General Carleton knew little about agriculture, and given his authoritarian temperament, no one ventured to advise him.

The hot sun and drought conditions withered most of the corn. Grasshoppers, worms, and severe storms devastated the melons and squash. The water was brackish, stagnant, and a breeding ground for mosquitoes. Carleton had few farm tools to give to the Navajo to cultivate the fields, and what he ordered were stolen by the Indian agents. Soon the Navajo were starving again, and many of them were stricken with malaria or dysentery. The soldiers at Fort Sumner infected many of the Navajo women with syphilis and gonorrhea, which in turn was transmitted among the Navajo men. Comanche Indians from Texas crossed the Rio Grande and raided the camp almost at will. The prisoners were on the verge of starvation most of the time and suffered from heat, malnutrition, and disease. Everyone who saw the camp said it was brutal and inhumane in the extreme. Charles Sumner of Massachusetts—one of the great opponents of slavery during the antebellum period—made a speech on the floor of the Senate, denouncing both the governor of New Mexico and General James Carleton for practicing "Indian slavery."

Throughout the years of the Civil War, the US government was spending more than $1 million every eighteen months on the Navajo imprisonment ($50 million in current dollars). When pressed in 1868, General Carleton said it was cheaper to imprison the Navajo than to fight them. He blamed the excessive expense on the corruption of the Indian agency that administered the camp. Indian agency superintendent Steck pressured Carleton to release the prisoners based on extreme hardship, the inability of the settlement to become self-sustaining, and its extraordinary expense. Carleton insisted that Steck should clean up the corruption in his own service.

In a long-running bureaucratic battle, General Carleton and Indian superintendent Steck fought over supplies, rations, budgetary responsibility, and bureaucratic turf. Carlton sent his own team to monitor a delivery of supplies from the Indian agency to the Navajo prisoners. "Rusty, old-fashioned, unserviceable, unsaleable plows, soft-iron spades, rakes, hoes, knives and hatchets, thin shoddy cloths and blankets," the army sutler recorded. George Gwyther, the fort's doctor, weighed the blankets and reported them "a full pound less than army issue and twice as expensive." Carleton's team figured that $100,000 shipment to be worth $30,000, a $70,000 profit for various politicians and purchasing agents.

Because the Navajo camp never became self-sustaining, at the end of 1868 Carlton was relieved of command and General William Tecumseh Sherman, fresh from his Civil War victories, was sent to Fort Sumner to negotiate the terms of a treaty with the Navajo. "Better send the Indians to a Fifth Avenue Hotel to board," Sherman reported to Secretary of War Edwin Stanton about the tremendous cost of the camp.

At first Sherman tried to convince the Navajo to move to Indian Territory in Oklahoma. Their leaders refused. Then he finally agreed to negotiate a strip of reservation land overlapping the Arizona and New Mexico border, extending to Canyon de Chelly. Even at the time it was recognized as being far too small and arid to support seven thousand Navajo. In the five years of the Navajo imprisonment, white settlers had moved into their old lands. Their previous economy and agriculture had been completely destroyed. On their old lands they found charred hogans, fields overgrown with brush, and corrals that had to be rebuilt. All that was left of the beautiful peach orchards of Canyon de Chelly were blackened stumps.

According to the Bureau of Ethnography's *Indian Land Sessions in the United States*, the treaty was never formally signed, but the Navajo agreed never to wage war against the United States in exchange for being released to their old lands. In turn, the government agreed to supply the Navajo with food and livestock to get them through the first few winters. But somewhere between the Indian Bureau and Fort Wingate, the shipments of supplies disappeared without a trace.

Few of General Sherman's promises were kept. The Navajo moved far beyond the paper boundaries marked out in the treaty map. The Navajo pushed on. They went north beyond Shiprock, northwest to Monument Valley and Navajo Mountain, and to the valley of the San Juan River. They went beyond the Hopi villages into the interior of Black Mesa. The government never did meet their terms of the treaty to provide them with the promised sheep and cattle to rebuild their economy.

The problem with the construct of the "centuries-old Navajo-Hopi land dispute" was that it was not centuries old. The actual history of the Navajo settlement and reservation negotiations would have provided a different historical context. Except for a one-paragraph summary,* the story of the Navajo reservation was not made part of the

---

* Summary of Bosque Redondo and subsequent Navajo reservation in *Healing v. Jones:* "Additional land was added to the southwest corner of the Navajo reservation by another executive order issued on January 6, 1880. Despite the vast size of the Navajo reservation at that time, this semi-arid land was considered incapable of providing support for all of the Navajos. Moreover the boundaries of the Navajo reservation were not distinctly marked. It is therefore not surprising that great numbers of the Navajos wandered far beyond the paper boundaries of the Navajo reservation as it existed in 1880. By 1882 Navajos comprising hundreds of bands and amounting to about half of the Navajo population had camps and farms outside the Navajo reservation, some as far away as one hundred and fifty miles."

Hopi-Navajo court case in *Healing v. Jones*. As a practical matter, the 1882 Executive Order Reservation of thirty-nine hundred square miles was useless in marking usable borders between the people of the two reservations. The Parker-Keam line established in 1891 and known as the "sixteen-mile limit" established with the cooperation of both Hopi and Navajo leaders was honored by most tribal members. This inter-tribal agreement facilitated by Thomas Keams, an Indian trader who gave his name to Keams Canyon, stood in practice and principle un-til 1958, when legal claims were filed by John Boyden on behalf of the Hopi against the Navajo.

By 1974 the Hopi Land Settlement Act had passed both houses of Congress and was awaiting President Ford's signature. When con-cerned citizens wrote to the Interior Department asking for informa-tion about the Hopi-Navajo dispute, Interior sent them a pamphlet prepared by the Peabody Coal Company. The final bill that passed had been introduced by Wayne Owens, a freshman congressman from Utah, but had been written by John Boyden. When Owens failed to win reelection, he joined John Boyden's law firm in Salt Lake City, now located in new offices in the Kennecott Building overlooking Temple Square in Salt Lake City.

John Boyden and Stewart Udall and Peabody Coal/Kennecott Copper needed leasing rights, coal, and access to the aquifer. It might have been theft, but it was all done legally. By passing new laws, Black Mesa became a crucial resource colony for the expansion of the New West. Water and energy were key to the massive population shift of the 1970s and '80s that, in the eight years of Ronald Reagan's presi-dency, transferred increasing political power from the East to the west-ern states.

PART III

CHAPTER 9

LEARNING FROM LAS VEGAS

The temperature was 112 degrees on May 15, 1905, when Senator William Clark came to establish the new town site for his railroad depot. He had bulldozed forty acres clear of desert scrub, laid out the main streets in a grid, and announced an auction to sell numbered lots on a map. The bidders were speculators from Los Angeles and agents for eastern investors. Some bidders brought their own tents. Others stayed in a tent hotel named Hotel Las Vegas. The auction platform was erected roughly where the Plaza hotel-casino stands today in the old downtown.

The investors were bidding on twelve hundred parcels. Each lot was 25 feet wide and 140 feet deep, marked out on a large map. Some offerings were double lots. These lines on paper represented a future town with streets, stores, saloons, housing, churches, schools, electricity, plumbing, and a septic system. In the spirit of Gilded Age speculation and the town's gambling future, Senator Clark's auction drew the speculators into a frenzy of bidding for numbered squares on a map at grossly inflated prices. The chance to buy property—even if it was only on paper—in a new railroad depot town was the equivalent of buying into a hot IPO stock offering today. Senator Clark was the forerunner of the real estate capitalists that built the urban Southwest. When the auction was over, Clark had earned $250,000 in profit ($6 million in today's dollars). He had paid Helen Stewart $55,000 ($1,275,000) for her ranch and its water rights at Big Springs.

Helen Stewart was the unlikely owner of the land and water rights from the original Mormon settlement, a missionary colony that Brigham Young had sent out in 1855 to a desert oasis that the Spanish called *las vegas* and Anglos called The Meadows. Like Tuba City, the site had abundant water sources from a large aquifer that had been collecting snowmelt and water runoff for a thousand years. The Mormon mission had lasted less than two years, done in by Paiute hostility, the poor desert soil, and too many people for the small agricultural base. (The restored old Mormon Fort can still be seen on Washington Street in Las Vegas.) Helen Stewart's husband had taken over the ranch from Octavius Gass, who had successfully farmed and ranched in the same spot for twenty years. But in the late 1870s Gass was seized by gold fever. After the Comstock silver strike near Reno, everyone in Nevada was filing gold or silver claims in the surrounding mountains. Even today Nevada has a major mining industry and is the fourth-largest producer of gold in the world. In 1880 Gass took out a $5,000 mortgage against his ranch and went off into the mountains to seek his fortune in precious metals. But he never struck gold and defaulted on the mortgage. His banker, Helen Stewart's husband, foreclosed.

Stewart moved to Las Vegas with Helen and their four children to fix up the ranch and sell it. Unfortunately for Mr. Stewart, he misjudged the temperament of his Las Vegas neighbors, and when he went to retrieve one of his horses that they had stolen, they shot and killed him. The newly widowed Helen Stewart, already with four children, was pregnant with a fifth. She knew little about ranching and had never wanted to come to Las Vegas in the first place. Yet she was in no position to move.

At first she stayed to fix up the ranch to sell. Then she discovered she had a talent for business and for managing a ranch. She also had five children to raise. One of the original Mormon buildings was incorporated into her ranch house. She raised cattle, grew vegetables and peaches, and started a vineyard that produced good wine (drought-resistant vines) that many farmers and ranchers in the Las Vegas Valley came to buy. She hired Paiute Indians as workers. When the State Land Act offered land at $1.25 an acre, she bought additional landholdings until the ranch grew to more than twelve hundred acres. Her ranch included the original water source that had irrigated the Mormon agricultural plots. The Las Vegas valley floor had several places where springs came to the surface and was filled with mesquite trees, willows, cottonwoods, and saltgrass. The major springs were known as Big Springs, Middle, and Little. The Stewart Ranch included Big Springs. (One spring was located beneath the lake in front of the Bellagio casino-hotel and formerly watered the golf course for the Dunes resort. Another of the original springs is at the Springs Preserve.)

In 1901 Helen Stewart sold more than a thousand acres of her ranch—excluding four acres of the family cemetery and another section she gave to her Paiute workers—to the new railroad venture headed by Senator William Clark. Senator Clark of Montana needed a supply depot for the new railroad line that he was building between Salt Lake City and Los Angeles; Las Vegas was a logical depot. It had the key resource he needed: water. With its springs and underground aquifer, Las Vegas had the huge amounts of water needed to supply the steam engines of the era. Clark set up the Las Vegas Land and Water Company and controlled the water from the three artesian springs. But the new residents who came to work on the railroad found that if they drilled down about three hundred feet, they too could strike water.

Geologically, Las Vegas is located in the Mohave Desert in a south-tilting bowl surrounded by mountains. The bowl held a natural water supply that was fed by mountain snowmelt and stored in a closed basin that did not run off into streams or rivers. Thousands of years of snowmelt poured down from the surrounding mountains and sank through sand, gravel, and rock to collect in underground aquifers, porous rock formations that stored water in the desert. In places where the water was trapped between layers of impermeable rock, it was under pressure, and springs bubbled to the surface through fissures in the rock.

These permanent artesian springs were a life-giving resource in the middle of the Mohave Desert. The oasis, first pointed out to the Spanish by their Paiute Indian guides, was well marked on the Spanish maps of the 1600s, maps that the Mormon leadership studied carefully. The Spanish named the spot *las vegas*, "the meadows," because of the green vegetation that sprang up in the gray-beige desert. It was a life-saving watering hole in the desert and a crucial stop for any pioneer party on the trail to Southern California.

Only seven years after arriving in Salt Lake City, Brigham Young sent thirty Mormon families on a mission to settle the Meadows. The Paiute Indians who had used the waters for eons were alarmed by this group of settlers who did not move on. They were used to the Spanish priests going to their missions in California, followed by various wagon trains that passed through, staying at the oasis for days or even weeks, then heading north to Red Rock Canyon along the Old Spanish Trail. But this new group built houses and a wall. They were still there after an entire year and then two years. In response to the worsening relations with the Indians, the Mormons surrounded the cabins, kitchen gardens, and the creek with an adobe wall.

Summer heat, Paiute incursions, and the alkali soil that produced stunted crops brought an end to the Mormon settlement. Brigham Young had overburdened the small mission with a party of miners he sent to look for minerals in the surrounding mountains. The miners overtaxed the food supply. Some of the Mormon settlers didn't return all the way to Salt Lake and settled in what would become Mesquite at the Nevada-Utah border or St. George, Utah.

Although the original Las Vegas settlement was a colony that lasted less than two years in the mid-1850s, the always-industrious Mormon settlers remembered their early history in Las Vegas, and many came back to work on the railroad.

Like many of the early railroad ventures, the big profits came not from running the railroad itself, but from land sales and town sites located along the routes and from controlling water rights. The Salt Lake, San Pedro, and Los Angeles Railroad was no exception. Senator Clark's partner in the venture was Senator Kearns of Utah, owner of the Silver King mine in Park City, Utah.

Senator Clark had a name for being a dishonest businessman. His unsavory reputation derived from documented accounts that he had bribed Montana state legislators to appoint him senator; the profusion of legal suits brought by former business partners who accused him, with good evidence, of cheating them out of profits; and his marriage to a teenager forty years his junior who had been a ward in his home. Senator Clark was from Butte, Montana, and had made his first fortune in copper smelters.

Mark Twain, who first came to Nevada in 1861 when his brother was appointed secretary to the governor of Nevada Territory, later wrote about Senator Clark and judged him to be considerably worse than the average Gilded Age robber baron: "He is as rotten a human being as can be found anywhere under the flag; he is a shame to the American nation, and no one has helped to send him to the Senate who did not know that his proper place was the penitentiary." Although Clark County, which includes most of southern Nevada, is named for the dodgy senator, there is no statue of this Las Vegas founding father anywhere to be seen. There is, however, a statue of Helen Stewart at Springs Preserve Park, a local park that preserves early Las Vegas history, both natural and man-made.

One day I asked the concierge at Treasure Island hotel-casino, where I was staying, for directions to the Nevada State History Museum. She twirled a Rolodex as big as a basketball several times and shook her head. I asked how come she couldn't find a state history museum. "No one has ever asked before," she told me.

"How about the Mormon Fort? I know that's not so far from here. Maybe they can tell me where the museum is." She gave a few more twirls of the Rolodex and came up with the address of the Mormon Fort. "No one has ever asked me for that either," she said.

When I finally got to the Mormon Fort, it was noon in June, and I tried to imagine the pioneer women living in those tiny cabins in summer temperatures, raising children, growing vegetables, and cooking in the summer heat. No wonder they all packed up and headed back to the border, I thought.

LAS VEGAS HISTORY

History is not a big subject in Las Vegas. As a rule, the hotels don't like visitors leaving the gambling center. The casino owners, who make up the most powerful lobby in the state, don't like the idea of historical tourism. Except for the Atomic History Museum, which is in the middle of the gambling district, museums are hard to find. I realized this only after I found that all the maps I could easily get at the hotel stopped at the outer edge of the old downtown. I had to go to the American Automobile Association office to get maps of Greater Las Vegas.

Today Las Vegas has fourteen of the largest hotels in the world, many with more than four thousand rooms, several designed by world-famous architects. It has dazzling light displays, themed casinos, big-name entertainment, Broadway shows, and celebrity-chef restaurants. Most of these, however, are not within the Las Vegas city limits. They are outside the city line, because the town-site survey set up by Senator Clark stopped at the north end of the Strip. The Strip is actually on what was called the Old Los Angeles Road in an area called Paradise. Clark County, however, named for Senator Clark, comprises most of southern Nevada. Two-thirds of the Nevada population now lives in southern Nevada. Sixteen of the twenty largest employers in the state are located in Clark County.

Senator William Clark's railroad dominated the future growth of Las Vegas because it controlled the water supply and jobs. Photographs of the town from the 1920s show a Spanish mission–style railroad depot (now torn down but located roughly behind the Plaza Hotel), extensive freight yards, butterfly sheds, an ice plant, a handful of stores, and the Arizona Club—which was a restaurant, bar, brothel, and hotel. Some streets have stucco houses with wide porches, others rows of small bungalows built for railroad workers, and many streets are interrupted by patchwork lots of scrub and desert. Until 1930 Fremont Street was the town's only paved street.

Many Mormons moved into Las Vegas to work on the railroad or to explore mining claims or to ranch or farm. A Church of Latter-day Saints was built at the outer edge of downtown. Then in 1921 a torrential summer rainstorm washed out a hundred miles of track. The railroad had to shut down. When the track was rebuilt, the railroad was under control of a new owner, E. H. Harriman's Union Pacific, and Las Vegas was no longer the supply depot. The new depot was 150 miles to the north, in Caliente, Nevada. The railroad prosperity had lasted barely fifteen years. Southern Nevada became known as "the empty quarter." The town settled back into desert torpor.

When Warren Bechtel came to Las Vegas in 1930 to scout the location where he and his partners were about to build a dam, thirty miles south, on the Colorado River, the town had fewer than 4,000 people. In 1922 Nevada, with a total population of 80,000, had been the first state to sign the Colorado River Compact, an agreement that divided the waters of the Colorado River among seven states and Mexico. At the time it was considered a coup that Nevada got 300,000 acre-feet* of water from the compact because of the state's sparse population. (California had 3.4 million people.) The dam would mostly benefit California, although Nevada and Las Vegas would get much-needed electricity from the dam's hydroelectric plant. Arizona refused to sign.

A Damn Big Dam

Although the Bechtel Corporation would emerge as the named builder of Hoover Dam, and still highlights the dam as the signature megaproject on its website, at the time it was two Mormon brothers from Ogden, Utah, who actually spearheaded the project. Edmund, known as "E. O.," and William "W. H." Wattis were the heads of Utah Construction, the largest construction company west of the Mississippi. The two brothers began by grading railroad bed in Canada at the turn of the century and grew into a major construction company, interrupted by intervals of sheep ranching when there was little railroad work. Within a decade they became the major builder for the Union Pacific Railroad and expanded into dam building, including the dam that created the controversial Hetch Hetchy Reservoir north of San Francisco. They subcontracted tunneling, grading, and laying track to many other construction companies in the West and knew everybody in the business.

---

* An acre-foot is 326,000 gallons or the amount of water need to cover a football field (roughly an acre) with a foot of water. One-acre foot is generally calculated as enough water to supply two families for a year.

They liked Warren Bechtel and gave his W. A. Bechtel Company a lot of business, but like many Mormons, the Wattis brothers preferred doing business "with their own kind," that is, with other Mormons.

Their preferred partners for bidding on the Hoover Dam project were Harry Morrison and Morris Knudsen of Boise, Idaho—former Bureau of Reclamation engineers, frequent partners with Utah Construction, and fellow Mormons. Bidding construction jobs was an art form in itself. As the saying went, "Estimate too high and you lose the job; estimate too low and you lose your shirt." Morrison and Knudsen had recently hired Frank Crowe, a legendary dam builder from the Bureau of Reclamation, to help them with the bid. Crowe had done the government's estimates for what was then called Boulder Dam. (Its original location was to have been in Boulder Canyon, twenty miles upstream, but the site was moved to Black Canyon because of accessible bedrock, a wide wash at the mouth of the canyon, and its proximity to rail lines in Las Vegas. Habit and inertia kept its name as the Boulder Canyon Project, until 1950, when President Truman renamed the dam for President Herbert Hoover, who negotiated the distribution of the river's water among seven states and under whose presidency the dam was bid and construction begun.)

Crowe was their best insurance that their bid would both get them the job and make them a profit. The Wattis brothers' intent was to bid the job with only Morrison and Knudsen as partners, but one member of their board, Marriner Eccles, insisted that the job was too big, the insurance bond of $5 million too large, and the risks too great. He insisted they needed to bring in more partners to spread the risk. Eccles didn't need to mention age and disease. William Wattis, age seventy-two, was ill with cancer, irritable, and hard to convince. Edmund, age seventy-six, had Parkinson's disease and was hardly more amenable. They were testy, tough, obstinate, and described by one person who had been on the losing end of a negotiation as "mean as snakes." (Neither man lived to see the completion of the dam.) The outspoken board member of Utah Construction, the remarkable Marriner Eccles, age thirty-eight, was the son of David Eccles, the wealthiest Mormon in Utah and the person who tithed the most to the Mormon Church.

Eccles Sr., Utah's leading industrialist and banker, had amassed controlling investments in mining, lumber, and land throughout the West.

Eccles Sr. had two families by two wives, the first with thirteen children, the second with nine. Marriner came from the second family, and when David Eccles died suddenly without a will, the sons of the first family, according to Utah state law, got 70 percent control of seventeen corporations, dealing in lumber, sugar, railroads, construction, and banking. They proved to be untalented stewards. Their younger half-brother Marriner had inherited his father's genius for business and soon leveraged his 30 percent share into a division of the Eccles holdings that left him with controlling interest in the Eccles banks and a seat on the board of Utah Construction.

In the end, however, young Marriner Eccles's views prevailed because the $5 million bond that had to accompany each bid was too large for the Wattis brothers to raise alone, even with Morrison and Knudsen. They began looking for additional partners with financial depth and experience in diversion tunnels, waterline construction, road building, and reinforced concrete. The dam project on the Colorado River had been in the works for more than fifteen years, budgeted at $50 million, and was the largest civil engineering project in US history. It would also be the first dam on any major river in the world. (The hydroelectric plant was budgeted at another $50 million and bid separately from the dam.) In February 1931 all six principals along with their lawyers and bankers met at the Engineers Club in San Francisco to work out the contractual details of their partnership. Marriner Eccles represented the Wattis brothers. (Four years later Franklin Roosevelt appointed Eccles chairman of the Federal Reserve Board, a post he held until 1948, concurrent with his role as president of Utah Construction.) The partners named their consortium Six Companies, after the Six Tongs of San Francisco's Chinatown. Every partner had to put in between $500,000 to $1 million of his own money to be held as insurance. It was not a consortium that inspired confidence in the insurance company that wrote their $5 million insurance bond.

Charlie Shea of Shea Construction, an Oregon company that laid out San Francisco's water-supply system, was using the San Francisco

Palace Hotel as his business address; Alan MacDonald of MacDonald Kahn of San Francisco, builder of sewers, storm drains, and the Mark Hopkins Hotel, was known to have been fired from a dozen jobs before starting his own company; Pacific Bridge of Portland, Oregon, with a specialty in underwater construction, was known to be having trouble meeting its cash obligations; E. O. and W. H. Wattis had to include twenty-five thousand cattle and thirty thousand sheep in their list of assets in order to meet their percentage of the insurance bond; and Warren Bechtel and Henry Kaiser, who had paired with Warren Construction of Boston, had to step up and cover the Warren share when the Warren brothers dropped out at the last minute. With $1.5 million invested, Bechtel and Kaiser were the largest investors in Six Companies.

When the bids were opened in March 1931, Six Companies had the lowest bid, almost exactly, thanks to Frank Crowe, the government's own estimate. They were $5 million lower than the next competitor and only $24,000 higher than the government's number. On the day of the announcement in March 1931, reporters and photographers went to William Wattis's hospital room at the St. Francis Hospital in San Francisco, where he was being treated for cancer. "Now this dam is just a dam, but it is a damn big dam," he told them with a smile. Downplaying the difficulty of the project, he said, "Otherwise it is no different than others we've thrown up in a dozen places." Many people thought the partners would go broke, but when the dam was completed in 1935, two years and three months ahead of schedule, every partner became a multimillionaire. Even in the middle of the Depression, each partner earned an extra $3 million in profits ($50 million in current dollars). William Wattis died in September of the same year, never having visited the dam site. His brother died in 1934, before the dam was finished.

The same month as the award announcement, on March 19, 1931, the Nevada Legislature passed a bill that legalized gambling, making Nevada the first and only state in the country where gambling was legal. The same year brought two men to Las Vegas who gave a hint of the future. One was Warren Bechtel, senior partner in Bechtel

Construction; the other was Tony Cornero, a Los Angeles bootlegger who, with a nice sense of history, planned to build a classy hotel-casino nightclub called the Meadows. In future decades, Warren Bechtel's company would become a global corporation and dusty Las Vegas would become the gambling and entertainment capital of the world.

WARREN BECHTEL

Warren A. Bechtel grew up on a farm in Peabody, Kansas, at a time when he saw many men missing an arm or a leg from service in the Civil War. He was born in 1872, nine years after Henry Ford, and like Henry Ford, he hated farming. He liked tools and equipment and was said to be able to diagnose and fix any piece of mechanical equipment that broke. He disliked the tedium of farm animals, the dawn-to-dusk labor every day. His father, a German immigrant, owned a prosperous farm as well as a grocery store in the town of Peabody. Warren was fifteen years old when the first railroad train cut through the county. During high school summers, he did road construction work and learned how construction crews were organized and how machinery could cut the time of a job in half. Although he dated the founding of W. A. Bechtel Construction to 1898, when he was twenty-six, his actual equipment for the first years of his construction career consisted of two mules, a slip grader, and a strong back. Walking along behind two mules grading railroad bed was not so different from walking behind two mules plowing fields. When he arrived in Las Vegas in 1931, he saw men grading roadbed using the same kind of old-fashioned Fresno grader (invented in Fresno, California, for grading irrigation ditches). They were extending Fremont Street out into the desert for some thirty miles to the edge of the canyon of the Colorado River. By then, however, he was president of a large construction company that owned a lot of heavy equipment and one of the two senior partners in the Six Companies consortium. Like the Wattis brothers, he had never gone to college or engineering school.

His first construction job was laying railroad track from southern Kansas into Indian Territory, soon to be known as Oklahoma. Known as a good manager who ran an organized construction site, he was promoted to supervising construction crews in Wyoming, working as a gang foreman, an estimator, supervisor of a shale quarry—all jobs that contributed to his understanding of materials, cost estimating, and how to write a contract to make a profit. Called a "natural engineer," his talent in managing men, machinery, and money was a rare combination. By the time he got to Reno, Nevada, he was twenty-seven and married with two small sons, and the family lived in a converted railroad boxcar. (Today, a more luxurious version of the railroad car, called Watateeka, sits outside Bechtel world headquarters on Beale Street in downtown San Francisco, a reminder of the firm's humble beginnings.) When his brother, Arthur, eleven years younger, joined him in 1897, Warren rented, and then bought, with the help of a loan from his father-in-law, one of the first steam shovels, a Model 10 Marion, the model developed for digging the Panama Canal. He had "W. A. Bechtel Co." stenciled on the cab door and never looked back. He and his steam shovel were in demand largely for building railroad lines. But he also expanded into building bridges and dams, one of them, the Bowman Dam in the Sierra Nevada, the largest rock-filled dam in the West. Many of Warren Bechtel's most lucrative jobs came as a subcontractor for the Wattis brothers. When he took on a partner, he chose Henry Kaiser, who had a sand and gravel business and was younger by ten years. By the time the Bechtel-Kaiser partnership became the largest investor in the Hoover Dam, the Bechtel family lived in a large Victorian house in Oakland, Mrs. Bechtel was on the board of the San Francisco Opera, and Warren Bechtel had four adult children, one of whom, Steven, was to become the full-time purchasing agent for Hoover Dam, a job second in importance only to that of the job superintendent, Frank Crowe.

The Great Depression

Although Hoover Dam is generally believed to have been a great public works project of the New Deal administration during the Depression, it was actually a construction project built by private enterprise, funded by the government, and put in motion by the business-oriented Hoover administration to help the landowners of the Imperial Valley of Southern California. When the head of the Reclamation Bureau, Arthur Powell Davis, made his full report on the Colorado River to Congress, the report was officially titled "Report on Problems of Imperial Valley and Vicinity."

What made the Hoover Dam project different from any other construction project that any of the partners had ever worked on was that the entire country was in the depths of the Great Depression. The economy was stagnant, and the cost of materials had been cut in half. Labor was limitless. With a national unemployment rate of 25 percent, one out of every four workers was unemployed. People were living in their cars. Families had lost homes, jobs, and their savings, and they needed everything—housing, health care, schools, jobs. By 1931, the year construction started, more than ten thousand unemployed workers from across the country converged on Las Vegas to fight for fifteen hundred jobs. Instead of the young miners they expected to hire, the Six Companies employment office in Las Vegas faced long lines of workers of every age and every background—some in three-piece suits—from all over the country. Many arrived with families and children and were living in tents or cars if they had them. They set up tent colonies along Boulder Highway and shanties adjacent to the federal reservation where workers were housed (actually, workers were also in tents because housing was still being built). The unemployed patiently waited for someone to die or be fired.

And during that first summer, as temperatures soared to more than 120 degrees and 130 degrees on the floor of Black Canyon and never went below 100 even at night, many did die. The medical teams did not know how to treat heat prostration or extreme dehydration. The stupefying heat was so relentless that workers could not replace the amount of water their bodies lost. Body temperatures went to 104 degrees, and workers went into comas. Even with the extreme summer heat, men tried to sneak into the dam site to ask for employment. Every worker had to have an official pass, or else they were turned away at the gate and told to apply at the main office in Las Vegas.

One desperate but resourceful unemployed father cut the small rectangular photo label off the front of his son's cereal box because the design was similar to a worker's identification pass. He hitched a ride down Boulder Highway to the job site with four employed workers and flashed the cereal-box cutout when the guard at the gate peered through the car windows and scanned their identification. The guard nodded and waved them all through. With a wife and four children, the youngest nine months, living in a tent along Boulder Highway, he didn't leave the job site until he had attached himself to a crew, been hired, and been given a real pass.

Organized crime figures already ran illegal gambling in Reno and Carson City, but advocates for legal gambling argued that it would provide an important source of recreation for the dam workers as well as revenue for the state. Gambling and prostitution were a fact of life in Nevada's hundreds of mining towns. No one thought in terms of legality or illegality. And even though the Volstead Act was still in effect, Prohibition was barely enforced in Nevada.

As the Great Depression deepened, unemployment in America continued to grow. America had 98 million people, less than a third of its population today, and a fourth of its workers were unemployed. Las Vegas became a magic name, the one place in the country where that elusive element called "a job" still existed. Thousands made their way to Las Vegas, by bus, train, car.

TONY CORNERO

Tony Cornero arrived in Las Vegas in 1931, the same year as Warren Bechtel, except that he came directly from prison. Cornero's real name was Anthony Stralla, and he was a talented promoter and liquor "wholesaler." He was also smart, a sharp dresser, and ambitious. Based in Los Angeles, he supplied Las Vegas clubs with good-quality imported liquor that he got from Mexico and Canada. Known for "the real stuff," not the liquor made in local stills or Las Vegas bathtubs, Tony Stralla Cornero was also known by the nickname of Admiral Cornero because he brought liquor in by boat from Mexico or Canada, transferring it into smaller boats before dawn and then unloading the cargo in small coves along the coast. The liquor went by truck to the many local saloons in Las Vegas, where it was said that every second or third building on Fremont Street was a sawdust saloon or a gambling hall—the Golden Camel, the Nevada Club, the Tivoli Bar, the La Salle Club, the Barrel House, the Silver Club. If the club's owner paid off the local sheriff—"dues" rather than a bribe—there was no problem with Prohibition enforcement. The only problem came when federal officers came to town.

Tony Cornero was ahead of his time. Although author James Roman called him "the original wise guy," he also was a good businessman with a vision of a high-class establishment for the visitors who would come to Las Vegas to see the dam construction. He wanted to build not only a hotel and a casino and nightclub but an airstrip that would bring a wealthy clientele to Las Vegas to gamble. He wanted to bring Los Angeles nightclub acts to Las Vegas. The luxurious Arizona Biltmore hotel had opened in the empty desert outside of Phoenix in 1929 and was attracting many wealthy Hollywood people to its private gambling and entertainment. Planes made it possible.

As a convicted felon—Tony had been arrested during the unloading of one of his Mexican-rum import operations—he was ineligible for a license. His brothers, Frank and Louis Stralla, secured one of Las Vegas's first gambling licenses, and Cornero named the place the Meadows. He and his brothers bought land outside the Las Vegas city limits at the intersection of East Sahara and Boulder Highway on the theory that it was a location where they could attract visitors going both to and from the dam as well as regulars from Las Vegas.

The Meadows opened in May 1931, and according to John Cahlan, who attended the launch, "It set the stage for all future openings in the city of Las Vegas." Everyone was expected to wear a tuxedo, even though "there were very few people outside the Las Vegas Elks Lodge who had tuxes. So there was a grand scurrying to get the tuxes in for the opening." The Meadows was the classiest place in Las Vegas, a social center for the locals and the place where the executives from the dam project went for recreation.

Another Las Vegas resident, Thomas Wilson, remembered a New Year's party the Stralla brothers invited him to. "They sent me an invitation to their black-tie New Year's party. The youngest brother Louis, introduced me to his guests, his brothers, some of the gals in the chorus . . . and then he said 'I gotta identify you, right?' And he drew with a pencil a badge on my shirtfront and put 'U.S. Prohi' [federal Prohibition officer] lettered on the shield. They thought this was funnier than hell! I had a wonderful time—all the scotch in the world, all the champagne in the world—all these crazy characters. . . . It was sort of like being on the set of a grade B gangster movie." Local business and civic leaders expressed appreciation for the new business and sponsored a ten-page supplement about the Meadows in the local newspaper: "Potent in its charm, mysterious in its fascination, The Meadows, America's most luxurious casino, will open its doors tonight and formally embark upon a career which all liberal-minded persons in the West will watch closely."

Tony Cornero introduced a few other innovations. He used silver dollars rather than chips at the gambling tables. He said that if anybody tried to heist them, they couldn't get away with much because a bag of silver dollars weighed too much.

He was prescient in seeing possibilities in Las Vegas that were different from the dusty construction site that it was at the time. He built the landing strip for small planes that did bring many wealthy people from Los Angeles. He brought in showgirls from Los Angeles and launched a popular nightclub act and entertainment. And he experimented with air-conditioning. As the *Las Vegas Review-Journal* wrote in a profile of Cornero, "He saw a Las Vegas of classy, carpeted casinos, quite distinct from the tiny places with sawdust on the floor, which opened after the gambling bill was signed into law."

Yet there were problems. Four months after the opening, the hotel part of the Meadows complex burned down. Because the building was outside the city limits, the fire department got to the city line and wouldn't go any farther. There was no county fire department. Then a story emerged that Cornero had made a deal with members of the leading law firm in town to arrange for the closing of Block 16, where all the brothels were located, so that Cornero would have the monopoly on prostitution at the Meadows. That did not happen. Block 16 remained the prostitution district of Las Vegas. Then another story went around that the fire was arson because Cornero refused to pay protection money to Meyer Lansky's syndicate that controlled the racing wire in Las Vegas.

Tony Cornero left his brothers to run the Meadows and went back to California and opened two of the hugely profitable gambling boats that operated outside the three-mile limit off Santa Monica Pier. When law enforcement agencies closed the gambling boats in the 1940s, he came back to Las Vegas, worked at the Apache Club, and began putting together the money and backing to build the Stardust casino-resort.

A Deadly Work Site

At the dam site construction surged forward, even before there was any housing constructed for the workers. Warren Bechtel had negotiated significant performance incentives into their contract. The faster they finished key phases of the dam, the larger the bonus they earned. Six Companies also had much lower costs than originally estimated. It was the depth of the Depression, and the cost of labor, materials, and equipment had fallen through the floor. For every cubic yard of earth excavated, the government contract paid $8, while the actual cost to the builder was $5.50. The contract stipulated $850 reimbursement for the houses built for the workers; it cost Six Companies $145. The workers were paid $4 a day instead of the $5.50 that had been estimated. The final contract called for nonunion labor and barred Asian (Chinese) workers.

Thousands of unemployed workers converged on Las Vegas to apply for construction jobs. Along with the miners and construction crews they expected to hire, the Six Companies employment office saw men in suits, men with families, men who had no construction experience whatsoever. Some took jobs with Union Pacific, grading railroad bed and building the thirty miles of railroad track that would carry materials and equipment to the dam site. They laid track to the edge of the canyon and then blasted six miles of switchbacks out of the canyon walls to bring the track down to water level. Others built the concrete plant on the Arizona side of the river, where the concrete would be mixed with aggregate and shipped by truck to the dam site. (The concrete plant is now underneath Lake Mead, and boaters say the old smokestacks of the plant are starting to poke through to the surface and nudge unlucky boaters.) Others got jobs at Boulder City, where housing for the workers and dam executives was being built. Experienced miners were able to get jobs blasting out the diversion tunnels on either side of the canyon in order to reroute the river and create a dry dam site on the floor of the canyon almost a mile long.

In August 1931 some fourteen hundred workers, almost two-thirds of the workforce at that point, threatened to strike. Workers on the canyon floor were surrounded by thousand-foot walls of solid black rock that absorbed the sun's heat. Temperatures during the day went as high as 130 degrees. The workers wanted free ice water on the floor of the canyon (they had water, but had to pay for ice water) and $5 a day in pay instead of $4, half of which was deducted in advance to pay for meals and lodging. (The pay scale ranged from $3.50 a day to $6 for truck drivers, welders, and skilled machine operators. Unskilled labor was at the bottom of the scale.) The workers also demanded payment in real money, not company scrip. Scrip, company paper usable only at Six Companies stores, was a common practice, but illegal on federal contracts. The workers wanted helmets instead of baseball caps that that been coated with hardened tar, because a pebble that fell from the top of the canyon to a worker at the bottom gained enough velocity to kill or cripple him. Frank Crowe, as project superintendent, fired all fourteen hundred men in the morning and began hiring a new workforce the same afternoon. The labor pool was bottomless.

In San Francisco W. H. Wattis called a press conference from his room at St. Francis Hospital, where he was still being treated for cancer, and attributed the strike to the work of communists and the hated Wobblies (International Workers of the World). As quoted in the *San Francisco Examiner*, Wattis declared, "They will work under our conditions or they will not work at all." There would be no unions tolerated at Black Canyon. Although Wattis died the following month, no unions took hold at the dam site. Anyone advocating for a union was soon fired and run off the job site.

Ten months into the construction, the Nevada superintendent of mines cited Six Companies for illegal practices such as using gasoline-fired engines in unventilated closed spaces and for returning men to the diversion tunnels in fifteen minutes instead of sixty after dynamite blasts. Warren Bechtel soon showed up with a lawyer and said they weren't a mining operation, so Nevada mining laws weren't applicable. The air in the unventilated tunnels was thick with carbon monoxide from the idling trucks. Many truck drivers who cleared debris from the tunnels became ill from carbon monoxide poisoning, a potentially fatal lung disease that the company denied and instead called "pneumonia." The ill workers, who claimed that the toxic gases in the tunnels were worse than coal mines, were soon fired or laid off. Although more than a hundred workers died on the job, from heatstroke, falls, explosions, or being struck by heavy equipment, no one was listed as dying from "pneumonia." Six Companies settled at least fifty cases of carbon monoxide poisoning out of court.

Warren Bechtel succeeded Wattis as president of Six Companies, and his son Steven took over as vice president. Steven Bechtel, later known as Steve Sr., was in charge of purchasing, a job that controlled expenditures of $10 million and was second in importance to that of Frank Crowe, the overall project superintendent. The prominence of the Bechtels, father and son, contributed to credit going to the Bechtel Company after the project's completion. Warren Bechtel also died before the dam was finished, which placed Steven Bechtel in a position of greater authority. "Hoover Dam," said Steven Bechtel years later after he became president of Bechtel, Inc., "put us in a prime position as being big-time thinkers, real thinkers."

In the 1932 election the economic depths of the Depression and the skillful campaign run by Franklin Delano Roosevelt defeated Herbert Hoover. President Roosevelt's new secretary of interior, Harold Ickes, investigated the workers' complaints at Hoover Dam, and, since it was a federally funded project, he filed more than a thousand labor violations against Six Companies. In 1933 Warren Bechtel quickly dispatched Henry Kaiser to Washington to launch a public relations campaign and to lobby Congress to keep funds flowing. At the time many congressmen argued that in the midst of such devastating economic times—the national unemployment figure was close to 13 million people—the federal government should not be spending money on a dam in the West that would benefit mainly California.

Kaiser had visited the dam site only once, succumbed to heat prostration, and never went back. In Washington, however, Kaiser was a brilliant and indefatigable public relations man, revealing a genius for working the press and shaping public perception of America's greatest construction project. Kaiser deserves credit for the popular view of Hoover Dam as a great civic undertaking.

He quickly made the case that public works projects like Hoover Dam were necessary for providing employment in desperate economic times and that funding for the project should not be cut. Zane Grey, the most popular western novelist of the era, wrote a novel called *Boulder Dam*; Edmund Wilson, known as America's preeminent man of letters, went to Las Vegas and wrote a series of articles for the *New Republic*, describing the towering man-over-nature dimensions of the project. Magazines like *Time* and *Life* and *Forbes* ran repeated stories about the dam's innovative construction techniques. Henry Kaiser succeeded in turning the construction of the dam—then called Boulder, later renamed Hoover—into one of the great heroic accomplishments of Depression-era America. In the public mind it became an enduring symbol of America's technological genius and resilient national character. During the economic hard times in the Great Recession of 2008–2013, President Obama was said to be looking for "his Hoover Dam," an inaccurate metaphor, since Hoover Dam was not a public works project or a great civic undertaking but was built by private companies whose profits are estimated to have been more than $18 million ($307 million in current dollars) in the midst of the Depression. The workers who built it under brutal working conditions did not share in the rewards. This symbolic version of Hoover Dam is largely due to Henry Kaiser's skills in public relations and media.

Kaiser used old-fashioned persuasion, and he pioneered modern lobbying techniques. He wooed congressmen and senators at lavish lunches and dinners. He fascinated them with stories of technological innovations like the multilevel drilling platform named the Jumbo from which men drilled the dynamite holes for the fifty-foot-wide diversion tunnels; he showed photographs of bold engineering innovations such as the concrete delivery system and cooling pipes embedded in the concrete and filled with ice water. He went on the radio and depicted the heroism of the "high-scalers," men hanging like human flies on vertical walls a thousand feet above the canyon floor, pounding rock loose from the walls with pneumatic drills. (One photograph of the high-scalers showed most of them to be Native Americans.) He described the quality and quantity of the food at the famous Anderson mess hall that could feed five thousand men three meals a day. He described the ideal workers' town being built at Boulder City for twenty-five hundred men and their families. He talked about the school that Six Companies built for the workers' children and the excellent education they were providing; he praised the courage and morale of the men who worked in stupefying desert heat and explained in layman's terms the special equipment and drills that had been designed and manufactured especially for dam construction. Long newspaper articles described the concrete plant and the steel reinforcement and the overhead buckets that would pour the concrete. He described the 115-square-mile federal reservation site and how the river was rerouted through diversion tunnels to create a mile-long dam site. He claimed, and he was probably right, that Hoover Dam would be the most significant single structure ever built in America. He went on speaking tours, commissioned a quick book on the dam, talked with reporters, lobbied congressmen, gave a weekly radio show, and asked for the country's support. He got it.

At the actual site the government had to send in troops from Utah to keep order. In Washington Secretary Ickes ordered Six Companies to pay its workers in dollars, not scrip; charged them with seven thousand counts of unfair labor practices; and imposed a fine of $350,000. Kaiser's political efforts got it reduced to $100,000.

When the dam was finished it was a seamless curve of concrete across the Colorado River, from foundation to crest, higher than the Empire State Building. It was the first dam on any major river in the world. Its actual structure was like a truncated pyramid, 660 feet thick at the base, tapering to 45 feet thick at the top. On either side of the dam the intake towers rose gracefully from platforms that had been blasted halfway up the canyon walls. In describing the construction for the Smithsonian archives, Frank Crowe wrote, "Twelve hundred men with modern equipment had in 32 months built a structure whose volume is greater than the largest pyramid of Egypt, which according to Herodotus required 100,000 men 20 years to complete." In actual fact closer to ten thousand men worked on the dam over the five years of construction because only a few lasted beyond one summer.

On September 30, 1935, President Roosevelt traveled to Black Canyon, accompanied by Interior Secretary Ickes and a retinue of reporters, governors, and congressmen from most of the Colorado River basin states. Roosevelt began his address, which was broadcast live over the two major national radio networks, "This morning I came, I saw and I was conquered, as everyone would be who sees for the first time this great feat of mankind." Even Ickes, who had been Six Companies' most vocal opponent, was won over by the power of the achievement and recorded in his diary, "It is a marvel of engineering."

Hoover Dam did transform the West, but its main beneficiary was California. California got most of the water, the electricity, and the budgeted canals and aqueducts. When John D. Rockefeller Sr., who owned almost 50 percent of almost every mining operation in the West, was asked why he didn't invest more in western industries or land development in California, he said it was because he didn't think the western states had enough water or electricity to sustain their own manufacturing base. He saw the West mainly as a source of minerals and energy resources for eastern industry and believed that the western states would always be dependent on the East for its manufactured goods. Until Hoover Dam began operation in 1936, he was right. The dam, its huge reservoir—named Lake Mead after Elmore Mead, the first head of the Bureau of Reclamation—and the accompanying hydroelectric plant provided the western states, but mainly California, with the water and electricity to break free of the East and to develop their own industries. Within thirty years California, by itself, had grown to be the fifth-largest economy in the world and the most populous state in the nation. That could not have happened without the water and power provided by Hoover Dam. Other states such as Arizona and Nevada, with tiny populations, saw that they would need more water and more electricity in order to grow.

The dam on the Colorado River changed Las Vegas by giving it reliable electricity from the hydroelectric plant and 300,000 acre-feet of water from Lake Mead. At the time Las Vegas didn't need the water because it still had its own aquifer, but by 1955 it had lowered the groundwater level by 200 feet and started pumping its Colorado River water allocation into the city. Although the dam was accepted by the government in 1935, postconstruction repairs continued until 1947, with the crews staying on in Boulder City and Las Vegas. The bedrock in which the dam was anchored was found to be riddled with fissures and faults through which water was seeping. For the next nine years a repair project went forward from inside the dam in which new rows of boreholes were drilled into the bedrock, one of them 480 feet deep. The project required $2 million and twelve thousand tons of cement. Although seepage began pouring into the dam's galleries and grouting went on for years, this was not public knowledge.

Tourists came from all over the country to see the dam. By the late 1930s, America's leaders were preparing for war and commissioning Army Air Force training bases in the Nevada desert around Las Vegas to train a new generation of pilots and soldiers. Bechtel teamed up with Utah Construction and Morrison-Knudsen to get contracts for military construction. During World War II they built military bases in Nevada, Arizona, and California as well as in war zones around the world. The West Coast was the staging area for the Pacific theater of the war and the beginning of a large population shift. Bechtel expanded to new projects (oil refineries, marine ports, pipelines, road systems, airports, tunnels, generating stations), but it also never left Nevada. In 1943 with the beginning of the Manhattan Project, it built storage plants for nuclear materials. When nuclear testing began, it built the "Doomsday Town." In 1950 it helped construct the Atomic Test Site, located sixty-five miles from Las Vegas. Bechtel-Nevada became a permanent subsidiary. (Today Bechtel is also the manager and operator of the privatized nuclear research labs at Los Alamos in New Mexico and the Lawrence Livermore National Laboratory in California.)

In today's Las Vegas, just a few blocks east of the Strip on Flamingo Road, is the Atomic Testing Museum. The museum documents the technical story of nuclear testing at the Nevada Test Site using interactive exhibits, videos, and a theater that replicates the sound and flash of a nuclear blast. A brass plaque in the lobby of the museum lists the founders and major donors. The largest donors all have the name Bechtel in the title:

- The Bechtel Foundation
- Bechtel Nevada Corporation
- Bechtel Science Applications International Corporation

Even though a line item in the 2012 federal military budget makes the Atomic Testing Museum an affiliate of the Smithsonian, the exhibits barely mention the social or cultural aspects of America's atomic project—the dangers from testing, the problems with fallout, the cancer levels among "downwinders," the treatment of Navajo uranium miners, and the thirteen hundred abandoned nuclear mines still blowing radioactive dust on the Navajo reservation.

Today Bechtel is also manager of the Nevada Test Site for the Department of Energy. With some three thousand employees, the test site is southern Nevada's largest nongaming employer. Until 2010 it had another large workforce hollowing out Yucca Mountain, also at the edge of the test site, the location that was supposed to become the nation's national nuclear waste depository. The same day I went to the Mormon Fort I also found the Nevada State Museum and met two men in the lobby who were there for a Bechtel meeting in the museum's auditorium. They worked for the Yucca Mountain Project, at that time budgeted at $18 billion. Its funding was stopped during the Obama administration because of local opposition and questions similar to the ones that a reporter for *Innovation America* asked Frederick Tarantino, president of Bechtel-Nevada, in 2004. "How do you reconcile the proximity of projects involving nuclear waste, hazardous materials and rocket launchings so relatively close to what is arguably America's greatest tourist destination, Las Vegas?"

His answer was that sixty miles of desert between Las Vegas and the border of the Nevada Test Site was plenty. "There's a lot of desert between here and there that's really not developed. There aren't very many remote places like the Nevada Test Site any longer." Many people in Las Vegas came to believe that when it came to nuclear materials, sixty miles wasn't anywhere near remote enough, especially when the spent nuclear fuel rods from 104 nuclear reactors from thirty-one states would be traveling by rail and highway through Las Vegas on their way to Yucca Mountain. Although the state's political culture is focused on small government and individual self-reliance, some 280,000 federal employees live around Las Vegas.

In the atomic age, Las Vegas, like America, was on a new path.

CHAPTER 10

CHINATOWN 2

In an arid climate water assumes a mystical power. Nothing is possible without water. It is why water is made to seem easily accessible in Las Vegas. Most Las Vegas casino-hotel entrances have fountains spouting jets of water, lit by colored lights, forming shapes of fish and dolphins. Hotel swimming pools are larger than New England ponds. One nightclub is built entirely around a pool. Steve Wynn bought and imploded an entire resort-casino, the Dunes, in order to create the eight-acre mini Lake Como in front of the Bellagio with fountain jets that dance in computerized perfection to Broadway show tunes.* Some of the jets shoot 250 feet in the air. Treasure Island used to have a lake large enough so that two pirate ships could conduct a mock battle every hour on the hour. Golf courses are designed with mini lakes, waterfalls, and greens with water holes. The Venetian has canals with gondoliers rowing guests around a mock St. Mark's Square. The most famous entertainment in Las Vegas, however, is Cirque du Soleil's water show, O, as in *eau*, the French word for water, billed as an "aquatic masterpiece" and staged in a specially built theater and tank. The sensuous qualities of water are heightened in the desert.

Talk of drought and water shortages is not encouraged. Criticism of water policy issues is limited to reader comments at the end of articles in the *Las Vegas Review-Journal* and on local cable channels. The

---

* The Bellagio hotel-casino is now owned by the small oil-rich Middle Eastern country of Qatar. The Qatar Holding Company, a subsidiary of Qatar Investment Authority, bought the Bellagio for $4 billion in April 2013.

theory is that anything that touches on climate change or water limitations will put off the tourist industry. "It was amazing to me when I first got into this job," said Pat Mulroy, the general manager of the Southern Nevada Water Authority, "how sensitive the tourist market is to water stories in Southern Nevada." "Water stories" refer to the visibly distressed Lake Mead, the shrinking Colorado River, lack of conservation, the location of a wastewater treatment plant only six miles above the water intake pipe, and the legally binding agreements that relate to the state's share of the Colorado River's flow. Although the water authority has been vigilant in promoting a conservation program in which they pay residents to tear up their lawns and replace them with desert plantings, there are still 39 million visitors a year who are taking showers and flushing toilets. No officials are suggesting that anyone tear up the grass on the more than fifty golf courses in Las Vegas. Las Vegas has the highest per capita use of water in the country.

Although some people still believe that Las Vegas sits on top of a limitless aquifer and that natural springs feed the lush green golf courses, the reality is that Las Vegas's unallocated groundwater was mostly pumped out by the 1960s. Today, 90 percent of Las Vegas water comes from the three hundred thousand acre-feet allocated from Lake Mead and the ever-diminishing waters of the Colorado River. Pat Mulroy and Las Vegas water planners have already looked to alternative sources and have spent more than a decade formulating new water schemes and buying up water rights in two valleys 200 miles to the north. The plan, which some have dubbed the Grand Scheme, involves running a pipeline at least 200 miles from northern Nevada to Las Vegas.

The model for Las Vegas's future water supply took place a century ago in Los Angeles with the construction of the aqueduct that brought water from Owens Valley, 250 miles away, to Los Angeles. Although Roman Polanski's classic movie *Chinatown* was based on true events that took place in 1913, the movie placed them in the 1930s—better clothes, better cars—and hit a few of the high points of the collusion between city officials and private landowners, but left out much of the political stealth involved, including federal involvement that reached to Teddy Roosevelt in the White House in 1908. The title *Chinatown* referred to layers of deception that were so convoluted it was impossible to trace an accurate story line. As Marc Reisner wrote in *Cadillac Desert*:

> Everything the city did was legal (thought its chief collaborator, the U.S. Forest Service, did indeed violate the law). Whether one can justify what the city did, however, is another story. Los Angeles employed chicanery, subterfuge, spies, bribery, a campaign of divide-and-conquer, and a strategy of lies to get the water it needed. In the end, it milked the valley bone-dry, impoverishing it, while the water made a number of prominent Los Angeleans very, very rich. There are those who would argue that if all of this was legal, then something is the matter with the law.

It may be legal, but it isn't moral or sustainable. The more sophisticated concept for today's new water wars is "legal theft." From 1908 to 1913, during the five years that Los Angeles was building the 233-mile aqueduct from Owens Valley, Fred Eaton, the mayor of the city, along with Harrison Otis, *LA Times* publisher Harry Chandler, and a syndicate of friends were buying up lands in the San Fernando Valley in anticipation of future irrigation water from the Owens Valley. When the aqueduct opened in 1913, the first use of Owens Valley water was not for Los Angeles citizens, but for irrigating the new farms of San Fernando Valley and the fortunes of millionaires. Within ten years, by 1924, the Owens Valley Lake had been pumped out. William Mulholland, the chief engineer of the Los Angeles Water and Power Authority, today's Los Angeles Department of Water and Power (LADWP), began buying up groundwater rights and valley farms in order to drain the Owens River. By 1928 Los Angeles owned 90 percent of the water rights in the valley. The lake disappeared, the river disappeared, vegetation disappeared, and finally Owens Valley had huge alkali flats at the north end where the lake used to be. The entire valley ecosystem had been devastated. The valley produced a poisonous dust named "particulate pollution" that was a toxic mix of fine sand, arsenic, and assorted metals that measured twenty-five times federal health standards. On days with high winds, local emergency rooms filled up with asthmatic children. Winds carried the Owens Valley dust for hundreds of miles, clouding national parks and marring the one hundredth anniversary celebration of the Los Angeles Aqueduct on November 5, 2013. "Wicked dust storms spun through Newall Pass during the centennial celebration of the Los Angeles Aqueduct," a reporter wrote. "The winds shuddered against the tent that held hundreds of LADWP workers and sent blinding poofs of dirt into the faces of the civic dignitaries seated onstage. It was an ominous sign."

Los Angeles is an arid city at the edge of the Mohave Desert. Today Los Angeles is looking for more water sources.

Chasing Water

Lake Mead, 30 miles south of Las Vegas, is the reservoir behind Hoover Dam that fills the canyons of the Colorado River for 110 miles upstream of the dam. It is the largest man-made body of water in the world. The appearance of a huge lake in the middle of the desert drew new residents to southern Nevada and turned desert dwellers into boaters and weekend fishermen. On average the Mohave Desert in southern Nevada gets four inches of rain a year. It is a desert often compared with the Sonoran and named "the hottest desert in North America." Consequently, a lot of evaporation takes place from the reservoir's surface.

Overton is about 40 miles north of Hoover Dam on the edge of Lake Mead. I went there because a woman I met in Las Vegas told me about the "red sand and white sands" of Overton, where her father had been a mining engineer for forty years (one sand was silica and is still being mined). She said the town was worth visiting because it had a museum about the largest pueblo settlement in Nevada. Overton was once the site of a thirteenth-century Anasazi settlement (now underwater), with hundreds of villages and cliff-side pueblos tucked into the canyon walls. As the river backed up to create Lake Mead in the 1930s, all the archaeological ruins were flooded, but some of the artifacts and petroglyphs were saved and preserved in the museum.* She also mentioned the Overton Marina.

The north branch of Lake Mead, called the Overton Arm, used to extend into the channels of the Muddy and the Virgin Rivers. So one Sunday in February 2010 I left Las Vegas, traveling on Las Vegas Boulevard, heading north. On my right I passed Nellis Air Force Base (not to be confused with Nellis Air Force Range) and, a few miles later on my left, the Las Vegas Motor Speedway. (The speedway offers a NASCAR 1.5-mile supertrack, a drag strip, and a promotion for what the owners call "the most exciting experience in Las Vegas," should you want to pay $299 to drive five laps around the track in a Ferrari.)

Had I thought to check the national park website, I would have learned that Overton Marina had been moved three years earlier and relocated 15 miles south to Echo Bay. This far north there was neither a marina nor Lake Mead. The Overton Arm had silted up. Thirty years earlier, in 1981, the US Geological Survey published an infrared satellite map of southern Nevada, and even then the Overton Arm was already silting up in its northern reaches. By February 2010 the Overton Arm had retreated so far from the shore, I couldn't see it, because Lake Mead had dropped more than 130 feet.

Since I was on my way to Overton, I took the access roads to Interstate 15. For the next 40 miles I sped through a landscape ranging from gray to beige—the Mohave Desert is known for having no color—interrupted only by the occasional railroad freight line and billboards advertising casinos, bail bondsmen, bankruptcy lawyers, strippers, and magicians. As I got closer to the Arizona-Utah border, the billboards changed to ads for golfing in St. George, LDS churches, and housing developments. The Las Vegas–Salt Lake railroad line is still operational, but not for passengers—freight and minerals only. Nevada's

---

* The Heye Foundation in New York did most of the excavation and saved many artifacts. George Heye established the Museum of the American Indian at 155th and Broadway in New York and financed the expeditions to the Anasazi sites near Overton. Its collections are now part of the Smithsonian.

two largest industries are still gambling and mining. I turned off the highway for Route 169, passing through Valley of Fire State Park and its astonishing landscape of brilliant red sandstone carved by wind and water. Guidebooks say that it looks like it is on fire when seen at sunset. A few miles later I emerged on the national park road at the edge of Lake Mead. There I stopped to recheck my map. At this juncture I was supposed to see the Overton Marina and Lake Mead. "Boat Slips Available" said the sign in front of me. Boat slips? I was looking out at a single date-palm tree growing out of cracked hardpan, dried-up lake bed stretching as far as the eye could see. What happened to the water? What happened to the marina?

The move of the Overton Marina to the south proved to be a temporary solution because the reservoir continued its relentless retreat. Soon both Echo Bay and Overton Marinas had to be moved another 20 miles south to Callville Bay.

The National Park Service continued chasing water, moving docks and extending roadways until the marinas on the Overton Arm were no longer viable. Finally, all the marinas were consolidated at Hemenway Wash, now called Hemenway Marina, only 7 miles upriver from Hoover Dam. Before going back the way I came, I went to the museum in Overton, bought some silver and turquoise jewelry, looked at the exhibits, and then turned around and drove 40 miles south to Hemenway Marina, where Lake Mead still is deep enough to launch boats of considerable size.

Elmore Mead, whose name was given to the Hoover Dam reservoir, was the first head of the Bureau of Reclamation—reclaiming lands from flood and building dams for irrigation and paying for them through hydroelectricity. He was also the man who, in 1905, told the growers of the Imperial Valley of Southern California that their destroyed diversion canal could not be rebuilt. In 1905 the Colorado River, the steepest-running river in North America, was in full flood and broke through the farmers' irrigation canal, jumped its channel, and began to flow north into the Salton Sink. Before it was rerouted, the river had created the Salton Sea, the largest lake in California.

As Joan Didion points out, farmers in California are called grow-ers. They are not called farmers because most of the growers are large landowners and run their agricultural operations like corporations. In 1905 the Imperial Valley landowners included the Chandlers, Harrison Otis, and E. H. Harriman, whose Union Pacific Railroad owned a lot of the land and carried most of the freight and agricultural produce of the valley. For two years the Union Pacific transported every possible timber, rock, and construction material to block the rampaging river and send it back into its natural channel. The Imperial Valley growers beseeched President Teddy Roosevelt to have the new Bureau of Recla-mation rebuild the destroyed irrigation system and the diversion canal because it would wash out in another flood. Elmore Mead refused to re-build the diversion canal and insisted that control of the Colorado River in the south required a dam farther up in the canyons of the north.

In 1908 the same plutocrats of Los Angeles began the Owens Val-ley project to secure Los Angeles's water supply. They created the Los Angeles Aqueduct and a new agricultural empire in the San Fernando Valley. A dam on the Colorado River was for the future.

California, however, did not have one river that contributed to the flow of the Colorado River. What it did have was more than half the population of the West and the political clout that went with it. The six states whose rivers did flow into the Colorado were still underpopu-lated: Wyoming, Arizona, Nevada, and New Mexico were still lightly inhabited (Nevada had fewer than eighty thousand people). Colorado and Utah each had a hundred thousand people. Before Congress would authorize a dam—only the federal Treasury could finance such a proj-ect—the waters of the Colorado River had to be appropriated among the states through which it flowed. Commerce secretary Herbert Hoover was a Californian, a Republican, and a former mining engineer who had worked all over the world, including China. He was selected to under-take the task of apportioning the waters of the Colorado River.

For eleven months in 1922 representatives of all seven states met in Santa Fe, New Mexico, with Secretary Hoover to apportion future use of the Colorado River. Because of western water law—western states allocate water on the basis of the "prior appropriation" doctrine, under which water that was used earliest has higher priority, as in "first in time, first in right"—everyone was afraid that California would take far too much water and keep it. The Bureau of Reclamation measured the river's flow at 17.5 million acre-feet, a measurement acknowledged, then and now, to be much too high. Then Secretary Hoover divided the states into two artificial groups, the Upper Basin (Utah, Colorado, Wyoming, and New Mexico) and the Lower Basin (California, Arizona, and Nevada) and divided the river and the states at the artificial division point of Lee's Ferry. The states of each basin were to allocate 7.5 million acre-feet of water among themselves. In the Lower Basin, California was to get 4.5 million acre-feet, Arizona 2.5 million acre-feet, and Nevada 300,000 acre-feet. At the time Nevada was more interested in electricity than water. Most of Nevada's citizens lived in the north, and Las Vegas had artesian springs. Arizona felt that far too much water was going to California and refused to sign the compact. Hoover then changed the ratification process so that if six out of the seven states signed, it was a legally binding agreement.

Pop Squires of Las Vegas represented Nevada on the Colorado River Commission negotiations and reported regularly to the governor. He was the editor of Las Vegas's only newspaper and had also started its telephone company and its electricity company. Because Las Vegas still had its aquifer and springs, Nevada was seeking hydroelectric power more than water. Mexico was allocated 1.5 million acre-feet because Mexican farmers had prior use. The Colorado River ran through two Mexican counties for ninety miles and had irrigated Mexico's agricultural fields long before the diversion canal to Imperial Valley. The final document, known as the Colorado Compact—also called the West's Constitution—was signed in 1922.

The same year Arthur Powell Davis, director of the Reclamation Service, presented Congress with an inclusive report on taming the Colorado River. Referencing its early California roots, it was called "Report on Problems of Imperial Valley and Vicinity" and encompassed flood-control dams, storage reservoirs, and hydroelectricity to fully exploit "the American Nile." The report was translated into congressional legislation called the Boulder Dam Project Act. For the next six years, the bill to authorize the money to construct a dam, a hydroelectric plant, and an aqueduct to the Imperial Valley was introduced in Congress, and every year it was successfully defeated in the Senate by Carl Hayden of Arizona. The California growers understood the need for a stronger political hand, so they decided to run their own candidate to be the first US president from the West. Their candidate: Herbert Hoover. As soon as Hoover's election was announced in November 1928, the Boulder Dam bill passed the Senate. Access to the White House was too important a carrot for senators to continue to support Arizona in its opposition.

By 1938 Hoover Dam had been built and declared the greatest structure in America. The reservoir behind the dam provided water for millions of people in Greater Los Angeles and irrigated more than 1 million acres in the Imperial Valley in Southern California. California was getting much more than its allocated 4.5 million acre-feet of water because Arizona couldn't tap its allocation because it didn't have the infrastructure. Las Vegas didn't get to use its allocation until the 1960s when it built a pipeline from Lake Mead, so California was probably using Nevada's water as well.

As a practical matter California was going to get as much water as it wanted because the aqueducts and canals and pumping stations to deliver the water to the Upper Basin states had not yet been built. Until there was a second dam farther upriver, the Upper Basin states had no stored water to tap. At the time it didn't seem significant because the mushrooming population growth of Phoenix and Las Vegas was still in the future. It was only after World War II when the advent of commercial air-conditioning coincided with the homecoming of millions of war veterans, who had trained at military bases in the West and began looking for a new start in a sunny climate, that the full potential of the Colorado River was exploited. By the beginning of the twenty-first century, more than 30 million people were dependent on the waters of the Colorado River. At the same time its flow was diminishing every year.

By the time I was driving along the shrinking Lake Mead in February 2010, the lake was on its way to its lowest point since the reservoir had been filled. I had been told that people in Las Vegas bet on the numbers of the water level of Lake Mead, like the point spread on a football game. The numbers are posted every day on the Lake Mead Bureau of Reclamation website.

The important numbers to keep in mind are these:

- 1,219 feet above sea level. This marks the high-water level when Lake Mead is full, and it was reached in June 1941. It wasn't seen again until 1983.
- 1,083.3 feet above sea level, the water level in February 2010 when I was chasing the water south from Overton to Hemenway Wash, approximately a 130-foot drop.*
- 1,075 feet above sea level, the number at which mandatory water cuts go into effect for California, Nevada, and Arizona.
- 1,050 feet above sea level, the top of the Las Vegas upper intake pipe, a pipe installed in 1971 and from which the 2 million people of Las Vegas get 90 percent of their water. Below this level there is not enough water to run Hoover Dam's generators that supply more than 1 million people with electricity. The hydroelectricity also pumps water over the mountains into California.
- 1,000 feet above sea level, the top of Las Vegas's second intake pipe, built in the mid-1990s, which has a problem with quagga (zebra) mussels.
- 895 feet above sea level, at which point Lake Mead is declared a dead pool in which evaporation exceeds inflow. Downriver water delivery to California stops. Electricity generation has already stopped.
- 863 feet above sea level, the top of the third Las Vegas intake pipe currently under construction (scheduled for completion in 2014 but delayed until 2015). A special machine,

---

* The current chart of Lake Mead water levels shows that number for the month of October 2010.

built in Germany, is boring through solid rock a half mile
out beneath the surface of the lake. At this level the intake
pipe will be draining the dregs of the lake.

In February 2010 I did not understand the significance of these
numbers because my quest was simple. I was trying to find a place
where I could sit close to water. And as an easterner the complexities
of western water law were still murky to me. (I have since learned that
water law is often also murky to westerners.) At Hemenway Marina I
saw the unmistakable element that testifies to the 130-foot drop of the
reservoir, an 80-foot white ring that marks every surrounding canyon
wall and every island jutting up from the lake. "The bathtub ring," locals call it. Some of the islands are entirely white, which means that
they were once entirely underwater. The white ring is a magnesium
deposit left behind as the water levels of Lake Mead slowly dropped.
Another jarring element is the silted-up side canyons and stretch of
dry land that surround the marina.

The Hemenway Marina has an RV trailer park, cottages, a public
launch ramp, restrooms, a fish cleaning station, a restaurant, a long-
term trailer village, a fuel station, and hundreds of boat slips filled with
cabin cruisers and sailboats, large and small. Over the past ten years
the National Park Service has had to extend roads and build ever-
longer docks to chase the retreating water. As the level of Lake Mead
kept dropping, the Hemenway Marina incorporated several other marina facilities that simply ran out of water access.

• • •

"DON'T WRECK YOUR BOAT!" I read in the headline of a National Park
Service newspaper as I sat at a table in a little open-air restaurant
and bar out at the end of the pier. The headline was accompanied
by a drawing of a motorboat hitting a rock beneath the surface and
a warning: "Water levels at Lake Mead change frequently. *Please be
aware of launching hazards, shallow reefs and recently exposed islands
and rocks.*"

At the edge of the dock, huge schools of inedible carp the size of small bulldogs fought for popcorn fed to them by children. They covered the surface, squirming like eels and making the water boil. I did not want to fall off the dock into that water.

"I won't go out on that lake," said the woman at the table next to me. We had struck up a conversation after I leaped up from my table in a panic when two of the ugliest birds I had ever seen waddled up to my table. The mutant birds had large black bodies, small heads, and red wattles. They looked as though they could neither fly nor swim. "Don't worry about them," she reassured me. "They're the mascots of the marina."

I learned her name was Doris and she was from Detroit, visiting her son and daughter-in-law, both of whom worked at one of the big casinos. "They have a big cabin cruiser, and they're out there fishing right now," she told me. "The lake is stocked with trout, but I told 'em I'm staying right here on the dock." She was emphatic. "Last time we went out we hit something. And we were in the middle of the lake going fast. A REALLY BIG thump." She again nodded emphatically as she told me this. Out in the middle, Lake Mead can be a mile or two from shore.

In *About a Mountain*, John D'Agata wrote about the strange items starting to poke through the surface of Lake Mead, among them the smokestacks from the old concrete plant from Hoover Dam construction. These remnants of the dam's construction were submerged when the reservoir filled, but are starting to reappear. The National Park Service has also started to write about the rocks and reefs that are beginning to change the boating pleasures of Lake Mead. It has put a more expansive explanation on its website, instructing boaters in how to think about the new low water levels of Lake Mead. "Low water doesn't mean *no* water," it begins.

> Even as Lake Mead's levels decline, the beauty and splendor of the lake and surrounding desert landscape remains. As a reservoir, Lake Mead is designed to fluctuate in order to provide the southwest with a reliable source of water during times of drought, such as is being experienced now.

Boaters should treat the lake as if they are visiting it for the first time *every time they visit* as Lake Mead's water elevation drops. Unmarked reefs are exposed or lurk just below the surface of the water. Boating at night or at faster speeds can be dangerous. Special care also needs to be taken on launch ramps, as temporary extensions may not provide the best traction.

Why is the water going down?

Lake Mead stores Colorado River water for delivery to farms, homes and businesses in southern Nevada, Arizona, southern California and northern Mexico. About 96 percent of the water in Lake Mead is from melted snow that fell in Colorado, Utah, New Mexico and Wyoming.

Each year, Lake Mead receives a minimum amount of Colorado River water from these states, known as the "Upper Basin" states. And each year, a specific amount of water is released from Lake Mead to users in Nevada, Arizona, California and Mexico. In an "average" year, the amount of water flowing out of Lake Mead exceeds the amount of water flowing into Lake Mead. In some years, Lake Mead receives much more than the minimum amount of water from the Upper Basin, but the amount of water released from Lake Mead does not vary much from year to year.

The water level in Lake Mead is lower than it has been in over 40 years. The water is going down because the Colorado River runoff from snowmelt over the last decade has been far below normal. This has combined with increased evaporation from rising temperatures.

CLIMATE CHANGE

Depending on who is measuring, overall median temperatures in the Southwest have increased by almost two degrees Fahrenheit. This may not seem like much, but think of it in terms of the human body. If you have a two-degree fever, your body temperature is 100.6 and chances are you don't feel so well and may go to bed. Another four-degree increase, you have a fever of 104.6 and you are probably in a coma. In other words, two degrees of temperature increase are significant and have a disproportionate effect on weather patterns. The problem in the flow of the Colorado River begins in the smaller snowfalls of the Rocky Mountains.

As the Park Service bulletin states, drought has increased the amount of evaporation and decreased the amount of snowfall in the Rockies so that the overall flow of the Colorado is considerably less than the numbers Herbert Hoover and the states put into place in 1922. The Park Service doesn't mention that the drought has come from climate change in which wet climates are getting wetter and dry places are getting drier. The entire Southwest is a dry place. The other problem at Lake Mead is the buildup of silt flats at the ends of the reservoirs.

The word *Colorado* means "colorful" in Spanish. The river used to be known as the red river, or "Old Red," because it carried enormous amounts of silt drawn from those red-rock layers that make up the wonderful canyons and mountains it drains. During the building of Hoover Dam, construction workers had to let water settle in a pool before they could take water to drink or boil. Reclamation engineers were worried about silt from the minute Hoover Dam opened in 1936. Their worry was the reason for the tens of thousands of Navajo sheep and cattle slaughtered in the 1930s supposedly to prevent the silt runoff from overgrazed areas from flowing into the river. It was in fact a tiny part of the problem. The real solution was the construction of Glen Canyon Dam at Page in 1963. That second dam caught much of the silt that used to build up behind Hoover Dam. (Lake Powell is at 48 percent of capacity.) Even so, the silt flats are still growing in Lake Mead.

In the 1960s John McPhee arranged a famous rafting trip down the Colorado River for Floyd Dominy, the legendary head of the Bureau of Reclamation, and David Brower, then head of the Sierra Club. The question of the moment was Brower's opposition to Dominy's proposed building of a third dam on the Colorado River at Marble Gorge.

This proposed dam was going to provide the hydroelectricity to power the fourteen pumping stations of the Central Arizona Project and finally provide Arizona with its share of Colorado River water. During the trip McPhee recorded the two men's exchange over the issue of silt.

> "They said Hoover Dam was going to silt up Lake Mead in thirty years," Dominy said. "For thirty years, Lake Mead caught all the God-damned silt in the Colorado River, and Hoover has not been impaired."

> Brower's answer:
> "No, but when [Lake] Mead is low there are forty miles of silt flats at its upper end, and they're getting bigger."

David Brower and the Sierra Club won that argument with Dominy, and the Marble Gorge dam was never built. Unfortunately, the Sierra Club's victory would prove disastrous for the Hopi and Navajo of Black Mesa because the Bureau of Reclamation would substitute coal-fired electricity for hydroelectricity. The Department of the Interior under Stewart Udall authorized the construction of a 2,250-megawatt power plant, the ironically named Navajo Generating Station (no ownership by the Navajo, and half of Navajo families don't have electricity), from which the Bureau of Reclamation would purchase a fourth of the electricity in order to run the fourteen pumping stations that would pump the Colorado River up over three mountain ranges 330 miles into Phoenix and Tucson. This Arizona aqueduct was called the Central Arizona Project, or CAP, and in 1973 a second coal-mining site opened on Black Mesa, the Kayenta Mine, to supply coal for the new power plant.

Finally, after forty years, Arizona would be able to use its full allocation from the Colorado River. The Navajo Generating Station is the only coal-fired power plant in the country that is majority owned by the federal government through the US Bureau of Reclamation.

The energy for the fourteen pumping stations, siphons, and tunnels of the Central Arizona Project still comes from Black Mesa coal.

The urgency for the water and the substitution of the power plant for the hydroelectric dam contributed to the inability to modify the legislation that set in motion the mass removal of Navajo like Roberta Blackgoat. Neither conservative Republican Barry Goldwater nor liberal Democrat Stewart Udall was going to do anything that might endanger water for the parched desert cities of Phoenix and Tucson. Phoenix had five dams high in the Superstition Mountains on the Salt River, and it had pumped out all its groundwater. Was the rerouted Colorado River into CAP the only possible new source for water?

The Central Arizona Project

I drove to the outer edge of the Phoenix city limits to arrive at Thunderbird Road and the headquarters of the Central Arizona Project, the world's most expensive water system. Apart from the $8 billion required to build it, it also requires 750 megawatts of electricity to run the pumping stations that move the water through tunnels and siphons, over mountains and across canyons. Just as the Mohave plant was famous for its slurry-pipeline delivery system, the Central Arizona Project was famous for having the highest pump lift of any water in the world. The project includes fourteen pumping stations, three tunnels, ten siphons (pipes), and sections of open-air aqueducts that run for 337 miles across terrain of high mountains, deep canyons, and desert. At one point outside of Phoenix the aqueduct tunnels beneath the Salt River. The water goes to irrigation for agriculture, to municipal water for the city of Phoenix, and to provide 1 million gallons of water a day for each of Phoenix's 247 golf courses.

The CAP headquarters are in a building complex designed by Taliesin West, the Phoenix branch of the architectural firm founded by Frank Lloyd Wright. Seen from an airplane, the Central Arizona Project appears to be a ribbon of white concrete with a sunlit flash of water in the middle. From its control room on Thunderbird Road, it is a computer room filled with men sitting in the dim glow of computer consoles, tapping keys, adjusting screens, and monitoring messages. With a few taps of the keys one man at a computer can open the gates to an irrigation ditch that releases thousands of gallons of water to irrigate agricultural fields or to provide drinking water to a municipality. It reminded me of a video game.

When I visited, the operations supervisor introduced himself as Freddy, formerly from Attleboro, Massachusetts, and twenty-eight-year veteran of the Navy. He explained the complexity and the uniqueness of the system. "It is the only project in the world that lifts water twenty-nine hundred feet," he said. The pump lift from the Havasu reservoir to Phoenix is twelve hundred feet; the pump lift from Phoenix to Tucson is sixteen hundred feet. Instead of storage reservoirs, they use pumping plants. At the Havasu Pumping House, Hitachi and Mitsubishi did the motors. He listed the major contractors and said Bechtel Corporation built the pumping plants. He explained the multicounty water districts and the role of the independent board of directors, the repayment system, the unique dam construction of the New Waddell storage dam, the modification of the Roosevelt Dam, the problems with subsidence, the price per acre-foot to the water districts, the competing water claims from mining interests, Indians (Pima, Papago, Apache), the projected amounts of groundwater replenishment, other competing claims of the Arizona Department of Water Resources, per-person water consumption (Phoenix 250–270 gallons, Tucson 150 gallons), actual water flow of the Colorado River (15.8 instead of 17), changing names for different sections of the aqueduct (Hayden-Rhodes, Goldwater-Fanin, Udall), the experimental desalinization plant built for Mexico, the marketing agreement for the electricity from the Navajo generating plant, the seven-mile tunnel on the Tucson stretch, the number of employees (370 on the CAP payroll and 700 Bureau of Reclamation), the water treatment plant needed for city users and the objections by Tucson residents for the high cost, wildlife bridges and the migration patterns of animals blocked by the aqueduct, cameras on mountaintops and buried cable, and all their security systems. He was anxious to tell me about all their security systems because I had arrived with a letter of introduction from Senator John Kerry of Massachusetts (now secretary of state), so Freddy wanted me to reassure the senator about how secure and how safe the overall installation was. Actually, the letter had been written by his environmental legislative aide, and even though I explained that I was doing research on the Navajo Generating Station and the source of the electricity that provides the energy to run the pumping stations—and who was paying for it—he kept returning to the subject of security. Arizona is a state where anyone is allowed to carry a gun anywhere, even into a bar on a Saturday night unless a "No firearms allowed" sign is posted. Many institutions have the overall feel of a military base, and I suspect there are many retired military running things in Arizona. So security is a central topic.

Climate change has changed the meaning of security. *Normal* is a word constantly subject to redefinition. Two sets of data, tracked in multiple decimal points, are continuously being fed into computers: one set tracks the recorded water volumes of the Colorado River; the other tracks ambient temperatures in the Southwest. The higher the temperatures, the greater evaporation, and the lower the water volumes tend to be. Over the past thirty years the ambient temperatures in the Southwest have risen by 1.7 degrees Fahrenheit (1 degree Celsius). This means lower snowpack in the Rockies, from which the Colorado River draws its water. Only in the Arctic are there more dramatic indications of climate change. As William DeBuys has written in *A Great Aridness: Climate Change and the Future of the American Southwest*, "We are on the verge of a new form of desertification. It won't be the result of overgrazing, failed agricultural schemes, or other familiar forms of land abuse. Instead, it will ensue from industrial society's abuse of the atmosphere." The trend lines are heading in only one direction—higher temperatures, lower water volumes. The combined trend lines suggest the water volumes of the Colorado River are not coming back to "normal." The water levels of Lake Mead are on their way to even lower levels.

FRIENDS IN HIGH PLACES

Searchlight is a former mining town in the mountains between Las Vegas and Laughlin. Today there is not much to see (population 539), but when Harry Reid was growing up there, it was still a mining town and his mother worked as a laundress for the local brothels. A newspaper profile of Reid says that the town had five gold mines and sixteen brothels. His father was a hard-rock miner and an alcoholic. Teenage Harry Reid hitchhiked sixty miles to high school in Henderson (a section of Las Vegas), stayed with an aunt who introduced him to Mormonism, became a baptized Mormon, and graduated from high school. "Oh yes, I remember having Harry in high school," said Gene Segerblom, a former teacher and Nevada assemblywoman, who was honored during Nevada Women's History Celebration of 2010 by Harry Reid's chief of staff from his Las Vegas office. She presented Mrs. Segerblom with a special letter of recognition from Senator Reid. His education and political career were greatly helped by another high school teacher, his boxing coach, Mike O'Callaghan, who later became governor of Nevada.

In 1970 O'Callaghan was running for governor and tapped Harry Reid, just turned thirty and now a lawyer, as a candidate for lieutenant governor. They both won. After the lieutenant governorship, Reid ran for the Senate (lost), he ran for mayor of Las Vegas (lost), and his father committed suicide. In 1977 Governor O'Callaghan selected him to head the Nevada Gaming Commission, from which many Nevada politicians get their start. The Gaming Commission is responsible for issuing gambling licenses throughout the state. It is distinct from the Nevada Gaming Control Board, which is the agency that oversees the tax and revenue reporting from the casinos. As head of the Gaming Commission, Reid had a job that required both political finesse and awareness of the outsize economic role the gambling industry plays in Nevada. Both came into play when the commission had to decide whether to give a gaming license to Frank Sinatra. Sinatra had previously had a license at the Sands, but he had lost it because of too many public associations with known gangsters such as the Fischetti brothers, Sam Giancana, and others.

But in 1980 Frank Sinatra applied again, this time with better references and at a time that Las Vegas needed a public relations facelift. The MGM Grand Hotel casino had just opened the city's first huge luxury hotel, twenty-three stories high, with twenty-one hundred rooms. Not long after opening, it had one of the worst fires in American history. When the electrical fire broke out, there was no sprinkler system, fire department ladders reached only to the ninth floor, and toxic black smoke filled the upper floors. People jumped out of windows; 85 people died and 650 were hospitalized. It turned out that Las Vegas had lax fire codes. At the same time, high gas prices were discouraging weekend gamblers from driving from Los Angeles, and Nevada was no longer the only state with legal gambling. New Jersey had licensed casino gambling. Eastern gamblers were going to Atlantic City rather than flying to Las Vegas. The return of Frank Sinatra to Caesars Palace could do a lot to help lure tourists back to Las Vegas. On the other hand, he did have a lot of connections with known mobsters.

Sinatra's political connections outweighed the gangsters. Ronald Reagan of California had just been elected president on a conservative Republican platform very similar to that of Barry Goldwater, and Sinatra had raised $5 million for the Reagan campaign. He had also produced Reagan's inaugural gala. One of his character witnesses before the Gaming Commission was US Attorney General William French Smith, who said he was "totally unaware of any allegations about Frank Sinatra's background." Soon Harry Reid and members of the commission granted a new gaming license to Sinatra, and he was performing again at Caesars Palace, drawing crowds back to Vegas.

Within the year Harry Reid's political fortunes took a decided upswing. In 1982 he was elected to the House of Representatives and in 1987 to the US Senate. Although he was a Mormon and Mormons don't approve of gambling, it did not seem to be a problem. "Representing gaming is as basic to being a senator from Nevada as it would be for a senator from California to champion Disney," wrote historian Michael Green in the *Las Vegas Sun* about Reid's reconciliation of Mormon faith and gambling interests.

At the same time Las Vegas took on a new public image in which the Mob-connected casinos had supposedly been scoured clean of crime connections. Casinos were now public companies being traded on the New York Stock Exchange. By the 1990s when the Steve Wynn era arrived, casinos were renamed "gaming enterprises," and Las Vegas was being rebranded as a convention and family-vacation destination.

Las Vegas's population was doubling and tripling every year, and in the 1990s the city had become the fastest-growing metropolitan area in the country. A time-delay sequence series of satellite images since 1970 to the present shows how Las Vegas's city limits kept expanding into the desert like amoeba multiplying in a Petri dish. Water continued to be an issue. No one liked to talk about conservation because it discouraged growth. Las Vegas continued to have the highest per capita water use in the country. The Southern Nevada Water Authority began paying people to tear up their lawns and use desert landscaping. The authority also built a water treatment plant and began recycling water, an arrangement that allowed the city to increase its annual use of the water in Lake Mead. For every gallon of treated water it put back into Lake Mead, it was allowed to take another half gallon out. (The treatment plant is only six miles upstream from the intake pipe for the city's drinking water, and from the air a visible clouded plume runs between the two. Water quality is an issue. Former Las Vegas resident germaphobe Howard Hughes had his aide write to the governor to try to stop the project.) The water authority now says that annual per capita water use is down to 250 gallons. But there are still many developments such as Summerlin and Anthem where green lawns, golf courses, and lush landscaping are standard. Part of the problem is that the land-development companies did not attract new buyers by telling them about the need for a desert aesthetic and water conservation. The hedonism of the Strip infiltrated the rest of the city.

A Savage Thirst

"The verdict is in for the Las Vegas Valley's main water source and it is as grim as expected." The headline on the August 2013 *Las Vegas Review-Journal*'s article read, "Federal Officials Cut Water Delivery for Lake Mead, Speeding Reservoir's Decline."

The only other major source of water for Las Vegas is hundreds of miles to the north in the rural counties of Lincoln and White Pine. In the 1990s the project of taking groundwater from rural Nevada and piping it to Las Vegas from the north was always described as a last resort. Today the project is under way. Like the building of the Owens Valley Aqueduct in Los Angeles in 1913, the political leverage to import distant water into Las Vegas became an imperative with the drop in Lake Mead for 2014. Spring Valley is in White Pine County. It is a valley 100 miles long and roughly 12 miles wide and contains an aquifer fed by Mount Wheeler snowmelt. From the point of view of someone sitting in the manager's chair in the Las Vegas Water Authority, Spring Valley is an irresistible water opportunity.

Two obstacles had to be surmounted: obtaining the rights to pump water out of the Spring Valley aquifer and obtaining a federal permit for a pipeline right-of-way across federal lands some 270 miles to Las Vegas. Even if the water authority were able to buy all the water rights, it would be unable to pipe it to Las Vegas without a right-of-way to cross federal lands. Although Nevada is a small-government, no-tax, individual-responsibility state, the federal government owns 80 percent of Nevada's roughly 70 million acres. The reason was that the state government did not want responsibility for lands that were not water supplied. The state government wanted areas adjacent to rivers and springs and left management of its vast desert and mountain ranges to the Bureau of Land Management. Then in 1998 Senator Harry Reid introduced a bill that would transfer 25,000 acres around Las Vegas from the federal government back to the state. The state would sell these lands and use the proceeds from the sales to go to the Nevada Education Fund (5 percent) and to the Southern Nevada Water Authority (10 percent), with the balance to the federal government. Then in 2002, 2004, and 2006 he introduced similar bills, adding more acreage for sale, but this time the lands were farther north in Lincoln and White Pine Counties. The proceeds went to the same two state agencies as well as wilderness preservation and federal parks, but the lands were now part of state territory.

Lincoln and White Pine Counties are in the heart of rural Nevada, where snowmelt from a circle of mountain ranges in the vicinity of Mount Wheeler, Nevada's second-highest mountain, is stored in an underground aquifer. The groundwater level in these mountain valleys is so high that it supports a system of springs, streams, and aboveground lakes. This section of the Great Basin is also known for its rich birdlife and pine forest ecology.

What could be more natural than that a desert city such as Las Vegas might want access to this vast water supply, untouched except by a few ranchers and alfalfa farmers in Snake Valley on the east side of Mount Wheeler and Spring Valley on the west? Snake Valley, however, is on the border with Utah and has one large landowner who has rights to forty thousand acre-feet of water. The Southern Nevada Water Authority, under the direction of Pat Mulroy, began applying for water rights to ninety thousand acre-feet of water in Spring Valley and fifty thousand acre-feet in Snake Valley. At that point the ranchers and farmers of the area cried "Owens Valley!" They claimed that Wheeler's snowmelt sustains pressure in the water table for hundreds of miles around. Pulling that amount of water out of the ground, they said, would suck the springs and streams dry, kill the vegetation, and turn the valley floor to dust. Then began a long series of hearings.

An Advisory Committee was charged with working out the mix of Las Vegas's water needs with those of the ranchers of White Pine and Lincoln Counties. But the scales seemed to tip in favor of Las Vegas. One local member of the Advisory Committee, Gary Perea, reported, "The thing I kept hearing was that MGM Mirage employs more people than live in White Pine County."

The locals requested a detailed water study that was never done. White Pine rancher Dean Baker, who had rights to forty thousand acre-feet of water in Snake Valley, decided he didn't want to share it with Las Vegas casinos. (Forty thousand acre-feet is roughly a seventh of Las Vegas's entire allocation from the Colorado River.) Meanwhile, Pat Mulroy's Southern Nevada Water Authority started buying up ranches in the adjacent Spring Valley, spending $22 million for one ranch and eventually $78 million for a dozen more. Once one ranch sold, other ranchers in the valley began to sell, figuring that once the city started pumping water out and the water table fell, their land would be worthless. After buying the ranches, the Las Vegas Water Authority was in the business of alfalfa farming in Spring Valley. Dean Baker, the rancher in Snake Valley, decided to hold out.

Up until this point the struggle was between southern Nevada and northern Nevada. Then Utah entered the picture when Utah senators introduced similar land bills and wanted to be able to use the proceeds for construction of a new pipeline from the Colorado River to St. George. (Utah does not use its full allocation of Colorado River water.) St. George, a Mormon town just over the Nevada border, is called the Mormon Dixie because of its mild climate. The town was the winter home for Brigham Young, and the Mormons grew cotton there during the Civil War. (It also has a classic Mormon church designed by Miles Romney.) These negotiations were taking place in 2006 before Nevada's great real estate collapse that began in 2008. Utah, however, had something Las Vegas did not—a debate about the true costs of development and a slow-growth movement. Nonetheless, the state wanted a pipeline.

Harry Reid's position as majority leader in the Senate helped delete the Utah land provisions from the bill, and the White Pine County Land Bill passed as a rider on the Tax Relief and Health Care Bill of 2006. It should be noted that Reid's old mentor, Mike O'Callaghan, was against pulling water from rural Nevada to supply Las Vegas. As editor of the *Las Vegas Sun*, he sided with the ranchers of White Pine County and wrote, "[This] isn't a new idea. . . . Big bucks and the drought have dragged it out of hiding again."

The ongoing hearings related to the pipeline project produced mind-numbing testimony about greasewood plants, water mining (illegal in Nevada), dust storms, water-table levels, Ice Age aquifers, "phreatophytes," Great Basin cold desert, cheatgrass, grazing rights, recreation land, shallow pumps, "wet valleys," rabbitbrush, and much more impenetrable language on water models. However, in testifying before the US Senate Committee on Energy and Natural Resources, Pat Mulroy gave one very clear statement of assurance: "An Owens Valley cannot and will not occur in Nevada."

The one remaining obstacle was for the city to obtain a federal right-of-way to build the pipeline to transport the water. The Bureau of Land Management owned hundreds of square miles that lay between the northern valleys and Las Vegas, so the pipeline would have to cross 250 miles of federally owned land. For the next six years the political efforts to stop the northern Nevada pipeline focused on stopping the federal permit for a right-of-way. As Lake Mead dropped farther in each passing year, the more likely it was that the Bureau of Land Management would approve the pipeline.

Two days after Christmas, on December 27, 2012, the Bureau of Land Management authorized a right-of-way for the Southern Nevada Water Authority to build the 263-mile pipeline that would run from Lincoln and White Pine Counties to Las Vegas. It allows for an 84-inch pipeline (7 feet in diameter), 272 miles of power lines, plus several pumping stations, electricity infrastructure, and a buried water-storage reservoir—all granted "in perpetuity." Nevada's state engineer granted the Southern Nevada Water Authority the right to pump up to 84,000 acre-feet of groundwater from the rural valleys. The US Fish and Wildlife Service issued an earlier finding that the project would not "significantly" affect a dozen threatened or endangered species. Estimates of the pipeline cost range from $3 to $15 billion. The board of the Southern Nevada Water Authority has not yet voted to proceed because the cost estimates and the funding for the project have not yet been determined.

When Bechtel built the Central Arizona Project, it was originally budgeted at $1.8 billion and ended up at $8.5 billion. When Bechtel built the Central Artery Project in Boston, it was originally estimated at $2.75 billion and ending up at $16 billion.* When they built the Black Mesa pipeline that has been pumping 4,300 acre-feet of water out of Black Mesa for forty-three years, it was subsidized with a $3 billion federal research and development grant.

Although Pat Mulroy assured a Senate committee there would be no Owens Valley syndrome in Nevada, this is a guarantee she cannot make. The future is out of her control. The city will grow, and there will be a new head of the water authority. Like Los Angeles and the Owens Valley, Las Vegas will need more and more water. Like Los

---

* The state of Massachusetts continues to find it difficult to fund infrastructure projects, upgrade its transportation systems, or fund new transportation projects because of the debt service on the cost of the Central Artery Project.

Angeles, growth is a goal in Las Vegas. In September 2013 the Bureau
of Reclamation announced that it would reduce its release of water to
Lake Mead by 750,000 acre-feet. This meant that Lake Mead could
drop another 25 feet by the fall of 2014, putting the water level in the
danger zone below the Las Vegas intake pipe and triggering automatic
reductions in water withdrawals. Pat Mulroy immediately went to
Washington, met with Harry Reid, and made headlines when she said
the drought on the Colorado River was a natural disaster no different
from Hurricane Sandy and that Las Vegas was as deserving as New
Jersey and should be declared a disaster area and eligible for federal
aid. She later backpedaled, but some believed that this was the opening
argument for federal dollars to help build the Northern Nevada Water
Pipeline Project.

The pipeline from northern Nevada promises to be the most
expensive public works project in Nevada history. As the *Las Vegas
Review-Journal* pointed out, "Pat Mulroy was in Washington this week
meeting with U.S. Senate Majority Leader Harry Reid in search of
federal money for the cause."

One of the many unasked questions about true costs in an age of
climate change is this: Why should the water that supports the Cirque
du Soleil's famous aquatic production, *O*, be drawn from an Ice Age
aquifer in northern Nevada and in the process destroy a landscape and
ecology that took thousands of years to create?

CHAPTER 11

THE BECHTEL FAMILY BUSINESS

Just before the Bally's video sign on the Strip, at the corner of Flamingo Road and Las Vegas Boulevard, a chain-link fence encloses an electricity switching station the size of a city block. Tall, stately electrical transmission towers emerge from the switching station. The towers cluster like masts of sailing ships before they march across the Strip, their fat cables drooping with electricity. Then they separate and fan out to the giant casinos—south to Bellagio and City Center (not a city, not a center), north to Wynn Resorts and the Venetian. One column, however, crosses the Strip and heads due west along Flamingo Road past the Playboy resort and continues for a dozen miles to what used to be the end of the city and the edge of the desert, but is now another switching station sending electricity to an endless sea of gated housing developments, none of which have solar panels on their roofs.

When a visitor points out the transmission towers to a friend who has lived in Las Vegas for thirty years, she says, "Funny. I never noticed them before." The electrical towers are visible only in the daytime. At night, with the lights at full megawattage, a visitor is wrapped in a nimbus of light. The Bally's corner marks the point of maximum illumination in the Las Vegas desert night sky, so bright that the electrical glow identifies the city to astronauts some 285 miles in space. At night, a driver approaching Las Vegas from 40 miles away on Route 15 sees the surreal glow rise out of the darkness like something from a science fiction movie.

The dazzling lights of the Strip distract a visitor from any awareness of anything but the pulsing immediacy of the twenty-four-hour party spread out around him: gambling, girls, fun, music, clubs, restaurants. Billboard trucks drive up and down the Strip, advertising euphemistic "escort" services: "Hot Babes—College Girls, Asian Girls—in 20 minutes." Prostitution isn't legal but isn't illegal either. Men on the street pass out pornographic business cards to anyone with a hand to take one, including children. Taxi drivers recommend casinos and nightclubs according to their passengers' budgets: Wynn Resorts for the wealthy, Circus Circus for the thrifty, Treasure Island for office workers on a spree. The name casino resorts are owned by a handful of players—Steve Wynn (Wynn Resorts), Sheldon Adelson (the Venetian), Kirk Kirkorian (MGM Grand)—and are all traded on the New York Stock Exchange. No more worrying about the Teamsters Pension Fund to get money for expansion.

The promise of Las Vegas is rarely realized, even for the rich and famous. Tiger Woods, who is known to have celebrated a golf tournament win with a $75,000 Methuselah-size bottle of Cristal champagne at the nightclub XS (pronounced "Excess"), found his VIP "escorts" in Las Vegas; Michael Jackson, his final doctor. Growing up in Las Vegas has its downsides. Nevada Stupak, the son of the man who built the Stratosphere, the highest building in Las Vegas, once reflected on what happened to his father, a hard gambler who was once offered $160 million to sell the Stratosphere, but hung on too long. "He had offers for $90 million, then $60 million, $38 million. Eventually the stock went down to zero. In the end he died alone and depressed and worth basically nothing." Kenny Baker described some of the girls in his high school class: "This is a city of fifty-year old men with eighteen year old girls."

Las Vegas is a city designed to alter perceptions: gambling substitutes for income, night is interchangeable with day, the scale of excess denies the idea of limits. Residents do not seem curious about where they get their electricity or water or the political entities that control their infrastructure. Or who pays for it. Las Vegas history is framed in present tense.

Hoover Dam was the engine for Las Vegas growth, although the senior men who built it did not live to see the era that it created. W. H. Wattis succumbed to cancer in 1931, and E. O. Wattis followed him several years later; Warren Bechtel died of a diabetic attack in August 1933 while on a trip to the Soviet Union; Tony Cornero died of a "supposed" heart attack at the gambling tables in 1955, although rumor said he was poisoned. (The glass he was drinking from disappeared; there was no autopsy; the body was sent to Los Angeles. Moe Dalitz took over the Stardust.) Henry Kaiser started his own company, Kaiser Industries, becoming a tycoon with investments in concrete, aluminum, insurance, automobiles, health care, and shipbuilding.

Although several of the Six Companies made the transition, as *Fortune* put it, from contractors "whose offices were in their hats" to big-shot industrialists with contracts running into the billions, it was Bechtel that exploited the brand of having built Hoover Dam. Steven Bechtel, Warren's middle son who worked as purchasing agent during the dam's construction, teamed up with John McCone, a former college classmate from whom he had purchased millions of dollars of steel during dam construction, and formed a new company called Bechtel-McCone. The big new opportunities were in the energy and war industries that were looming over the horizon. Contracts for construction of naval bases began in 1938.

Steven Bechtel and John McCone marketed their services to the large oil companies, particularly Standard Oil of California, or SoCal. They planned to build full-service energy facilities—refineries, pipelines, tank farms, loading areas, port facilities. Although the company had not been in the oil construction business before, by 1939 Bechtel-McCone had ten thousand employees and was building refineries, chemical plants, and pipelines at project sites from Montana to Venezuela. "We will build anything, any place, anytime," advertised Steven Bechtel, later known as Steve Sr. "The bigger, the tougher the job, the better we like it."

Bechtel-McCone became the construction arm for SoCal. At the same time, a mere twenty years after the close of World War I, the second installment of the war loomed; World War II was a global war because of the colonies in Africa, India, and Southeast Asia held by the European countries. The US government issued contracts to build shipyards and military training bases. Bechtel-McCone opened three shipyards in California, one in collaboration with Henry Kaiser's Cal-Ship operations. At first the shipyards were to build ships for the British navy in a lend-lease arrangement, then they were to supply the US Navy with ships for war in the Atlantic, and after 1941 and the attack on Pearl Harbor, they were to supply ships for naval operations in the Pacific.

As the war progressed, logistics took precedence. Airplanes, tanks, ships all needed fuel to run. Harold Ickes, Roosevelt's secretary of interior, who had slapped Bechtel with a large fines for labor violations during the Hoover Dam project, was in charge of compiling a report on the locations and amounts of all of America's energy reserves, particularly oil. Supply logistics were key to winning the war. One surprise was how much of America's energy resources lay beneath Indian reservations in the American West. As Marjane Ambler illustrates in *Breaking the Iron Bonds: Indian Control of Energy Development*, 30 percent of America's untapped reserves were located beneath the Indian reservations in Arizona, New Mexico, Colorado, Utah, Wyoming, South Dakota, North Dakota, and Montana. A new mineral resource of particular importance was uranium. With the beginning of the Manhattan Project in 1943, uranium mining began on the Navajo reservation, although the Navajo miners were not told that there was anything unusual about the ore they were being asked to mine, nor were they given protective clothing.

Although Texas and Oklahoma had a lake of oil underneath, much of it had not yet been developed. Worried about American oil reserves, Secretary Ickes ordered Standard Oil of California to exercise the oil leases they held in Saudi Arabia and Bahrain and start pumping oil. (The Bahrain wells were productive, but Standard Oil drilled many dry wells in Saudi Arabia before they struck a lake of oil.) In 1944 SoCal (later the Arabian American Oil Company, or ARAMCO) took Bechtel with them into Saudi Arabia to build a pipeline, refinery, and port. Other projects followed for the Saudi royal family. Bechtel-McCone spun off International Bechtel, a firm that became the major engineering and construction company in Saudi Arabia. As more and more oil was discovered, more engineering and construction projects followed.

When ibn Saud's son Faisal visited San Francisco, Steve Sr. established such a good rapport with him that King ibn Saud gave International Bechtel the contract to build a four-hundred-mile railroad across the desert from Riyadh to the port of Damman and another contract for a road system. The road project was to be in collaboration with the king's favorite builder, a contractor from Yemen named Mohammed Bin Laden. (This collaboration later became Bechtel–Bin Laden and ended on September 12, 2001, or, if it didn't end, at least disappeared from the Bechtel website.) With oil royalties pouring in, the Saudi king had the financial resources to designate more projects to a company with Bechtel's experience—electricity for his palace, city power plants, sewer systems, airports, and roads. Soon Bechtel was entrenched in Saudi Arabia and had developed excellent relations with the Saudi royal family.

The war in the Pacific required construction of many military bases and Air Force training bases, among them the Army's Modification Center for the fleet of B-54 bombers in Birmingham, Alabama; a series of military airports in Alaska; and multiple bases on islands in the Pacific for the Navy. Domestically, Nevada was a good site for expanded military bases because the Department of the Interior's Bureau of Land Management already owned 80 percent of Nevada's land. Named for Joe Nellis, a local war hero, Nellis Air Force Base expanded far out into the desert in chunks of real estate the size of Connecticut. Sections of it were used by the US Army and Navy air divisions, and, after 1947, the newly established US Air Force.

When atomic testing began in Nevada in 1950, other government agencies took charge of vast tracts of Nellis. The Atomic Energy Commission (now the Department of Energy) had control of Yucca and Frenchman Flats and the Atomic Test Site where more than 950 atomic tests took place in the 1950s and '60s. The CIA controlled another Maryland-size parcel around Groom Lake, where it tested the U-2 spy planes and several generations of high-altitude surveillance planes. Only the strange lights seen in the night sky around the town of Rachel made people suspect that this was the area where the US military kept outer-space visitors. This section of Nellis was called Area 51.

Nellis Area 2, on the north side of Route 15, is home to the largest aboveground weapons storage complex in the United States. When atomic tests were taking place, Area 2 was where the atomic weapons were stored.

The Nevada Test and Training Range—separate from the Nevada Test Site—is the largest contiguous air- and land space available for peacetime military operations in North America. It has five thousand square miles of land and twelve thousand square miles of restricted airspace. According to the Nellis website, "The 12,000-square-nautical mile range provides a realistic arena for operational testing and training aircrews to improve combat readiness. A wide variety of live munitions can be employed on targets on the range."

The postwar period was a time of both a heightened sense of external threat and ideological certainties about the nature of the Soviet Union. The National Security Act of 1947 established the national security state and created the Central Intelligence Agency, the National Security Council, the permanent Department of Defense, the Pentagon, and the US Air Force. John McCone moved to Washington as deputy secretary of the newly organized Air Force. He was particularly involved in the shape of nuclear weapons systems in which the Air Force would play a central and decisive role.

As a trustee of the California Institute of Technology, McCone had remained in contact with the scientists who had played key roles in developing the atom bomb and those who were planning for peacetime uses of nuclear power. As a hard-line anticommunist and a strong Catholic, McCone believed that the atom bomb was a God-given means of defending the American way of life from godless communists. "He was a rightist Catholic," said journalist I. F. Stone. "A man with holy war views." Attracted to the decision-making power in Washington, McCone left Bechtel-McCone to help organize the newly formed Department of the Air Force and its highly controversial and top-secret nuclear Strategic Air Command, which put planes in the air twenty-four hours a day armed with nuclear bombs ready to bomb Russia if so ordered. As Eric Schlosser's book *Command and Control* makes clear, most of the danger that human beings faced from nuclear weapons in the Cold War period came from accidents involving airplanes, bombs dropped by mistake, an airplane loaded with a hydrogen bomb catching fire, missiles mistakenly released. As the United States shifted to a "permanent war economy," John McCone was temperamentally and ideologically suited to help shape America's new nuclear defense and the commercial nuclear power industry that accompanied it.

• • •

Although Bechtel went back to a single name, McCone's association with Bechtel helped to frame a new relationship between the company and the government, particularly in the field of nuclear testing and commercial nuclear-generated electric power.

In 1948, after officials decided that nuclear tests required another testing site in addition to the Marshall Islands (islands were destroyed and Japanese fishermen and Pacific islanders exposed to radiation), the Atomic Energy Commission began looking for new test sites. The scientists favored the Outer Banks of North Carolina, where fallout would drift across the Atlantic. But the Air Force already had huge air bases in the empty deserts of Nevada—and the population of Nevada was so small that they made the decision to locate the new Atomic Test Site some sixty-five miles north of Las Vegas. Bechtel expanded its Nevada offices to begin construction for the intricate apparatus for nuclear testing. Some of the structures and technology for atomic testing can be seen today at the Atomic Testing Museum in Las Vegas.

A new subsidiary company called Bechtel-Nevada, incorporated in Reno, was formed to do the construction work for the test sites in

Nevada.* (Other civilian contractors included EG&G of Boston, General Electric, and Westinghouse.) In 1957 President Eisenhower named McCone chairman of the Atomic Energy Commission, in charge of the test sites, nuclear research, mining, enrichment, and purchase of all uranium.

Three-fourths of the uranium used at the time was being mined on the Navajo reservation. In 1990 I was in Farmington, New Mexico, on my way to visit the Four Corners Generating Station (also built by Bechtel) on the same day that former interior secretary Stewart Udall was holding special hearings to try to help compensate former Navajo miners and their families for deaths and illnesses that came about from radiation exposure and uranium mining. Never informed of the dangers from the ore they were mining, the Navajo miners had contaminated their families by coming home wearing the same clothes dusted with radioactive ore from the mines. They had received inadequate treatment for the chronic health problems and cancers they, and members of their families, subsequently came down with. The Indian Health Service had not been told of the uranium mining, so they didn't know the source of the illness they were treating or how to correctly diagnose it. In addition, at a time when the Atomic Energy Commission was the only buyer of uranium, they were also paid shockingly low wages. As one of the Navajo wives said during the hearings, "It was the Cold War. Nobody dared ask questions. It was unpatriotic to ask questions."

During McCone's chairmanship Bechtel was chosen as one of the few American companies licensed to build nuclear power plants. (Another was Stone and Webster of Boston.) Bechtel opened its nuclear division, hired Ken Davis (the Atomic Energy Commission's director of nuclear reactor development), and began designing commercial nuclear reactors to sell to America's largest utilities. Bechtel's nuclear power division hired so many employees of the Atomic Energy Commission that Senator Abraham Ribicoff of Connecticut complained, "The nuclear industry was so incestuous that it was hard to tell where

---

* Organizational chart of Bechtel, Caspar Weinberger Papers.

the public sector begins and the private one leaves off." This permeable membrane between government and private industry became the rule, rather than the exception, in building energy infrastructure for the next half century.

The McCone connection continued to open up new markets for Bechtel, especially after 1962, when McCone became head of the CIA. Joseph Kennedy Sr., who knew McCone from their shipbuilding days during the war—Kennedy Sr. had the contract for the Quincy shipyards in Massachusetts—suggested to his son President John F. Kennedy that he appoint McCone to replace Allen Dulles as director of the CIA, under whose disastrous direction the Bay of Pigs in Cuba had taken place. By then the CIA was already involved in testing spy aircraft like the U-2 from its base at Area 51 inside Nellis and was involved in new surveillance aircraft like Oxcart.* (Pilot Francis Gary Powers, the U-2 pilot who was shot down over Russia in 1960, said KGB interrogators asked him about the spy-plane base north of Las Vegas.) Area 51 of Nellis Air Force Base became home to a lot of activity. The town of Rachel saw many mysterious sightings of unusual aircraft.

NEVADA NIGHTS

One moonless night in northern Nevada, writer John McPhee and his geologist friend Ken Deffeyes were returning from exploring a scavenger silver mine** when a white sphere of blinding light shot across the sky in front of them. As the light kept expanding in volume and brightness, they pulled their truck over to the side of the road and got out to get a better look.

Standing by the side of their vehicle, staring at the heavens, McPhee described what followed as outside anything he or his colleague had

---

* In an oral interview at the Kennedy Library, the interviewer did not ask McCone about Oxcart because the project was still secret information.

** A scavenger mine is a former commercial mine whose claim has run out, but may still have a lot of valuable ore that could be extracted using small-scale, modern mining processes.

ever seen before. "The 'white sphere' kept expanding 'like a cloud' until a smaller spherical object moved out from the larger one, possibly from behind it." Although McPhee was a writer for the sophisticated *New Yorker* and his friend a world-famous geologist, they were no different than anyone else in rural Nevada who witnessed the same phenomenon. They suspected they were seeing extraterrestrial visitors in a flying saucer.

The next day the *Nevada State Journal* reported on the "mysterious ball of light" and gave similar descriptions from other random observers. Two hunters at another location not far from McPhee's said, "As we looked back we saw a smaller craft come out of the right lower corner. This smaller craft had a dome in the middle of it and two wings on either side, but the whole thing was oval shaped." A third observer reported, "It looked like a star. Then a ring formed around it. A kind of ring like you'd see around Saturn. It didn't make any noise and then it vanished."

The Nevada landscape is so scoured, so mathematical in its stately procession of mountains, followed by flat, empty desert basins, that extraterrestrial sightings seem plausible. But as I was reading McPhee's account of the inexplicable spacecraft sighting in his *Annals of the Former World*—a book about the geologic history of the entire North American continent, including a detailed chapter on the basin and range creation of Nevada through seafloor spreading—it occurred to me that he did see a spacecraft of sorts, but not from outer space.

McPhee and his friend were more likely to have seen a test flight of one of America's top-secret spy planes, probably followed by a chase plane—or even a drone version mounted on the back of an M-21. These top-secret stealth planes were launched from Area 51, a CIA-operated base about eighty miles north of Las Vegas. Some were designed in elliptical shapes to avoid radar detection and engineered to travel at heights up to one hundred thousand feet (almost twenty miles) for high-altitude surveillance missions. Like the famous Oxcart, which was constructed of light-reflecting titanium, they could travel at speeds of two thousand miles per hour, often with one or two trailing chase planes. Desert optics—sunlight bouncing off dust particles in the air—could account for the circular light rings and the perception of expanding light. Flying-saucer sightings usually occur within an hour of sunset when the earth's surface is in darkness but the sun's rays are still lighting the atmosphere at higher altitudes. Pilots of commercial jets flying at twenty-five thousand feet sometimes look up and see a spheroid object streaking above them and report yet another unidentified flying object, or UFO. Forty years ago when McPhee was writing, the archives for U-2 and Oxcart development had not yet been opened to the public. Flying saucers or UFOs were the only available explanations. Even the chairman of the Senate Armed Services Committee in the 1980s, Senator Barry Goldwater, said he believed in flying saucers and that the military was keeping space aliens at air bases in Nevada.

Thirty minutes later when McPhee and his friend reached the town of Lovelock, Nevada, where they were staying for the night, the plane they saw would have already crossed the Canadian border. It might have banked left, swung out over the Pacific, and an hour later circled back over Southern California in its approach to its home base outside Las Vegas, seeking a four-mile runway that bisected the dry lake bed of what once was Groom Lake. The runway lights came on only within minutes of the plane's approach.

The town of Rachel is high in the mountains at the same latitude as Groom Lake and lies within the twelve thousand square miles of restricted airspace, but outside the military-only perimeter. Located on Route 375, which residents have named "the extraterrestrial highway" because of long experience with strange lights in the sky, the town has created a cottage industry of guidebooks on UFO sightings. An artist-photographer with a powerful telephoto lens and considerable mountain climbing agility has spent a lot of time on the mountain peaks around Rachel and published long-range mysterious photographs of Area 51's hangars, warehouses, outbuildings, planes on the runways, and vapor trails in the sky. The drones that now operate in Pakistan and Afghanistan were tested there and look very much like the bat-shaped plane that was shot down and put on public display in Iran.

Area 51 is now the most famous top-secret installation in the world, so famous that the Atomic Testing Museum in Las Vegas is in the process of mounting an exhibit about the site and has an ongoing lecture series about it.

VIETNAM WAR CONTRACTS

Bechtel remained involved in military contracting and military-related construction. In 1964 President Lyndon Johnson, running against the conservative, hawkish Barry Goldwater in the presidential election, greatly expanded the war in Vietnam. The two prime contractors for building military bases in Vietnam were Bechtel and Brown and Root, a Texas construction firm that beginning in 1940 had helped to finance Lyndon Johnson's political career. The two firms built air bases, landing fields, military compounds, roads, ports, support facilities, and energy depots throughout Southeast Asia. In a postwar audit of expenditures, the Congressional Budget Office said that the two firms had billed the government for so much concrete that they could have put a concrete skin eight feet deep over the entire country of Vietnam. Thirty years later during America's ongoing wars in Iraq and Afghanistan, the two prime military contractors for the US government were once again Bechtel and Brown and Root, although Brown and Root had a new parent company, Halliburton, the former employer of Vice President Dick Cheney. Unlike other major engineering and construction firms, Bechtel did not become a public company. It remained a family business. Its business was megaengineering. It was the largest family-owned business in the world.

Steve Sr. retired in 1960, and his son Steve Jr. took over. A trained engineer with a master's in business administration from Stanford, he was, people said, "more of a numbers guy" than his father. But he was still politically connected. By 1970 the numbers in their nuclear power division, on which Bechtel had been focused for growth, were dropping. (The last nuclear power plant in the United States would be licensed in 1976.) For one thing, it took a long time to build nuclear plants and the cost estimates at the beginning were not the same as the actual costs at the end of a completed installation. Utilities were finding that nuclear electricity was far more expensive than originally estimated. The issue of disposal of spent nuclear fuel was still unresolved. And finally, reassuring the public about the safety of nuclear energy—even before Three Mile Island and Chernobyl—was becoming increasingly difficult.

Permitting hearings grew more complex as public groups educated themselves about nuclear power and raised more sophisticated objections to nuclear plants. The public distrusted government reassurances and raised the issue of failed accountability in the 1960s over strontium 90, a by-product released in nuclear testing that was carried by winds, fell to the earth in rain, was digested by cows, and reappeared in milk. Children, who drank a lot of cow's milk, came down with cancers and leukemia in alarming clusters unrelated to water supply. Epidemiologists could not find a common cause. The US government adopted a strategy of denial—no nuclear tests were taking place, there was no fallout, strontium 90 didn't exist, and even if it did it was unrelated to leukemia or cancer in children. (Eventually, strontium 90 was shown to be a direct cause of childhood leukemia.) As a result, public trust in government honesty regarding the promise of nuclear technology was difficult to restore.

The issue of nuclear waste disposal remains unresolved to the present day, even though for eight years Bechtel-Nevada was boring through Yucca Mountain, eighty miles north of Las Vegas, to create a National Nuclear Waste Repository. The cost to the American taxpayers has been an estimated $18 billion with penalties for not building up to another $21 billion (states and utilities are suing). The project was stopped in 2010 after appropriations were cut off, largely because of the opposition of Las Vegas residents and Nevada politicians who questioned the safety of transporting nuclear fuel rods from all over the country on rail lines and interstate roads that ran through Las Vegas.

By 1974 Steven Bechtel Jr. decided the company needed a new framework for strategic planning. Although Bechtel was still building nuclear plants throughout the noncommunist world, nuclear power was no longer a growth industry. What was the next growth industry for energy? Steve Jr. determined that the company needed some outside perspective and in May 1974 offered the position of executive president to George Shultz, President Nixon's secretary of the treasury. Shultz was the first outside president in Bechtel's history. As a former dean of the University of Chicago Business School, former secretary of labor, and former treasury secretary, he was known as a skilled analyst of business trends and as astute as any investment banker in buying up the companies needed to dominate a new industry.

Among Shultz's portfolio at Bechtel were the Metals and Mining Division and Bechtel Power. According to Laton McCartney in *Friends in High Places*, Shultz grilled the members of the Power Division about new coal technologies and the Metals and Mining Division about coal. America had stunning reserves of coal, and American utilities were still getting 60 percent of their electricity from coal. In short, Bechtel decided to buy a coal company, and the company it chose was Peabody Coal, America's largest coal producer. The new technology that could change the economics of coal was the coal-slurry pipeline, which Bechtel had built in the first place. No longer would utilities have to build expensive railroads to transport coal to their new plants. As it had done with nuclear plants, Bechtel planned on an international market. Russia and China had huge reserves of coal as well as plenty of rain and groundwater.

Although Kennecott Copper didn't want to sell Peabody Coal, a year after Shultz stepped into the president's office at Bechtel, the US Justice Department declared that Kennecott Copper was in violation of antitrust laws. Its ownership of Peabody Coal created barriers to entry in the coal industry and was in restraint of trade. Kennecott would have no choice but to sell Peabody Coal. Although there were not many suitors who both were big enough to buy it and would not be in restraint of trade themselves, a few came forward. The Tennessee Valley Authority was one prospective buyer; Amax Metals was another. Then came a bid from a new entity, a private holding company called Peabody Holding, a consortium of six companies that had been put together solely to purchase Peabody Coal. The companies were Bechtel, Newmont Mining, Boeing Corporation, Fluor Engineering, Williams Technologies, and Equitable Life Insurance. *Forbes* said the deal had been engineered by the president of Newmont Mining, but *Fortune* said it was George

Shultz who actually pulled it off when it looked as though the deal would come apart. Peabody Coal was sold for $1.2 billion, $800 million in cash. As a private holding company, Peabody Coal was now private, not obliged to issue profit-and-loss statements or public reports.

By the end of the 1970s Bechtel was in the unique position of having built four of the major power plants on the Colorado Plateau— Mohave, Navajo Generating Station, Four Corners, Coronado—and the Black Mesa coal-slurry pipeline, and it now owned the coal company that mined the coal that supplied two of them. Most important, it was about to begin building the $8 billion Central Arizona Project, the largest civil engineering project since the Hoover Dam, which would require the coal and electricity of the Navajo Generating Station to power the fourteen pumping stations that would lift the Colorado River over three mountain ranges into Phoenix and Tucson.

Like Bechtel, Peabody Coal had a substantial political presence. It owned coal mines in ten states, and the twenty senators and dozens of congressmen of those states were aware of the company's interests. In addition, in other states where they didn't have mines, Peabody supplied coal to some of the largest utilities in the country, and those utilities had political relations offices. As a result Peabody Coal had a significant government affairs department.

A new narrative began to appear in Sunday supplements in which the Hopi were good Indians who wouldn't turn off their power and the Navajo were the bad Indians who would shut things down. The dominant narrative was of an old-fashioned range war on these remote Indian reservation lands. Photographers were brought to see and photograph bullet holes in the signs on the Hopi reservation. The Navajo supposedly showed the corpses of dead sheep that had been killed by the Hopi. Much of the faux range war was orchestrated by Evans and Associates, a public relations firm in Salt Lake City that was on retainer to the same utilities that owned and operated the four generating stations, organized under the umbrella name of Western Supply and Transmission.

In 1980 the Bechtel Corporation was a major supporter and behind-the-scenes fund-raiser for the presidential candidacy of California governor Ronald Reagan. They were well rewarded for doing so. Caspar Weinberger, Bechtel's legal counsel, left to become Reagan's secretary of defense, and Ken Davis, head of Bechtel's Nuclear Division, was appointed assistant secretary in the Department of Energy. By then George Shultz was chief executive officer of the Bechtel Corporation, the most important of Bechtel's three operating companies,* and second only to Steve Jr. in authority. In 1982 George Shultz left Bechtel to become President Reagan's secretary of state. It was during the 1980s that all efforts to amend or soften the relocation law were defeated.

Many former Bechtel executives held lesser posts throughout the Reagan government, particularly in the Departments of Energy and Interior, particularly the Office of Surface Mining and Enforcement. Consequently, Bechtel's influential presence in Washington accounts for not only the difficulty the Hopi and Navajo had in presenting alternative views of the "range war," but also for the consistent failure, despite many efforts, by several prominent senators and congressmen to modify the original legislation. The narrow resource base of the West was a worry. The water and power infrastructure depended on cheap coal in distant locations. In the case of Arizona, the Central Arizona Project depended primarily on the massive coal beds that lay beneath the Hopi and Navajo reservations. The people who lived close to the coal would have to be moved. Coal strip mining and sheepherding are not compatible occupations. After the passage of the Hopi Land Settlement Act of 1974, the physical partition of the Executive Order Reservation and the removal of the Navajo seemed unstoppable.

The Navajo chairman, Peter MacDonald, was eloquent and effective in explaining conditions on the ground to the Senate committee as they considered bills to amend or reauthorize the relocation program that, although it was called the Navajo Hopi Relocation, primarily affected the Navajo:**

---

* The three operating companies are Bechtel Incorporated, Bechtel Corporation, and Bechtel Power Corporation.

** During the same hearings the head of the Relocation Commission, Hawley Atkinson, said that the commission had received 4,449 applications. Because the

I believe the performance of the Relocation Commission, however well intentioned, has made a more terrible situation than we started out with earlier. Everything is so bad. I know that you members of the committee sense this just by listening to your questions and also hearing the responses from the Commission. . . . They can't even give you a figure that they can agree upon as to how many people are really affected, what their needs are, where they are, what they are doing, what their problems are. . . . It has been that way for a number of years and I don't know that it is ever going to improve.

The Navajo legal services attorneys inform me that the problems we have seen in the past with faulty housing construction by contractors and incompetent inspection by the Commission continue to appear today. . . . [Among the] problems are concrete not level; holes in the foundation through which rodents enter; plumbing leaks; inadequate insulation; repairs costing $75,000, doubling the cost of the house.

In one instance the contractor was paid but abandoned the project with the home left roofless. . . . Contractors aren't bonded. They don't complete warranty work. . . . The Commission told the two relocatee families that they should sue the contractor. . . . Too many people are hurting. Too many people are dying because they are not able to find a way out of the situation in which we have put them.

Senator Dennis DeConcini of Arizona agreed. During an earlier public hearing, he had called the law inhumane. "There are many problems which have developed in the course of the effort to carry out this law, a law which, in this Senator's judgment *is not a humane law*. . . .

---

applications were from heads of households and the average number was 4 in a family, it meant that more than 16,000 Navajo were affected. The Hopi chairman said only 36 Hopi had applied for relocation.

I have argued for a change in the law for a long time. . . . I am still convinced that our moral obligation to these citizens of our country deserves nothing less than the most humane treatment. I will continue to push for that kind of change."

In the House, Congressman John McCain also agreed: "Congressman Udall and I offered a comprehensive settlement last year, but subsequently withdrew the bill [HR 4281] for lack of support." The congressional summary report noted that "support for the measure was not forthcoming from the [Reagan] administration or from Senator Barry Goldwater."

Senator Alan Cranston of California introduced a bill that would have placed a moratorium on the relocation of the Navajo for an eighteen-month period. Again the committee report noted, "Senator Goldwater took exception to this bill."

Soon Peter MacDonald was being investigated by the IRS, supposedly set in motion by Senator Goldwater, and then sued for fraud for having personally profited from a ranch that he bought with tribal funds. The first person to testify at his trial over tribal corruption was a vice president of Peabody Coal. By the time the Reagan administration was over, Peter MacDonald would be serving jail time, Peterson Zah was again Navajo chairman, and there were no more official objections from the Navajo Tribe to relocation. The Navajo resisters were on their own.

On the other hand, the Hopi chairman, Ivan Sidney, inadvertently testified that the coal and the land dispute were working out well for the Hopi: "I was honored to be in the same city and the same room three weeks ago signing the renegotiated contract with Peabody Coal that would bring more revenue to both the Navajo and the Hopi for the coal that we own jointly as a result of this land dispute."

COAL AND THE GRAND PLAN

The common denominator in the Grand Plan was Bechtel. A photographer took a rare picture of Steve Jr. and Secretary of Interior Stewart Udall outside the Four Corners Plant in Farmington, New Mexico, when the expanded plant opened in 1968. Although Utah International had built the first units, Bechtel had built two new giant units, which, at 2,250 megawatts, made Four Corners one of the largest power plants in the United States. The two new units were copies of the Mohave plant that was already under way in Laughlin, Nevada.

As soon as the Four Corners plant was completed, Bechtel moved its workers to the new power-generation plant in Laughlin, Nevada, and the site of the Black Mesa slurry pipeline that would supply it. Then a year or two later it moved its workers to a site near Page, Arizona, where it began construction of the Navajo Generating Station, which was completed in 1974. At the same time it shifted workers to St. Johns, Arizona, for construction of the Coronado Generating Station. All four power plants, along with two nuclear plants, were part of a larger energy design called the Grand Plan, organized by twenty-three utilities to provide electricity for the booming West.

The utilities of Western Energy Supply and Transmission, located in Los Angeles, were among the largest in the country and were designing the energy infrastructure for the next thirty-five years. The West in the 1960s had entered a state of permanent boom. West Coast ports had been the staging areas for the Korean War during the 1950s and for the Vietnam War in the 1960s. The infusion of military contracts, aerospace industries, and other military bases had provided the yeast for jobs, population growth, booming housing, and a speculative land industry. The economies of the western states were flourishing thanks to the US government and military. At the same time, the political culture of the population that grew in the new Sunbelt cities was conservative, focused on small government, self-reliance, and low taxes. As author Wallace Stegner said, the westerner's attitude toward the federal government is pretty much "Give us the money and leave us alone."

Despite the extent of the resources, no Indians were getting rich from resource extraction. Despite promises that leases for uranium, coal, oil, and gas would bring in millions of dollars to the tribes and create thousands of jobs, a visit to the reservation reveals the illusion of those promises. Authors Bob Gottlieb and Peter Wiley later characterized the Grand Plan as a failure, saying it marked "a raid on resources that would outstrip the 19th century and turn some of the most beautiful and scenic areas of America into a vast industrialized energy colony under the control of major corporations headquartered in cities hundreds of miles away."

By the time the Hopi and Navajo were coming to Washington to try to change the legislation that would affect the future of their lands and their people, they were dealing with a huge international company with contacts in Washington at the highest levels. Bechtel had forty thousand employees in twenty countries building the infrastructure of the free world. It was often described as a company with its own foreign policy, and soon its foreign policy was America's foreign policy.

It had no public stockholders, issued no annual report, and submitted no quarterly forms to the Securities and Exchange Commission. It was the twentieth-largest corporation in the United States but was still a family business. Many of its operations were viewed as opaque, even by its own employees. Complaints made outside the company were echoed inside. D. J. Hallett, controller of Bechtel Corporation, wrote a memo to Steve Jr. expressing his concerns about the attitude toward transparency and open communication: "The Bechtel organization wishes to operate with a 'low profile' [in its] exposure to the business world. I consider this low profile aspect, together with the general secrecy surrounding a private company, is often used as an excuse by management for not communicating essential information." He criticized the company culture of treating all information as confidential information. "As a multi-national company, we must improve overseas communications by developing managers who . . . understand customs and practices of the countries they are working in."

Operations on Indian reservations are like operations in a foreign country: pliable government agencies, lax environmental enforcement, lack of access to media, weak tribal structures. As the environmental movement grew in the 1970s and '80s, the company seemed to view environmentalism with the same hostility it viewed labor unions or communism. Therefore, when several nonprofit Indian and environmental organizations asked Peabody Coal for information about the terms of the leases on the Hopi and Navajo Indian reservations and the amount of water that would be pumped out of their land to transport coal, they could not get copies of the leases or the water rates. The Interior Department claimed the leases were confidential and not available to the public.

In the era of transnational corporations, the methods of separating indigenous peoples from their lands and resources are many, and often quite legal—at least to those making the laws. When native lands, like those of the Hopi and Navajo, hold important energy resources, the human rights and environmental impacts take place far from mainstream media.

Although northern Black Mesa and the Colorado Plateau might appear to be some of the most isolated land remaining in the United States, Bechtel has had a long and profitable history there. Hoover Dam made Bechtel an engineering legend and still looms large in its institutional memory. The dam created a small group of construction-company millionaires who understood long-range infrastructure planning and how to open the federal Treasury to execute it. Yet as Marc Reisner wrote in *Cadillac Desert*, "The Colorado River is a metaphor for our time. The age of great expectations was inaugurated at Hoover Dam—a fifty year flowering of hopes when all things appeared possible. And one could say that amid the salt-encrusted sands of the river's dried up delta, we begin to founder on the Era of Limits."

Unexpectedly, the era of limits began to be publicized by a small group of Navajo resisters who organized themselves into the Independent Diné Nation. Even though many of the signatures on their proclamation were in the form of a thumbprint, their understanding of the situation eventually became a larger awareness of climate change caused by carbon levels in the atmosphere and accompanying drought. "Our Mother Earth is continuously raped by the exploitation of coal, uranium, oil, natural gas. Our Father Sky has been contaminated by the poison from burning coal and the radiation from uranium mining. Our sacred water has been abused, so now there is no certainty for the future generations."

Although Roberta Blackgoat, Katherine Smith, Pauline Whitesinger, and the many Benallys, Yazzies, and Begays who signed the Declaration of Independence of the Big Mountain Diné Nation on October 28, 1979, were invisible to American media, over the next thirty years they became visible at the United Nations, at the European Parliament, and at the newly established Commission on Indigenous People in Geneva. They were emblematic of an international issue of native peoples with rich resources that global corporations wanted and successfully extracted. At the same time, many became aware that the decimation of land-based cultures and the knowledge of their people was a huge and irretrievable loss.

CHAPTER 12

ROBERTA BLACKGOAT'S WORLD

Roberta Blackgoat's sheepherding camp is gone now, but it was located some eighteen miles south of the Kayenta Mine in the area around Big Mountain, at seven thousand feet the highest point on Black Mesa. It was February 1991 when I first went to see her, driving from Flagstaff with her daughter Vicki Blackgoat, who skimmed along ungraded roads, skirted deep canyons, and at one point saw the road vanish entirely into a swiftly running stream. "Washed-out dam," said Vicki matter-of-factly as she gunned the accelerator and slammed into the stream and up the steep bank on the other side. Vicki, who was a graduate of Dartmouth College, had grown up on the reservation and seemed to remember every turn and rise in the road, although it had been at least fifteen years since she had lived there full-time.

At another point I looked over the edge of a deep canyon to see an Anasazi cliff house carved into the amphitheater of a canyon wall. As the sun was setting she told me we were finally getting close to her mother's camp and pointed out a series of earthen dams at the side of the road. "Those are to catch rainwater for the sheep," she said. "You can store up to two days of water in those little catch basins." In a region that receives only six to eight inches of rainfall a year, every means of storing water counts.

At dusk we finally pulled into her mother's camp, a cluster of buildings that included a three-room house (originally built by the Bureau of Indian Affairs, but now unfinished because her land had been designated as part of the new Hopi lands and she was not allowed to make any repairs), a round earth-covered hogan with an inviting plume of cedar smoke coming out of the center, a sheep corral made of split cedar rails, a henhouse, and in the distance two outhouses.

On that visit in February 1991, Roberta was seventy-four years old, a woman with round cheeks, a warm smile, and shrewd eyes. She was plainly delighted to see Vicki and welcomed me with a hug. I was fascinated with the dignified way she carried herself as well as her elegant Navajo silver necklace and a huge turquoise cluster pin. Somehow, I never expected someone who lived as a sheepherder to be so elegantly turned out. On the other hand, this was a woman who had succeeded in helping to bring the issues of Black Mesa before the United Nations and the European Parliament.

Both Vicki and Greg, an Anglo sheepherder sent by the Big Mountain support group to help her, teased her about the dazzling white sneakers that peeked out from under her long, tiered Navajo skirt and for refusing to remove the kerchief tied under her chin. She said it was to keep her hair out of her face. Long wisps of white hair escaped from under her kerchief because her hair kept coming out of the figure eight knotted at the nape of her neck. Her voice was high and raspy. I would learn that this was her voice in English; in Navajo it was low and authoritative.

"Why are we going to the hogan?" Vicki asked as we walked away from the house toward the sheep corral. It was February and it was cold. Greg explained that Roberta had been sick with bronchitis and she thought that sleeping in the hogan would help her get better. The land around her three-room house, hogan, and sheep corral contained an eclectic collection of objects: a pile of stacked cedar logs, several hundred-gallon barrels for hauling water, oil drums cut in half, plastic one-gallon containers, a set of iron grates in different sizes, a pile of shiny coal from the Peabody mines, and the skull of what I would learn was a coyote. It was too dark to see much else. The next morning I also saw an exercise treadmill (a gift from a visitor who thought Roberta needed more exercise, even though sometimes she walked nine miles a day taking her sheep out to graze) and ancient Anasazi pottery shards with vivid geometric designs scattered in the dirt of the sheep corral. Her lands had once held a large settlement of people called the Anasazi.

The next morning we were getting ready to go to Holbrook, where Vicki was to give a student talk about college preparation, when Roberta asked me to check the oil in her pickup truck. I leaned into the engine, found the dipstick, and pulled it out. We agreed it needed another quart. Even though she was the subsistence sheepherder and I was the urban dweller, I was certain she knew more about the workings of a combustion engine than I ever would.

When I went to the hogan to get the can of oil, I looked around at the interior in daylight and realized how complex it was and how superficially I had judged it the night before. From the outside it looks like a bubble of mud. (The *Healing v. Jones* court decision had described Navajo dwellings as "rude shelters known as hogans, usually built of poles, sticks, bark, and moist earth.") But from the inside it was substantial and intricate. The complex log frame was made of trees that were placed in the upright direction in which they grew. The door faced the east and the rising sun. In addition to being a perfectly organized one-room home, it was a miniature version of the Navajo cosmos. Many Navajo who moved to border towns around the reservation constructed hogans in their backyards. At the time three people were living and sleeping in the hogan—Greg the sheepherder, Vicki, and Roberta. At my request I slept in the unheated three-room house, mainly because the heat in the hogan was too warm for me to be able to sleep.

At the entrance was a box of cedar chips and logs that were used to feed the fire. Around the edge was a big cooler, which held perishable food, a fifty-pound bag of dog food, several metal folding chairs, a tool box, a coffee tin that—I knew from dinner the night before—had cookies in it, a kerosene lantern perched on a stool, Roberta's loom for weaving, and a box of automotive supplies that held the oil. The floor was covered with strips of denim over which were laid sheepskins.

On the wall, however, was the item that astonished me and that remained in my mind long after I left. A large Rand McNally map of the world was tacked to the curve opposite the entrance. Each continent had colored tacks that marked locations in Africa, Australia, Asia, and South America where other indigenous people were fighting global corporations, several of them the same corporations she was dealing with on Black Mesa. Roberta Blackgoat understood she was engaged in an international enterprise.

"Those are places like us," Roberta said, pointing to one of the colored tacks, explaining that they were locations where other indigenous people were being pushed off their lands by mining corporations. I found myself remembering the map because the people in the way of "development" in third world countries wasn't the way I had learned about "developing nations" in graduate school. The process by which Roberta was being removed from her lifetime land and home rested on a complex mix of laws, hearings, court cases, appeals, and ongoing lawsuits and was technically "legal," although, as Senator DeConcini said, "inhumane." The corporations had the ear of the government agencies, and tribal councils were often compromised. Corporate money was invested at every level of the process.

Together we walked back to the truck. Vicki put in the oil, got in the driver's seat, and motioned to me to get in the middle, and off we went. It was a cold February day, and a light dusting of snow muted the landscape into a vast expanse of chilly pastels. As we came up over a rise, I looked out at an oceanic vista of whites, blues, pinks where the sky and the land blended imperceptibly into one another. This is what infinity looks like, I thought.

On the drive to Holbrook I asked Roberta if she had any other children like Vicki who lived so far away. No, she said. "My other four children all live in Arizona." (Two daughters lived in Flagstaff and Tuba City; one son worked for Peabody Coal in Page; the other son taught Navajo language at the University of Northern Arizona.) She said the reason Vicki was able to travel and live so far from home was because she had given birth to Vicki at the Indian Health Service Hospital in

Tuba City. All the other children had been born on the land, and Roberta had buried their umbilical cords in the sheep corral to link them to the earth from which they came and the sheep that nurtured them.

THE INDEPENDENT DINÉ NATION

Roberta Blackgoat was famous among the Navajo and among Indian activists for her leadership of the Independent Diné Nation. Although she was one of approximately sixteen thousand Navajo being removed from their lands on Black Mesa, she was also chairperson of the population of Navajo who had formed the Independent Diné Nation and seceded from the authority of the Navajo Tribal Council. In 1979 she had helped organize hundreds of families to sign the Proclamation of the Big Mountain Diné (Navajo) Nation to declare their independence from the Navajo tribal government. Their proclamation made a demand for the repeal of the Hopi Land Settlement Act, Public Law 93-531, as well as a declaration of intent to present charges of genocide and racism to the United Nations. Although it was a radical act, to go outside the US legal system and present a case before the United Nations, it had a secondary purpose of preventing AIM leaders from coming in and taking over the resistance.

At the Indian school in Holbrook we sat at a large table of parents while Vicki gave a presentation to their children about a summer-school program that would prepare the Navajo students for taking SATs for college admission. At our table the parents went around to introduce themselves, and when Roberta said, "Roberta Blackgoat," everyone stared. "Are you really?" said one man in disbelief. It seemed to stop conversation. One woman later took me aside and said, "I certainly admire what she has done, but believe me we are not going back to sleeping on sheepskins."

Shortly afterward Roberta said to me, "Let's go look for some concrete." I drove her truck around Holbrook to different hardware stores while she explained to me the history of Arizona laws, US laws, the fate of Navajo chairperson Peter MacDonald, and what burning coal does to the planet. Thirty years before the Sierra Club's "Say No to Coal" campaign or Bill McKibben's 350.org, she was describing the permanent destructive effect that carbon would have on that membrane of air, land, and water where we all live. We did not yet have the term *biosphere* in popular usage. She wanted me to understand that she saw it as a much larger struggle than saving her personal sheepherding camp. In 1991 climate change was still known as the "greenhouse effect." She was describing a shift in patterns of air, groundwater, and temperature that made climate change a permanent condition. I asked her how she knew so much about politics and activism.

We Hold the Rock

In the mid-1960s Tuba City had a Legal Aid office staffed by an Anglo husband-and-wife legal team. Tuba City had about four thousand residents then (today it has nine thousand), a hospital, schools, a bank, and an office of the Bureau of Indian Affairs that kept track of Navajo livestock grazing permits. Other activities included a field office for the Atomic Energy Commission, a uranium mining corporation called Rare Metals, and a number of outlying uranium mines. The Navajo mines supplied more than three-fourths of the uranium used in the one thousand atomic tests held at the Nevada Test Site outside Las Vegas.* Tuba City still has an abandoned uranium mine on the outskirts of town with a tailings pile covered up with black sand, still blowing dust. I didn't know that when I bought an orange T-shirt that advertised "Tuba City: Home of the Best Navajo Taco in the West."

The Tuba City Legal Aid office opened the first Indian Welfare Rights organization in the country. Martha Blue, the Legal Aid attorney who ran the office with her lawyer husband, said she started the organization to help Navajo women negotiate the bureaucratic complexities of a federal program called Aid to Families with Dependent Children (AFDC). Navajo children who should have been receiving

---

* The most recent test was on December 7, 2012, at the Nevada Test Site. Mayors of Hiroshima and Nagasaki formally protested.

aid were being denied by the Arizona state administrators. AFDC was a federal program designed to help children in families living below the poverty line, which meant many families on the Navajo reservation should have been eligible. But Arizona state agencies routinely made it extremely difficult for Navajo women to get benefits.

One day a Navajo woman named Roberta Blackgoat came to her office seeking help. "From our first meeting," Martha Blue recalled, "it was clear Roberta was different from almost all the other Navajo welfare applicants that I'd represented. First of all, she was articulate in English. Second, she didn't seem daunted about challenging the state government or the Bureau of Indian Affairs." Roberta's case was a typical example of a case that shouldn't have been denied. Two years earlier Roberta's husband had been changing a flat tire by the side of the road and had been struck and killed by an automobile. Roberta was left with five children to support, with the youngest, Vicki, still in grade school. As the head of a traditional Navajo family who lived in the deep interior of Black Mesa, Roberta was barely getting by with sheepherding and subsistence agriculture. She needed cash for necessities such as gas and medicines and groceries. She had filed for welfare assistance through the AFDC program, and the Arizona Welfare Department denied her claim.

On what grounds? Martha asked. Roberta said the welfare office multiplied the number of her sheep by the market value and said her wealth was too great to qualify for the welfare program. Martha, who knew that a Navajo's sheep were like a bank account, also knew that sheep were not liquid assets and could not be counted as income. When she asked more questions, she found that they also ruled against her because of the value of her pickup truck. Much of Roberta's small cash income came from neighbors who paid her to drive them into Flagstaff or Holbrook, where they could buy groceries and supplies more cheaply than at the trading posts. Roberta charged them a fee for gas and transportation, and those fees were how she earned enough cash to make payments on her truck. The Arizona Welfare Department claimed that she was hiding income by running a "taxi service" with her pickup truck.

Interviewed years later, Martha Blue added, "It's also important to know she lived thirty miles away from the nearest paved highway, on an unimproved dirt road, sometimes no wider than a track, at an elevation of seven thousand feet. The nearest garage was probably a hundred miles away. She needed a reliable recent-model automobile with good brakes that wouldn't break down." Roberta already knew firsthand the tragedy that came from a broken-down vehicle at the side of the road. "Unlike a lot of Navajo families, Roberta always made sure she had a relatively new pickup truck and kept it in good repair."

Martha had traveled all over the Navajo reservation but described her one visit to Roberta's sheepherding camp as "the most isolated place I'd ever been on the reservation and on the worst dirt roads. I felt as though I had never been so far from the amenities of the white world. It was a profound experience to feel I was in the middle of nowhere, lost, and isolated."

"Roberta had had some high school education," she continued, "maybe even graduated. Because of her knowledge of English, she'd also served as chapter secretary for the Hard Rock Chapter. That was unusual for a woman at that time." As Martha came to know her better, she said, "I felt she also had a strong sense of fairness and an expectation that people would respond to reason."

Martha took Roberta's case, they appealed, and they won. This was in 1968. But the larger case was ongoing. Other welfare rights groups representing Hispanic and African American clients in Arizona had appealed to the federal government about Arizona's arbitrary and capricious administration of the AFDC program. As a result the federal Department of Human Services (then called the Department of Health Education and Welfare) scheduled hearings in San Francisco to determine whether Arizona was out of compliance with federal guidelines.

Although Martha Blue was not optimistic that she could get any of her Native American clients to appear as witnesses, because it was so difficult to get traditional people to leave their sheepherding camps for big cities and Anglo proceedings that they didn't understand, she did ask Roberta. To her surprise, Roberta said yes.

In August 1970 Roberta, along with a friend, Desbah Slender, a Navajo woman who did not speak English, traveled by bus to San Francisco for the first time, part of a bus caravan of welfare recipients from Phoenix. (Their lawyers took a plane.) They all, witnesses and lawyers, stayed at the YWCA.

It was in San Francisco that Martha Blue realized that Roberta was a person with unusual powers in front of an audience.

> When Roberta testified at the hearings, she was a star. Unlike many of the other women witnesses, she was not intimidated by the surroundings, the panel of lawyers running the hearing, or the aggressive questioning by the attorney for the Arizona welfare agency. She was a great witness. She was warm, self-assured, and completely Navajo. She was comfortable in whatever situation arose. Her English was excellent. When she was cross-examined, she remained unflappable. The opposition lawyer didn't ruffle her composure or get her to contradict anything in her testimony. She was matter-of-fact, clear, lucid, well-spoken.

Martha Blue remembered other unusual characteristics, such as her ease in strange surroundings with unfamiliar foods. When they went to a Chinese restaurant, for example, Roberta began eating with chopsticks without hesitation. She was curious about everything she saw. She didn't seem awed by anything, although she had never been to San Francisco before and never seemed disoriented or confused, as one might expect of a Navajo woman in her midfifties, a widow who lived a hard life in remote, isolated country. "And," Martha added, "she has that wonderful way of carrying herself."

Roberta's appearance and testimony gained positive newspaper coverage in San Francisco newspapers, and once again Martha and Roberta won their case. The hearing examiners found that the State of Arizona was out of compliance with federal welfare regulations. But the welfare hearing became only one part of Mrs. Blackgoat's San

Francisco experience. Roberta Blackgoat had arrived in San Francisco at the height of the 1970 Native American occupation of Alcatraz.

In November 1969 fourteen activists calling themselves the "Indians of All Tribes" occupied the island of Alcatraz in San Francisco Bay. The former prison had been closed and the island was empty, so the occupiers invoked an 1868 government agreement with the Sioux that granted Indians first rights to buy any government "surplus lands." The government had declared Alcatraz Island "surplus land." The occupying Indians offered to purchase the island for $24 in glass beads.

Their goal was to draw public attention to the history and treatment of all Indian tribes—the unmet terms of the 363 Indian treaties ratified by the US Senate and the more than 800 treaties that the US government had signed but never kept. They asked why, in exchange for the vast land cessions the Indians had made throughout the United States, the US government had never provided the promised payments, education, economic help, health care, or trust income promised by the terms. When the tribes were strong, the government signed treaties; when the tribes were weak, the terms of the treaties were forgotten. Who was to make the Bureau of Indian Affairs accountable if not Indians themselves?

In the spirit of the 1960s teach-in, in which minority groups taught their own history and investigated the stories omitted from mainstream history books, the Alcatraz Indians wanted Native American people to take pride in their own struggle against a powerful and predatory government. In this undertaking they successfully put Native Americans squarely in the historical and political mainstream, rather than the realm of anthropology. Their cause landed on the front pages of the nation's newspapers. The boldness of the Alcatraz occupation attracted hundreds of Native Americans and minority college students from across the country who poured into San Francisco. Some took up residency in the prison cell blocks; others became staunch supporters, handling logistics and providing the occupiers with food, supplies, funding, and help. They defied federal demands to leave the island. On the front of the entrance to the prison they posted a large handwritten sign that read:

We are Indians of All tribes! We are still holding the Island of Alcatraz in the true names of Freedom, Justice
and Equality, because you, our brothers and sisters of this
earth, have lent support to our just cause. We reach out our
hands and hearts and send spirit messages to each and every one of you—WE HOLD THE ROCK!

Among the occupiers was Wilma Mankiller, then a college student
in San Francisco and a Cherokee originally from Oklahoma who had
left with her family when she was five years old. She said later that until
the Alcatraz occupation, she knew neither her family's nor her tribe's
true history. At Alcatraz she learned the story of the "competency
commissions" in oil-rich sections of Oklahoma that had the power to
declare Indians incompetent to handle oil leases on their lands and
appointed local lawyers as their "trustees" who often separated the Indians from their royalties and their lands. This history so influenced
her that she later returned to Oklahoma, went to work for the tribal
government, and eventually become the principal chief of the Cherokee. Another person involved in the occupation was Lorraine "Rain"
Parrish, a Navajo social worker from the Navajo reservation who spoke
both Navajo and English and arranged for Roberta's visit to Alcatraz.

As it had with Wilma Mankiller, the Alcatraz occupation had
a powerful long-term influence on Roberta. She had arrived in San
Francisco at a unique moment in resurgent Native American activism.
Roberta was impressed by the boldness of the Alcatraz activists. Like
many, she had also been deliberately cut off from Navajo history and
her larger heritage. The boarding school she attended in Keams Canyon did not teach any Navajo history.

The Nixon administration—not wanting to create a violent confrontation and create even more publicity—took the position of waiting out the occupation, which it did. Even so, the Alcatraz leaders'
demands for government accountability marked a sea change in Indians' attitudes about their own identity, regardless of tribal affiliation,
and the nature of the US government. Alcatraz sparked a new Pan-
Indian movement of Native identity, tradition, and spirituality. By the

time the Alcatraz occupation ended in June 1971, a new assertive Indian movement had been born, one that was not afraid to take on Washington. The Paiutes of Nevada, for example, sued the Interior Department for the draining of Pyramid Lake, claiming, rightly, that Indian water rights were superior to those of either California or Nevada. The two states had signed an illegal agreement, allowing California to pay Nevada for taking water pumped from the lake. The Alcatraz occupiers organized a caravan of automobiles from San Francisco to Nevada to support the Paiutes. The publicity reached network television news. Soon the Interior Department was renegotiating the California-Nevada agreement and stabilizing water levels at Pyramid Lake.

In another Alcatraz-related event, the Taos Pueblo of New Mexico pressed for the return of the sacred Blue Lake. The legislation had been pending since the 1920s, when the corrupt interior secretary Albert Fall—of Teapot Dome notoriety—owned ranch lands adjacent to the lake and drained the water from the lake for his own use. With the help of John Ehrlichman in the White House, Congress finally passed legislation returning the lake to the Taos Pueblo. The same year the Alcatraz occupation ended, a mainstream New York press published Vine Deloria's groundbreaking *Custer Died for Your Sins: An Indian Manifesto*, a best-selling book that refuted many of the romantic notions about the American West and told the history of American expansion as a story of imperial power and conquest. Deloria, a lawyer with a graduate degree in theology, became an important voice of the new Indian movement. By 1972 America's official Indian policy of termination of Indian tribes—first introduced by Senator Arthur Watkins of Utah in the 1950s—had changed, and three years later Congress officially repudiated termination policy (but not before thirty tribes had been terminated) by passing the Indian Self-Determination and Education Act.

LEARNING HISTORY

During the long drive to and from Holbrook, I asked Roberta about her childhood, where she lived, her relatives, what she learned in school, how she learned about Martha Blue, why she had gone to jail. As we drove through Keams Canyon, I asked where the boarding school had been.

"There. That's where I went to school," she said, pointing to the opposite side of the road.

"I don't see anything," I said, noting only a small wood-frame building hardly big enough to be a school.

"Gone now. But that's where the Indian school used to be."

"What was it like?"

Roberta made a face of extreme distaste, as though she had eaten something sour. "Oh, I hated it," she said, shaking her head. "They cut our hair. They took away our clothes. We had to wear uniforms. So scratchy. We had to speak only English. If we spoke Navajo, we got punishments. We had to pray every day. I hated it," she repeated. "I got lots of punishments. Then," she added matter-of-factly, "I ran away."

When she was young, around nine or ten, her mother had died, and she went to live with her father's relatives. It was a time in the mid-1920s when services to the western Navajo reservation—health care and food supplements—had been curtailed. Families were starving, so her father's family sent her to the boarding school so she would get enough to eat. Each time she ran away, the family brought her back. She stayed for five years, until the ninth grade, and then was sent to the Indian school in Phoenix.* That was how she learned English at a time when most Navajo children of her generation were able to avoid boarding school. (That historic reality is noted in the signatures on the Independent Diné Nation proclamation with the column that calls for "a thumbprint" instead of a signature.)

As we passed through the canyon, I noticed a heavy concrete bureaucratic-looking building off to the right. "What's that?" I interrupted Vicki and Roberta, who were talking in Navajo.

"Hopi jail," answered Roberta.

---

* She was born in 1916 and attended the Keams Canyon boarding school, a K–9 school, from 1926 to 1931. She later went to the Phoenix Indian School, also a boarding school, in the 1930s.

"Jail? I thought the Hopi were the people of peace." ("The Hopi are a timid and inoffensive people, peaceable and friendly with outsiders," stated the 1962 *Healing v. Jones* case summary.) "Why would a small community of Hopi need a jail that looks as though it could be in Beirut?" It was squat, massive, a concrete fortress.

"For us Navajo," said Roberta, chuckling.

"That's where Mom was put in jail," said Vicki without humor.

Blackgoat and two other ladies had blocked a backhoe that was digging up land for the fence. "You'll have to scoop me out of the way to do this project," she told the construction crew. She ended up spending the night in jail. I started to ask what was important about that piece of land, but Roberta changed the subject and pointed to something else in the landscape. Later I understood that she was protecting places where ancestors had been buried or a site where ceremonies had taken place. The destruction was the equivalent of running a highway through the Gettysburg cemetery.

When the second piece of Hopi-Navajo land legislation passed Congress in 1974, the government began building a hundred-mile barbed-wire fence that looped like a hitchhiker's thumb deep into the interior of Black Mesa. The new Hopi lands included Roberta's sheepherding camp. Then came the administrative orders of implementation, one of which said that she could keep no more than seventy sheep—at the time she had four hundred—and she could not repair her house, even though the roof was leaking. Although the Hopi had never lived on these new lands, thousands of Navajo families would have to be moved. The real determinant of the new boundary line, as she learned, was access to the aquifer and the location of the coal seam. The Navajo lived over the coal. The Hopi lived thirty miles away, clustered in villages at the edge of Black Mesa.

In her short visit to San Francisco in August 1970, Roberta Blackgoat had received a full education in activism, media relations, public articulation of grievances, grassroots organizing, Indian history, Pan-Indian communication, and perseverance. She would use them all. Barry Goldwater was adamant about the physical division of the land and the removal of the Navajo. After Senator Goldwater's visit to Black Mesa in 1978, Roberta understood there would be no help coming from his office, or from the Navajo Tribal Council, which was legally obligated to enforce the law.

I asked her why the Navajo Tribal Council and its tribal chairman, Peter MacDonald, hadn't been able to help. She was silent at first and then shook her head sadly. "He speaks a wonderful Navajo. The old people like him," was all she would say. I asked about Peterson Zah, the new tribal chairman. She shook her head again. There was good reason for her sadness. While we were speaking in 1991 Peter Mac-Donald was being tried for various federal crimes and was on his way to a twelve-year prison term on various counts of fraud and inciting a riot. The charges were later found to be dubious, but soon Peter Mac-Donald was out of the way. He became an object lesson for any Native American tribal chairman who might want to be too aggressive in dealing with energy companies. After MacDonald's experience, neither Peterson Zah nor any other tribal official was going to help the Navajo destined for removal.

Bedo MacDonald

Peter MacDonald was the only four-term tribal chairman the Navajo ever had and was considered the most powerful Native American official in the country. Along with being the head of the Navajo Tribal Council, he had organized CERT, the Council of Energy Resource Tribes, composed of the thirteen tribes whose reservation lands held the largest energy reserves in the West. That initiative alone could have made him a target for the energy companies, which up until then had not had to negotiate with knowledgeable consultants, energy lawyers, or tribes that expected equitable participation.

By 1973 he was Navajo tribal chairman and was thinking in Pan-Indian terms. His point of view was that with the amount of oil, coal, uranium, and natural gas being mined on the Navajo reservation, the Navajo people should have the highest per capita income of any reservation in the country. Instead, the leases never seemed to work to the Indians' advantage or in their real interests. This was true of almost all the "energy tribes." With MacDonald's experience in business—trained as an engineer, he had been a vice president at Hughes Aircraft in California for more than a decade—and his insider experience with a huge corporation, he wanted to improve the Indians' bargaining position. MacDonald's template for the Council of Energy Resource Tribes was OPEC (Organization of Petroleum Exporting Countries) and the steps the Middle Eastern countries took to get out from under the control of ARAMCO and British and American oil companies. CERT's stated purpose was to hire legal experts outside the BIA, share information about different companies, renegotiate contracts, and increase lease royalties. This mission was not viewed as a popular institutional improvement by the energy companies or by the Bureau of Indian Affairs, who approved all the leasing arrangements. (And, it must be acknowledged, it was not popular with traditional Indians within the tribes who were against mining, regardless of the economic advantages.) MacDonald was almost uniformly described as "corrupt" in the white press, but part of his problem was that he thought the chairman of an Indian tribe could operate like an Anglo businessman; another part was that the energy corporations and the utilities were deeply involved in tribal elections, both by injecting money and by supporting candidates.

Born with the name Bedo of the Tsin Secadnii clan, he was named "Peter" by the white schoolteachers at the Teec Nos Pos school because that was the closest English approximation of his Navajo name they could pronounce. They translated his last name as "Donald." When his grade school classmates learned the song about Old MacDonald's farm, they started calling him Peter MacDonald, and that became his name. He came from a family that had been devastated by the livestock reduction of 1934 and '35 in the Utah part of the reservation. Trained as a medicine man, he enrolled in the Army at the age of sixteen and was trained as a Navajo code talker in World War II. After the war he graduated from the University of Oklahoma with an engineering degree and went to work for Hughes Aircraft in California, where he had a successful career and rose to vice president. Politically, he was a Republican and a friend of Barry Goldwater. Then in 1963 he took leave from his job to return to the reservation to run the Navajo Office of Economic Opportunity. His mission was to attract new businesses to the reservation. Ten years later his story took a Shakespearean turn.

In the beginning Peter MacDonald and Barry Goldwater were great friends. MacDonald was a Republican and liked the limelight. Goldwater wanted to showcase an Arizona Indian who was a Republican. He proposed MacDonald as a speaker at the 1972 Republican National Convention. But by then MacDonald had read the Hopi Land Settlement Bill and recognized that he was expected to preside over a disastrous relocation of thousands of Navajo. Knowing it would be a disaster for the Navajo, he hired new lawyers to lobby against the bill and defeat it. Sponsored by Goldwater in the Senate and an Arizona congressman named Sam Steiger in the House, the first bill failed.

MacDonald's invitation to be a speaker at the convention was soon rescinded. Goldwater spread the story that the invitation was recalled because MacDonald announced he was going to tell the bloc of Navajo votes to support George McGovern in the 1972 presidential election rather than Richard Nixon. George McGovern, however, told me in a telephone interview, "I never met Peter MacDonald, and I have no idea of who he or the Navajo were supporting in the '72 election."

Two days before the Christmas recess in 1974 and in the midst of the Vietnam War, another version of the Hopi Land Settlement Bill passed the House and Senate and was signed into law as Public Law 93-531. Sponsored this time by Goldwater in the Senate and by a Democratic congressman from Utah named Wayne Owens, the bill was presented as having bipartisan support. Owens was defeated for re-election and immediately joined John Boyden's law firm in Salt Lake City, which was moving its offices to the Kennecott Building, Peabody Coal's new owner.

By 1987 when relocation was well under way, Navajo chairman MacDonald was unsparing when he testified before Congress about the lack of humanity in the bill and the "botched-up" execution. He asked why no planning had been done for where these elderly sheep-herding families were supposed to go. Senator Goldwater appeared before the same committee and said that "the Navajo were trespassers" and shouldn't get any money or subsidized housing. Goldwater refused to support any money for resettlement and said it should come out of the Navajo coal royalties or other moneys the US government gave the Navajo.

MacDonald had lost his third reelection bid to Peterson Zah in 1982 but won again in 1986. By then at least three senators and Morris Udall had proposed bills to mitigate the relocation by providing a financial settlement or a land-exchange proposal. All three bills were opposed by Barry Goldwater and withdrawn. Goldwater also suggested that the IRS do a tax audit of the Navajo Tribe and Peter MacDonald's accounting practices, and MacDonald was charged with tax evasion.

Goldwater retired from the Senate in 1987, and the same year Representative John McCain ran for and won his Senate seat. It made no difference. There was no softening of the Navajo relocation law. Then in 1989 the debate suddenly went off on a new track. Arizona's senior senator, Dennis DeConcini, presided over an Indian affairs subcommittee hearing that was supposed to deal with the issue of how the oil companies defrauded the Indian tribes through rigged meters on their pumps and falsified royalty reports, aided by a corrupt contracting office inside the BIA. Instead, the hearing topic suddenly shifted to Indian graft and corruption *within* Indian tribal governments. The *Wall Street Journal's* page 1 subject was Peter MacDonald and his requirement for kickbacks from the corporations who wanted to do business on the Navajo reservation. The staff reporter referred to him as "an Oriental potentate" and Peter "MacDollar."

Suzanne Harjo, director of the Morning Star Foundation, said that two Senate staff members resigned over the changed focus of the hearings. Soon Peter MacDonald was charged with fraud over a ranch purchase that he had approved, misuse of federal funds, tax evasion, and inciting a riot in which two people were shot and killed. The charge of inciting a riot came about in 1989 when a divided tribal council put him on administrative leave while the charges were investigated. A group of MacDonald supporters stormed the council chambers. Two people were shot and eventually died. MacDonald charged Barry Goldwater with putting out a contract on him.* Although the Navajo Tribal Council later pardoned him, he served a jail sentence for eleven years.

In 1991 when some of the less salutary aspects of energy extraction on Navajo lands began to overtake the Hopi-Navajo centuries-old land-dispute narrative, the ownership of Peabody Coal changed yet again. In 1991 Peabody Coal became a British company.

LONDON, ENGLAND, 1996

Peabody Coal had been strip mining on Black Mesa for twenty-two years by the time Lord Hanson bought the company. It was not a take-over, but a purchase from the private holding company composed of six of America's largest corporations, all of whom had some connection to the exploration, mining, transport, or burning of coal.

Silk Street in London's financial district has echoes of the legendary Silk Road, the four-thousand-mile trade route that wound from China through India, Persia, and Turkey and into eastern Europe, mixing trade goods, tribes, and religions along the way. Lord Hanson chose Silk Street's Barbican Centre as the location for his 1996 annual stockholders meeting, because it was the year he would announce the restructuring of Hanson's and the plan for his eventual retirement. It was the most important stockholders meeting of his career.

Like the Australian Rupert Murdock or the American Ted Turner, Hanson had taken a modest business inherited from his father

---

* MacDonald would spend eleven years in tribal, state, and federal jails. One of the three men charged with Don Bolles's murder said that he had also been instructed to put a bomb under Peter MacDonald's car. Don Bolles was an investigative reporter who worked for the *Arizona Republic* in Phoenix and was killed by a car bomb in 1976 while he was investigating organized crime in Phoenix and a Mob-related operation called Emprise that had concessions at Arizona racetracks. Emprise and six individuals were later convicted of concealing ownership of the Frontier Hotel and Casino in Las Vegas. MacDonald was pardoned in 2000 by President Clinton after an appeal from Congressman Patrick Kennedy. The Navajo Tribe also dropped its charges.

and built it into an international behemoth of construction, tobacco, and energy. Hanson's Ltd. was a multinational conglomerate with subsidiaries on five continents. He was no longer Jimmy Hanson, but Lord Hanson, and moved in the highest echelons of Margaret Thatcher's England. In April 1996 he was bringing together two thousand of his wealthy shareholders, the international financial press, and some well-known celebrities and government officials. The days of the multifaceted conglomerate—owning everything from toasters to oil refineries—were over, and, as Lord Hanson explained in his prepared remarks, it was time to "de-merge."

The meeting opened as planned with a welcome and a documentary film. Known in the British press as the Takeover King or the Silver Fox, Lord Hanson was tall, silver-haired, and impeccably turned out in Savile Row tailoring. Belying his seventy-four years, Lord Hanson bounded to the stage while a huge video screen behind the podium projected his sleek silver hair and vulpine smile. Among his peers he was known as a diplomatic and skillful corporate politician; among his staff he was known as a tyrant who ruled by fear and who could dress down a subordinate on incidental matters of punctuality, dress, or manners. Sharing the stage with him were a handful of top Hanson executives and the preternaturally handsome Roger Moore, still world famous for his movie roles as James Bond, but who was now Hanson's spokesperson.

After welcoming the gathering, Lord Hanson gave a flick of his hand, and the meeting opened with an artfully produced documentary telling the "Hanson story." Roger Moore provided the mellifluous narration, explaining how Lord Hanson's acumen had led to profitable holdings on several continents: construction materials (Kaiser Permanente Sand and Gravel), tobacco (Imperial Tobacco), and energy (Peabody Coal, America's largest coal company).

Moore gave a regal wave, acknowledging the applause as the lights came back up. The meeting moved along with the tight pacing and scheduling that had taken hundreds of hours of staff preparation. Lord Hanson had every reason to expect that his decision to restructure the company and protect Hanson's future share price would be applauded by his stockholders. Following the business presentations, he confidently opened the floor for questions. Then he was surprised. He didn't like surprises.

A small delegation of Hopi and Navajo Indians was clustered behind one microphone, their brightly colored shirts and silver jewelry a splash of vivid color in the sea of beige and gray. The earlier documentary film about Hanson's business investments had described the American Indians as Hanson's "friends and business partners in Arizona" where Peabody Coal operated some of the largest strip mines in the world.

Each member of the delegation stepped forward to explain his or her experience of living with Peabody Coal in the high desert of northern Arizona. In their unmistakably sincere voices and slow cadences, they described the realities behind the stockholders' quarterly dividends: the toxic water that resulted from blasting the coal beds, polluted water holes that killed their sheep, coal dust in the air causing skyrocketing asthma and bronchitis rates, land stripped of all vegetation that could never be reseeded and reclaimed in the high-desert climate because of inadequate rainfall, mountainous slag heaps of gray earth that once had been valleys of piñon and juniper, thousands of ancient archaeological Anasazi sites destroyed in the dragline buckets, Hopi springs and Navajo wells going dry because of billions of gallons of water pumped out of an Ice Age aquifer to run a coal-slurry pipeline, increasing desertification, and, finally, the ongoing removal of thousands of Indian families, mostly Navajo, who lived too close to the coal. In short, they were telling the assembled shareholders about the "true costs" behind their investments.

The audience was riveted. Lord Hanson, however, was horrified and soon furious. His subordinates saw his rage as a gathering storm. Finally, he couldn't contain himself. "Are we going to have to listen to you all day?" he barked as an elderly Navajo woman began to speak. "Shut up! Nobody wants to hear what you have to say. You are a bloody nuisance."

The woman at the microphone was Roberta Blackgoat. Now in her late seventies, she was wearing her white hair knotted in the traditional loop at the back of her neck, a tiered Navajo skirt, and a heavy silver and turquoise necklace. Lord Hanson did not intimidate her. The hand that grasped the microphone was steady, and her eyes were canny. "I only wanted to offer a prayer for you," she said in her soft, raspy voice.

"Oh." Lord Hanson was momentarily disarmed. "I apologize," he said.

In her prayer Mrs. Blackgoat called for the well-being of the thousands of people gathered at the meeting and for "balance [to] be restored to the universe."

In 1996 climate change was still known as "global warming." The Hopi and Navajo, however, were describing shifts in patterns of air, water, and temperature that made climate change a permanent condition. They were describing the felt consequences of mining and burning coal and putting carbon in the atmosphere. Plants didn't reseed. Water holes were turning to mud. Only a few people in the lay public understood that second only to Arctic ice melt, the greatest weather changes were being tracked in the American Southwest. The Indians lived in the arid high desert as sheepherders (Navajo) or dry farmers (Hopi), and they understood what they were seeing. The members of the delegation were speaking independently of their tribal councils, which now faced public criticism for having silently signed the coal leases and water rights. Roberta Blackgoat's prayer was for the health of the planet and that narrow membrane of land, air, and water where all life takes place. Strip mining, she said, was no way to treat the earth. "Coal is the liver of the earth. When you take it out she dies," she concluded.

As soon as she finished, a dozen security men swarmed around the delegation and forcibly escorted them out of the room. Some in the audience cheered; others booed.

The turmoil was just beginning. Now members of the audience had new questions. When one well-coiffed Englishwoman took the microphone to object to the way Lord Hanson had dealt with the Indian people, he responded, "Madame, let me introduce you to a broker."

When another asked why Hanson's had to strip-mine on Indian lands, he answered, "Because I say so. Now belt up."

The next day's newspapers reported a meeting that is every corporate executive's nightmare. "Furious Hanson on the Warpath: Indians' Protest Wrecks Meeting" ran the *Daily Express* with a large photograph of Roberta Blackgoat. The caption read: "Apology." "Insults Fly at Hanson Meeting," announced the *Independent*, accompanied by a photograph of the silver-haired Lord Hanson.

Years later Lord Hanson's many obituaries recounted the jeers and tumult of his final stockholders meeting, although the cause was long forgotten. Long before Hanson's death, Peabody Coal had been sold again. Hanson's sold it to Citizens Power of Boston (now a Peabody subsidiary) and Lehman Brothers of New York. The investment bankers were restructuring Peabody Coal as part of a private equity fund.

Lehman Brothers, New York, 2001

The Lehman Brothers shareholders meeting on April 2, 2001, took place only weeks before Peabody Coal was to become a public company as Peabody Energy, Inc. (ticker symbol BTU). Another Hopi-Navajo delegation was in the audience. Roberta Blackgoat, now age eighty-five, and Arlene Hamilton, organizer of Weavers for Life and Land, had bought two shares of Lehman stock to gain entrance to the stockholders meeting. Other delegation members who spoke were a Lakota Sioux chief named Joseph Chasinghorse and Navajo Leonard Benally. They mentioned the spiritual bankruptcy of Lehman Brothers and predicted dire consequences if the investment bank did not stop the strip mining on Black Mesa and went ahead with its planned public offering for Peabody Energy, then and now the largest coal producer in the world.

The next day, April 3, 2001, all four members of the delegation appeared on the program *Democracy Now* to describe their "friendly takeover" of the Lehman Brothers annual shareholders meeting and the reasons it was necessary. A year later Arlene Hamilton was killed in a car crash in San Francisco, and Roberta died of unknown causes while she was there attending the memorial service.

Unlike the Hopi leader Emory Sekaquaptewa Jr., Roberta Black-goat did not get her obituary in the *New York Times*, but she did succeed in making Black Mesa an international name, a name that many Europeans know better than Americans.

In the winter of 1999, when the relocation of all the Navajo was supposed to be final, activists from the Green Party were demonstrating in front of American embassies in cities across Europe, objecting to the mass relocation of what by then amounted to fifteen thousand Navajo people. In February 2000 the European Parliament passed a resolution citing the United States for "Human Right Violations in Regard to Native Americans in the U.S.-Diné." That resolution, sent to the American secretary of state, Madeleine Albright, also requested a congressional investigation into the relationship between the strip mining and the Navajo removal. It also called for an investigation of environmental effects: the air and water hazards from coal strip mining, the draining of the aquifer to run the coal-slurry pipeline, the destruction of thousands of archaeological sites, and—still unmentioned in the American press—the nuclear contamination of the New Lands to which the government was sending many of the relocatees. The secretary of state did not respond.

Roberta understood the power of persistence. When she first began protesting, the Native American resisters had to stand on the street outside the United Nations with signs to present their message. By the time of her death, the United Nations had formed a Commission on Indigenous People and she had traveled to Geneva, Switzerland, to testify. Big Mountain Support Groups formed in cities across the United States, Europe, and Japan. Roberta appeared before members of the International Treaty Council when they met in Mashpee, Massachusetts, and became a worrisome presence to those who expected the Navajo to disappear quietly. "The Creator Is the Only One Who Is Going to Relocate Us" is the sign she wore before armed US marshals when they came to enforce many of the "final deadlines" for removal.

In English her voice was high and raspy; in Navajo it was strong and deep. She had an easy smile and twinkle in her eye as though she found nothing to surprise her. "I am doing this for all of us," she told

students at Harvard University in 1992, "your children and my children and their children." During her time at Harvard, she also managed to inform students of the Native American program that the Harvard faculty member who led their program was a partner in an economic consulting group that gave expert testimony for law firms and corporations seeking mineral leases on Indian reservations. She was talking about climate change years before we had the right vocabulary to name the peculiar chemistry of global climate and the impact of coal and carbon on its composition.

Her accomplishment was to provide focus and continuity to three decades of intense struggle—human and ecological—in an area of the United States virtually invisible on the political map. Viewed in a global framework, she took America's closed system of Native American policy into the international arena. Her leadership—recognized by a Martin Luther King Jr. Human Rights Award and the American Women's History Association's Unsung American Woman Award—extended from an era when the ability to cheat Indians out of land and resources was considered both good sport and a minor regional issue into a new era of global environmental activism as well as awareness of the corporate backing of the extraordinarily well-funded climate deniers.

As Daniel Peaches later said of her, "She was a hero to stand against the forces of the federal government, the Hopi Nation, and a big corporation. She did not compromise her belief or her dignity against overwhelming odds."

I always remembered the bumper sticker she had tacked up in her kitchen that read:

You NEVER Fail Unless You Quit Trying

EPILOGUE

At the Plaza, one of the small downtown casinos in "old" Las Vegas, a low-stakes blackjack game is in progress. Six players sit in an arc around the dealer. Brenda is a friendly African American woman who is chatting and trading banter with the regulars who call her by name. She is also explaining the betting rules to a novice who has just slipped into an empty seat. She deals the cards crisply, effortlessly, as though the cards were extensions of her fingers. Two cards land silently in front of each player. Even though the table minimum is only $5 a hand, one of the players is betting $100 a hand and then doubling his bets when he wins. He wears a chartreuse shirt with western embroidery on the shoulders and mother-of-pearl snap buttons down the front. The large stack of chips in front of him totals several thousand dollars. He's quiet. The man next to him—jovial, gregarious, and thoroughly enjoying himself—is losing.

Brenda deals her own hand, placing one card face down, the other face up. The players push their bets into circles outlined on the green-felt table. After all bets are made, the players show their cards. One player triumphantly unfolds a ten of clubs and an ace (counted either as one or eleven). Twenty-one. Blackjack!

Smiles and cheers all around. Winning chips are quickly distributed. The winner drops a $50 chip in Brenda's tip glass, gives another $25 chip to the waitress who brings him a bourbon, and signals for the next hand. The goal in blackjack is to assemble a hand of cards with a count total of twenty-one. Unlike the players, the dealer has to make a total of at least seventeen. Any hand over twenty-one loses. You can either ask for more cards or hold the cards you were originally dealt. Technically, it should be a simple game. It *is* a simple game. I remember playing it as a kid at camp. It's the betting that gets complicated.

• • •

When former mayor of Las Vegas Oscar Goodman showed up at public events, he often brought along two statuesque, stiletto-heeled, sequined showgirls, one on each arm. The girls made him the center of attention. In order to raise money for the city, he leased the old federal courthouse to the newly named "Mob Museum" and sold the old Las Vegas City Hall to Zappos.com, an online shoe retailer. Zappos was founded in San Francisco by two Harvard graduates, and they moved it to Las Vegas because they liked the idea that Las Vegas had what they characterized as a "call-center culture" and a 24–7 time frame. (They also liked the low tax rates, especially after they sold the company to Amazon for $1.2 billion.)

One of the former mayor's other idiosyncrasies was that he prominently displayed a large bottle of Sapphire Blue Bombay Gin in his office from which he always poured visitors a drink, regardless of the time of day. He had a contract to promote Bombay Gin. When term limits caught up with him, the current mayor, his wife, took over.

In this atmosphere politics is seen as a diversion, a sideline of entertainment. Governance is part of the "just the right amount of wrong" Las Vegas brand. When the former governor was investigated for attempting to sexually assault a woman in the parking garage of a well-known restaurant on Flamingo Road, the tapes from the surveillance cameras mysteriously disappeared. The political atmosphere of Las Vegas does not lend itself to reality, never mind hard choices. That the Lake Mead reservoir—from which Las Vegas gets 90 percent of its water supply—is dropping more quickly than anyone foresaw is an occasion for hard choices.

For the past four years a project to drill through canyon bedrock into the middle of Lake Mead to place an intake pipe in the center at its lowest level has encountered delays and is unlikely to be completed for another two years, even though the water surface of Lake Mead could drop below its current intake pipe. The backup plan is called the Great Basin Pumping Scheme. Over the past ten years the Southern Nevada Water Authority has succeeded in buying up water rights in mountain valleys two hundred miles away in northern Nevada. US Senate majority leader and Nevada senator Harry Reid has succeeded in obtaining a federal right-of-way to build a pipeline and pumping stations to pipe the water across federal land into Las Vegas. Almost everyone estimates that the Great Basin Pumping Scheme will cost at least $15 billion and will be the most expensive public works project in Nevada history. The question: Who will pay?

●　●　●

Meanwhile, at the Plaza the pace of the game speeds up. The average bet of the man in the chartreuse shirt is now $200 a hand. If he wins, he doubles his bets. The novice sitting beside him continues to bet the table minimum, $5, win or lose. In the next few hands the chartreuse man wins more than $1,000, an interval of time that takes no more than five minutes, maybe less. No one keeps track of time. There are no clocks and no windows in Las Vegas casinos. It is supposed to be a place of timelessness. Like church.

In the background the floor manager begins talking with the pit boss and watching the table. Brenda deals more quickly now. No more chatting or charming the customers. The stack of chips in front of the chartreuse man keeps growing. He is smiling, but more focused and concentrating on the cards being dealt. The most interesting thing about his play is its consistency. When he lost, and he did, he had a small bet on the table; when he won, he always had a large bet on the table. Was it possible the chartreuse man was counting cards?

Counting is a system that helps a player win in blackjack. In its simplest form, card counting involves keeping a running count of low-value and high-value cards. The player gives low cards (2 through 6) a value of plus 1, high cards (10 through king plus the ace) minus 1, and assigns 7s, 8s, and 9s a zero. Counting has been the subject of the movie

Bringing Down the House and an article in the *Journal of the American Statistical Association.* Blackjack is the one game where the player has the best odds against the house. It requires a certain mathematical ability and an understanding of probabilities.

• • •

The water situation in Las Vegas, Phoenix, and Los Angeles is two-edged. No one wants to be alarmist because it slows growth and keeps the tourists and their dollars away. On the other hand, there is cause for alarm. Thirty million people are dependent on the waters of the Colorado River. And if the Colorado River keeps shrinking, there will soon be need for federal money, a lot of federal money. Pat Mulroy, Las Vegas's water manager, rushed to Washington in September 2013 when the Bureau of Reclamation announced that 750,000 acre-feet *less* would be released into Lake Mead in 2013 and 2014. That could cause another 25-foot drop in the level of Lake Mead. She met with Harry Reid to talk about the possibility of having the president declare southern Nevada a disaster area in order to get federal disaster aid. She compared the effects of the southwestern drought to Hurricane Sandy. Then she backpedaled. The real underlying question is how to finance the Great Basin Pumping Scheme—a network of wells, pumps, and pipelines that will run for 250 miles or more from northern Nevada's mountain valleys into Las Vegas. How does a low-tax, no-tax state function when faced with a project that requires significant taxpayer-generated revenue? Who will pay?

One of the benefits of hiring a company like Bechtel is that not only does it have experience in building pipeline projects all over the globe, but it also has an unparalleled political and government relations department that knows how to work congressional committees and federal agencies. At the same time, other states might raise objections because Nevada does have two large industries—mining and gambling—that could pay significantly more in taxes. The mining industry has a tax rate that has been unchanged since 1863 and incorporated into the Nevada state constitution. Mining has a tax rate of 5 percent (of net). The mining industry likes to present mining as a thing of the past, all scavenger mines and ghost towns (a lot of photo exhibits of mining ghost towns), but mining is still a thriving industry. Twenty-five percent of the world's gold supply, for example, comes out of Nevada mines.

The gambling industry in Nevada has the lowest tax rate in the country, a maximum of 6.75 percent. In the rest of the country, the average gambling tax rate is 16 percent. According to the American Gaming Association, in Ohio the rate is 33 percent, in Illinois it runs from 15 to 50 percent, and in Massachusetts it will be 25 percent. (Racetracks and slots and table games are frequently taxed at different rates.) During the recent economic downturn and flat gaming revenues, the Nevada governor (the same one sued for the parking-garage assault) called for a 14 percent reduction in the state education budget. From kindergarten to university, teachers were laid off, budgets slashed, and state workers furloughed. No mention of adjusting the tax rates or auditing the net proceeds from mining companies.

Although Las Vegas is well known for having the highest suicide rates in the country, in 2013 its mental health policies became the subject of national headlines when San Francisco authorities noticed a sharp increase in its homeless population. Through what was called "Greyhound therapy," it seemed that Las Vegas mental health patients were being "treated" by putting them on a Greyhound bus with a bag lunch, a day's supply of medication, and a one-way ticket to San Francisco, where they joined the ranks of that city's homeless. San Francisco estimated it received at least fifteen hundred people from Las Vegas and is now suing the State of Nevada. Other cities such as Boise, Idaho, and Denver, Colorado, also realized that they too were recipients of Las Vegas's export of its homeless population.

The difficulty in Pat Mulroy's comparing the long-term drought of Nevada as a disaster that would warrant federal funding similar to the devastating effects of Hurricane Sandy on the East Coast is that for at least thirty years the process of desertification in the Southwest has been well documented, and reported, and increasing. Although a 1983 US government report confirmed that desertification in the Southwest is moving faster than that of Africa, pumping out groundwater and burning coal have only increased.

• • •

Even a player with a bad hand can win at blackjack. The chartreuse man was winning with hands totaling fourteen or even thirteen because Brenda's hand went over twenty-one. But it takes concentration, rationality, and a certain kind of mathematical memory to keep track of dealt cards. The gambling brain tends to magical thinking. The pit boss continued to watch the table. The chartreuse man had winnings far beyond anyone else, pillars of $100 chips stacked up in front of him. Soon Brenda was stuffing her tips into a table slot (all the dealers pool their tips) and packing up her chips, and a new dealer slipped into her seat. The new dealer had a face of stone, no chatter, and no charm. Before she started dealing, she removed all the old cards from the shoe and inserted six new decks. The chartreuse man stopped winning. With new cards there was no history. There was nothing for the chartreuse man to count. The odds returned to the house. Soon he too packed up his chips and left the table with what looked to be more than $5,000 in winnings. That's not much money in Las Vegas, but the house was going to make sure he didn't win any more.

• • •

As a practical matter, for decades the entire urban Southwest has been living off federal money for subsidized water. As Wallace Stegner observed, "The West has . . . become an empire and gotten the East to pay most of the bills." On Black Mesa we, as a society, are engaged in destroying some of our oldest sustainable Native American cultures so that people in Phoenix and Las Vegas can water their hundreds of golf courses, swim in swimming pools, and pretend they live in a desert miracle. The oligarchs who control decision making in Las Vegas may have realized that the long-term future of desert living is in doubt, which may be why Steve Wynn (Wynn Resorts) is trying to build a new huge, but "tasteful," casino in the brownfield marshes of Everett, about eight miles from my home in Massachusetts. That casino also means a new well-funded lobby in state politics.

When Robert Venturi, Denise Scott Brown, and Steven Izenour wrote their book *Learning from Las Vegas*, they were not writing about Las Vegas per se, but writing about symbolism in architecture. They were celebrating populist building design—like the fried-chicken stand in the shape of a chicken or the Las Vegas marriage chapel that looked like a wedding cake. They saw Las Vegas as a series of symbols and signs. Forty-five years later you can still interpret Las Vegas as "a series of signs." Those signs are about excess, about diversion, about scale. You see a city designed around odds and probabilities—a place where Big Bets are in play.

Meyer Lansky used to say there was no such thing as a lucky gambler. The only winner was the house. In this case, the house is nature. We're in the climate casino now. Who will win? Who will pay?

ACKNOWLEDGMENTS

I entered the labyrinth of this story in 1973 when I was still a speech-writer in the US Congress and realized I was uninformed about a version of American history that allowed for an accurate inclusion of Native American events. Belatedly I recognized it also required an education in energy economics, coal mining technologies, Indian law, congressional procedures in the Committee on Public Lands, water planning, population growth, real estate development, the gambling industry, Mormon religion, the railroads, mining, the politics of Indian Affairs, and the political dynamics of the 1960s and 70s that began shifting political power to the urban West. Most important it required placing the events of Native America in mainstream politics and history. Many people helped guide me through these areas of re-education. I take all responsibility for errors.

The idea of a book began with an article published in *Orion* magazine in 1998. I am grateful to *Orion* editors Emily Hiestand and H. Emerson (Chip) Blake who supported a point of view about Black Mesa that was at odds with a narrative storyline that had prevailed in the nation's press for more than twenty years. They championed the article ("The Black Mesa Syndrome: Indian Lands, Black Gold") on the web and nominated it for the John Oakes Award in Environmental Journalism, for which it became a finalist. Emily Hiestand has continued to act as a friend and valued consultant. During a Bunting Fellowship at Harvard's Institute of Advanced Study in 1992 and '93 I was fortunate to meet many Native American students in Harvard's Native American program and particular thanks go to Dr. Gabrielle Tayac and Professor Phyllis Fast, for their friendship, humor, and efforts to educate me in the complexities of current Native American policy and politics. Ever since I met Martha Blue "by accident" in the Hopi museum on Second Mesa in 1990, she has sent me clippings, answered questions, and corrected historical inaccuracies over the twenty-five years that I kept following Roberta Blackgoat's remarkable life and fascinating ability to challenge the power of the U.S. government and several huge corporations. The Blackgoat daughters, Vicki and Sheila, helped to keep the connection.

Editor Carl Bromley at Nation Books is that rare editor who actually edits and who gave me chapter-by-chapter notes, tactfully suggesting that a complete revision of my original draft would result in a much stronger book. He was right about both and I am deeply grateful for his superb guidance and editorial insights. Any remaining flaws of substance and style are entirely my own. My agent Don Fehr played a critical role at key junctures and I am indebted to his support and sense of humor.

I owe much to the marketing and production staff at Nation Books with particular thanks to assistant editor Daniel LoPreto for his initiative in marketing; to Sandra Beris, and Annette Wenda for their impressive skills in scheduling, production, and copyediting; and to Alex Christopher for her innovative ideas for promotion.

Books like this require access to a large library system and I am grateful to the librarians at the Library of Congress, Tozzer Library at Harvard University, Brigham Young University, State University of Arizona at Tempe, Lied Library at the University of Nevada Las Vegas.

Fellowships, grants and residencies were crucial to giving me time from my various jobs to travel, do research, or work on the manuscript. I am extremely grateful to the MacDowell Artists Colony, the Yaddo Corporation, the Blue Mountain Center, Mesa Refuge, and the Bellagio Center of the Rockefeller Foundation. The unique Black Mountain Institute Fellowship combined both a stipend and time at the Kluge Center of the Library of Congress and the University of Nevada Las Vegas. The fellowship was crucial to finally pulling all the pieces together.

Over the years many people in many ways have assisted me by explaining complex events, sharing their own experience, writing letters of recommendation, answering questions, requesting privileged xix **"This was a centuries-old land dispute":** Author notes from press conference.

xxi **Peabody Holding Company:** The member companies of Peabody Holding changed during the fifteen-year period from 1976 to 1991, during which Peabody Holding included the Bechtel Group, Newmont Mining, Williams Technologies, Fluor Engineering, the Boeing Corporation, and Equitable Life Insurance as the parent company for Peabody Coal. From 1991 to 1999 Peabody Coal's parent company was Hanson's of Great Britain. From 1999 to 2001 it was the private-equity firm of Lehman Brothers (now defunct) and Citizens Power of Boston. It went public in 2001 as Peabody Energy, now the largest coal company in the world.

xxiii **"The California settlement":** Joan Didion, *Where I Was From*, 24.

CHAPTER 1. EVERYONE COMES FOR THE MONEY

4 **A week before this performance:** On January 12, 2010, a magnitude 7.0 earthquake took place some 16 miles west of Port-au-Prince, Haiti's capital. More than 250,000 residences and 30,000 commercial buildings collapsed, including the presidential palace, the National Assembly building, and the headquarters for the United Nations Mission in Haiti. By January 24 at least fifty-two aftershocks measuring 4.5 or greater were recorded. An estimated 3 million people were left homeless, injured, or otherwise affected by the quake. The delivery of humanitarian and medical aid was hindered because of damage to port facilities and airport runways and collapse of electrical grids. The death count was estimated at 220,000. Morgues were overwhelmed, and tens of thousands of bodies had to be buried in mass graves. The tragedy was soon compounded by cholera that was accidentally introduced by UN forces. Yves Pierre-Louis, "Le choléra—MINUSTAH rebondit." See also Amy Willenz, *Farewell, Fred Voodoo: A Letter from Haiti*; and *NBC Network News*, October 8, 2013.

6 **"Event Annie":** Event Annie was an aboveground test in 1953 in which the military attempted to determine the feasibility of an atomic cannon for battlefield use. Two 280 mm cannons were brought to the Nevada Test Site from Fort Sill, Oklahoma, along with artillery crews, to test an atomic shell. On May 25, 1953, a cannon at Frenchman Flat fired an atomic shell with a yield of fifteen kilotons, marking the first, and last, use of a nuclear artillery shell. The cannon, nicknamed "Atomic Annie," returned to Fort Sill. Event Annie was one of a series of tests that were responsible for nearly one-quarter of all radiation exposure to people and livestock that lived downwind of the test site. Many families and communities in the Intermountain West, along with test-site workers and military veterans, reported cancers, tumors, and degenerative diseases. The US military did not admit radioactive fallout from tests carried by westerly winds into rural Nevada, Utah, and Colorado. Author and activist Terry Tempest William's book *Refuge: An Unnatural History of Family and Place* tells of seeing the light from a nuclear test blast as a child while driving with her family in Utah. She describes

information: John Peters, former commissioner of Indian Affairs for Massachusetts, Professor Karl Teeter, Florence Ladd, Inés Talamantez, Debra Spark, Elizabeth Graver, Jane Holtz Kay, Elise Boulding, and staff members in Senators Edward Kennedy and John Kerry's offices. Among the people I interviewed over a span of two decades special thanks to the late Senator George McGovern, Audrey Dowling and Jean Page who described Las Vegas in the 1930s and what it was like to be school teachers in 1933 during the construction of Hoover Dam. Maria Mangini spent hours explaining details of her experience on Black Mesa, Anita Parlow, Laton McCartney, Tim Giago, Kit Owens at the Four Corners Power Plant, Lowell Hinkins at the Black Mesa Pipeline, Paula Ellis at the Salt River Project, Manley Begay, Vine DeLoria, Vicki Blackgoat, Sheila Keith, Howard Wright, Arthur Jokela, George Hardeen, Bella Abzug as head of the Women's Environmental and Development Organization (WEDO). Special thanks to Dorothy Cole, who has been a one woman clipping service, Louise Steinman, who has been a supporter and long term reader-strategist, and my critical writing peers: Ben Brooks, Scott Campbell, Patricia Harrison, Jean Hey. Angelika Festa and Charles Eisenhardt, both knowledgeable about Native American history, generously took time read an entire draft and asked perceptive questions. Others who have helped at critical junctures include Beth Thielen, Rosemary Winfield, Amy Hoffman, J. R. Lancaster, Anne Leslie, Eleanor Ramsay, Tim O'Grady, Jane Midgley, Susan Indresano, Richard Cole, Maria Van Dusen, Anne Spraker, Cristina Garcia, Sara Rimer.

Some books and their authors have been hugely influential far beyond their presence on the bibliography page, and I must cite Barbara Freese's elegant book *Coal: a Human History*, and Patricia Limerick's *The Legacy of Conquest: The Unbroken Past of the American West*. Last, but certainly not least, I have to thank my daughter Cristina McFadden who has literally grown up with this project and helped in innumerable ways from carrying boxes of files out of the cellar, reorganizing my office, and acting as my driver through several trips through spring snows in northern Arizona and New Mexico on our trips to see, as she put it, "power plants, coal strip-mines and other scenic infrastructure."

NOTES

INTRODUCTION

xiii **In 1982 Robert Redford starred:** *The Electric Horseman* was released in December 1971, but all the publicity materials relating to the Hopi celebration used photographic stills from the movie. Along with *Butch Cassidy and the Sundance Kid* (1969), the film reenforced Redford's image as a cowboy-culture hero of the Southwest.

xiv **no one had ever accurately counted:** Author interview with Paul Tessler, August 10, 1990. Tessler was both legal counsel and executive director of the Indian Relocation Commission, or IRC as it was known in Arizona, located at 201 East Birch Street, Flagstaff, Arizona. At that time, he said that the total number of Navajo moved at that date was 7,292 (1,823 households counted as an average of 4 people). The total number of Hopi moved was 15 households, or 60 people. At least 2,000 applications were still pending. The commission continued its work for another fifteen years, going out of business only in 2006 after passage of a bill by Senator John McCain to cut off funding. From 1977 to 2006 the total number of Navajo moved, relocated, or disappeared from tribal roles was estimated at approximately 15,000, the cost to taxpayers in the billions. The relocated Indians remained poor.

xv **"The Black Mesa Field":** The *Keystone Coal Industry Manual* (Denver: Mining Media International, 1984), 479. (No longer published in print format.)

xvi **Susanne Page, who had just published:** Susanne Anderson, *Song of the Earth Spirit*. Anderson (Page) is also the photographer for *Hopi*, with Jake Page.

xvii **Steve had written a book:** Originally published as *Life in a Narrow Place* in 19[ ] it was republished in 2006 as *I Am the Grand Canyon: The Story of the Havasu[ ] People*.

xvii **I had proposed a short article:** The *Atlantic Monthly* was a Boston-based [mag]azine (since 1857) but moved to Washington, DC, in 2005 under new owner[s] and renamed the *Atlantic*. C. Michael Curtis was the longtime literary editor [who] gave the author the press credential, expressing some doubts as to whether *A[tlan]tic* readers were interested in the West.

herself as coming from "the clan of One-Breasted Women" because almost all the women in her family have come down with breast cancer, a result of Utah's downwind exposure to fallout from nuclear tests.

Another famous "event" was Apple-2, which involved dropping a twenty-nine-kiloton device from the top of a five-hundred-foot tower in Yucca Flat. An entire town and housing development were built around ground zero, using different materials and exteriors at differing distances, to test the aftereffects. Tours of the Nevada Test Site include the "Doomsday Town," remains of houses, shelters, steel frames, a bank vault, and other structures. www.onlinenevada.org/articles/atmospheric-nuclear-testing-nevada-test-site#sthash.2Z7Gbxdj.dpuf.

7 **"That radioactive groundwater":** Pat Mulroy quoted in David Thomson, *In Nevada: The Land, the People, God, and Chance,* 291. "In the new attention to the aquifer, it was found that in southern Nevada the water table had amounts of plutonium—leached in from the Test Site—that were moving far more quickly than had been thought possible before. Pat Mulroy said, 'The plutonium doesn't concern me because the flow pattern is not toward Las Vegas.' It was going toward Death Valley."

7 **Lake Mead has dropped 130 feet:** Lake Mead has an official capacity water level of 1,229 feet above sea level. The level fluctuates according to water volumes in the Colorado River, which in turn are determined by snowmelt from the Rocky Mountains. Water levels of Lake Mead are posted every day by the Bureau of Reclamation website. In the past decade the water level has dropped by at least 130 feet and in some months 140 feet. www.usbr.gov/lc/riverops.html.

Although the levels vary, an agreed-upon average, the figure of a 130-foot decline, has been used since 2009. "Lake Mead's Water Level Plunges as 11-Year Drought Lingers." See also Henry Brean, "Las Vegas Water Chief Seeks Disaster Aid for Colorado River Drought."

7 **Area 51:** The existence of Area 51 near Groom Lake, Nevada, was denied for years by the Pentagon and all military services. In 2008 the papers relating to the development of high-altitude spy planes such as the U-2, SR-71 (Blackbird), and Oxcart by the CIA at Area 51 north of Las Vegas were declassified. One of the many recent books on the subject is Annie Jacobsen, *Area 51: An Uncensored History of America's Top Secret Military Base.* In 2013–2014 the National Atomic Testing Museum in Las Vegas offered an ongoing Area 51 lecture series.

CHAPTER 2. GOLDWATER AND THE DESERT INN

9 **"the most elaborate gambling establishment in America":** Kefauver Committee Report, 10:907, quoted in Oscar Lewis, *Sagebrush Casinos: The Story of Legal Gambling in Nevada,* 201. Lewis, a sociologist, was writing in 1956 and said that the 1950 launch of the Desert Inn "is still looked on in Las Vegas as the most brilliant social event in the annals of the Strip." He described the hotel as having

four hundred rooms built around a big quadrangle that enclosed a swimming pool and spacious "terraces for lounging." The resort encompassed 170 acres, an eighteen-hole golf course, a health club and solarium, twenty-four-hour meal service, two main dining rooms, a series of specialty shops, cocktail bars, a nightclub, and a casino that "in size and luxury has few rivals anywhere." The cost was estimated at $5 million. Although Wilbur Clark's name was in neon in front, as "Wilbur Clark's Desert Inn," the real owners were Moe Dalitz and two associates from Detroit and Cleveland. The builder was Del Webb from Phoenix (also the builder of the Flamingo). In 1966 Howard Hughes returned to Las Vegas (supposedly to help with tests at Area 51) and took over the top floor of the Desert Inn; when Dalitz suggested it was time for him to move on, he bought the resort from Dalitz. In 2000 Steve Wynn bought the entire 170-acre property, imploded the hotel-casino, and built the two Wynn Resorts, today Las Vegas's most luxurious resort hotel-casinos.

9 **Designed by noted New York architect:** The New York architect was Jac Lessman, whose architectural designs are archived at the Avery Architecture and Fine Arts Library at Columbia University.

9 **The real template for the Desert Inn:** T. J. English, *Havana Nocturne: How the Mob Owned Cuba . . . and Then Lost It to the Revolution*, 289–290. "Havana will be a magical city," Meyer Lansky told Armando Jaime, his driver. "Hotels like jewels. . . . Fabulous casinos, nightclubs, and bordellos as far as the eye can see. More people than you can imagine."

10 **"the muscle behind the Havana Mob":** Ibid., xvii.

11 **Wilkerson looked at the land and wrote a check:** A copy of Wilkerson's check was included in a Las Vegas history exhibit at the Nevada State Museum and Historical Society at Twin Lakes Drive, June 2003. A copy is also archived in the Special Collections, Lied Library.

12 **on hand for the hotel's festive opening:** Sally Denton and Roger Morris, *The Money and the Power: The Making of Las Vegas and Its Hold on America, 1947–2000*, 151. The Goldwater family's ties with Las Vegas came through Del Webb, a board member of the Valley National Bank of Phoenix along with Bob Goldwater, Barry's brother. Walter Bimson's Valley National Bank was a major bank for the land-development oligarchy of Phoenix and saw Las Vegas as a good investment opportunity. Valley National was the source of the loan to Bugsy Siegel used to pay Del Webb to finish the Flamingo. Webb often told the story of how nervous he was in asking Siegel for money. Siegel told him, "Don't worry. We only kill each other."

13 **"Hoover formed a small group":** Steven Fox, *Blood and Power: Organized Crime in Twentieth Century America*, 337.

14 **He was murdered in his bed:** Gus Greenbaum was known as the "second toughest Jewish mobster in Las Vegas," the first being Moe Dalitz. His home was in Phoenix, where he ran the racing wire for Meyer Lansky and commuted to Las

Vegas to run the Flamingo (and later the Riviera). In 1958 Greenbaum and his wife were found in bed in their Phoenix home with their throats cut ear to ear, inaugurating a series of gangland-style slayings in Phoenix. Michael F. Wendland, *The Arizona Project*, 21.

14 **"I knew him only as a businessman":** Barry M. Goldwater with Jack Casserly, *Goldwater*, 133. Goldwater answered reporters' questions about why he attended Greenbaum's funeral. "The fact is," Goldwater wrote in his memoir, "[I was] a major Phoenix store owner and political figure. . . . I knew many people. Greenbaum had operated a Phoenix grocery store before taking over a Las Vegas casino. He was, after all, a local resident." Goldwater is the only source to have described Gus Greenbaum as "a former grocer."

14 **To have mobster friends:** Goldwater always tried to discredit journalists such as Ed Reid who, in *The Green Felt Jungle*, described Goldwater's frequent visits to Las Vegas, staying in plush suites at the Flamingo and enjoying the company of known racketeers, including Willie Bioff (later killed by a car bomb), Moe Sedway, and Gus Greenbaum.

16 **"I'm secretary of the corporation":** US Congress, *Hearings Before the Special Senate Committee to Investigate Organized Crime in Interstate Commerce*, 52, 61. When called to testify, Wilbur Clark explained that the Desert Inn was a corporation in which he held some stock, Moe Dalitz and Morris Kleinman held 74 percent, and many others such as Hank Greenspun (a local newspaperman) had points. The restaurants, nightclubs, motel, and hotel were a separate operating company managed by vendors. When asked about his background, he said, "I worked on the old gambling boats, on the Joane A. Smith, the Monte Carlo, the Tango." Meyer Lansky later gave Clark a job as director of entertainment at the Hotel Nacional in Havana.

16 **"You have the most nebulous idea of your business":** Ibid., 53.

16 **"that secret, indirect, revolving traffic":** Denton and Morris, *Power and Money*, 131.

17 **"Well, I didn't inherit a trust fund Senator":** *Hearings Before the Special Senate Committee to Investigate Organized Crime in Interstate Commerce*, 923.

18 **"the biggest mistake of my life":** Goldwater with Casserly, *Goldwater*, 55.

19 **"He'd get wound up":** "AuH2O," 43.

20 **"Gus Greenbaum was running the horse-betting wire":** Ibid., 73. Others wrote about Rosenzweig's links to "prostitution, gambling, and the police agencies that enforced the laws against them" as well as his ties with "mob-connected bookmakers and syndicate hoodlums who midwifed the birth of Las Vegas as the gambling capital of the nation." Robert Gottlieb and Peter Wiley, *Empires in the Sun: The Rise of the New American West*, 171.

21 **"That part of Northern Arizona":** John Dean and Barry Goldwater Jr., *Pure Goldwater*, May 26, 1952, 82.

24 **"I don't know what the hell I'd do":** Ibid., 79.

25 **"My aim," claimed Goldwater:** Goldwater with Casserly, *Goldwater*, 3.

26 **Las Vegas reporters noted:** Ed Reid and Ovid Demaris, *The Green Felt Jungle*, 155. In April 1962, "Senators Barry Goldwater, Howard Cannon (Nevada), Frank Moss (Utah) along with fifty Air Force Reserve members from Goldwater's unit arrived in JFK's official plane for an 'inspection tour' of Nellis Air Force base in Las Vegas. They stayed one half hour, gave no notice to the press, then changed into civilian clothes and disappeared into the Strip casinos. Goldwater [was soon] elevated to Major General in the Air Force Reserve."

CHAPTER 3. THE LADIES FROM BLACK MESA

28 **Mrs. Blackgoat explained:** Author interview, February 16, 1991.

29 **"replacing human beings with livestock":** Senator James Abourezk, *Congressional Record*, December 2, 1974, S20334, quoted in Jerry Kammer, *The Second Long Walk: The Navajo-Hopi Land Dispute*, 127.

32 **The Blair family had owned:** Author conversation with James Blair, August 29, 1990.

32 **"Anglo activists, most from outside Arizona":** Barry Goldwater with Jack Casserly, *Goldwater*, 85.

36 **"Our great ancestors are buried here":** Author conversation with Roberta Blackgoat, February 17, 1991.

37 **"He is a man":** Congressman Steiger introducing Goldwater during House hearings, May 14–15, 1973, US Congress, House Committee on Interior and Insular Affairs, Subcommittee on Indian Affairs, *Partition of Navajo and Hopi 1882 Reservation*, 42.

38 **A photograph taken during Goldwater's visit:** Kammer, *Second Long Walk*, 172 (photo inserts).

39 **"There has been no decision":** *Navajo Times*, August 31, 1987, quoted in ibid., 164.

39 **"No money has been appropriated for relocation":** Ibid.

39 **"I can tell you right now":** Ibid., 165.

40 **"the people here have suffered":** Ibid., 165.

40 **"I've lived here fifty years":** *Navajo Times*, August 31, 1978.

41 **"I had hoped":** Goldwater statement, hearings, Navajo-Hopi dispute, May 14–15, 1973, US Congress, House Committee on Interior and Insular Affairs, Subcommittee on Indian Affairs, *Partition of Navajo and Hopi 1882 Reservation*, 42.

42 **Black Mesa was home to the first:** Lowell Hinkins, interview with the author, Black Mesa Slurry Pipeline office, March 15, 1990.

42 **Bechtel designed and built the coal-slurry pipeline:** According to Laton McCartney, *Friends in High Places: Bechtel, America's Most Secret Corporation and How It Engineered the World*, 15, Peter Flanigan, a business adviser to President Nixon, helped get a $3 billion grant for Bechtel to build the pipeline. After leaving

the Nixon administration, Flanigan went to work as a managing partner at Dillon Read investment bank, in which Bechtel had a controlling interest. See also McCartney, *Friends in High Places*, 174n; and obituary, *Boston Globe*, August 2, 2013.

CHAPTER 4. FOUNDING MYTHS: LAUGHLIN, NEVADA

46 **No water is left in the Colorado River:** *Chasing Water*, a film by Peter McBride (Bullfrog Films, 2011). See also *The Colorado River* by Peter McBride and Jonathan Waterman, 2011.

48 **The huge development of Summerlin:** Eugene P. Moehring and Michael S. Green, *Las Vegas: A Centennial History*, 234–235.

50 **Lowell Hinkins, an operator at the slurry-pipeline office:** Interview with the author, Black Mesa Slurry Pipeline office, March 15, 1990.

52 **A series of films on YouTube:** "Nevada Real Estate Crash #19," www.youtube .com/watch?v=479bdfv1WHg.

53 **The water-table level had dropped from 10 to 70 feet:** Marjane Ambler, *Breaking the Iron Bonds: Indian Control of Energy Development*, 222.

54 **"The water is more valuable than the coal":** US Department of the Interior, Office of Surface Mining Reclamation and Enforcement, *Environmental Impacts and Proposed Permit Application for the Black Mesa–Kayenta Mine, Navajo and Hopi Indian Reservations, Arizona*, May 1990, letter from Marilyn Maseyevsa, 24; 1:1–14 refers to "minor water impacts."

55 **The 1985 accident:** J. D. Dolan, "Anniversary of a Disaster," *Los Angeles Times*, June 9, 2010.

56 **Kit Owens, the public relations director:** Interview with the author, March 14, 1990.

58 **Thousands of archaeological ruins:** The artifacts and ruins in the Black Mesa mining area were photographed and documented by the Center for Archaeological Investigations, Southern Illinois University, Carbondale.

CHAPTER 5. GILDED AGE LAND GRABS

61 **the fractious Republican convention of 1880:** Thomas C. Reeves, *Gentleman Boss: The Life of Chester Alan Arthur;* Justus D. Doenecke, *The Presidencies of James A. Garfield and Chester A. Arthur*.

62 **diplomatic recognition to the Congo Free State:** Adam Hochschild, *King Leopold's Ghost: A Story of Greed, Terror, and Heroism in Colonial Africa*.

63 **"Proposed Reservation for the Moqui [Hopi] and Other Indians":** National Archives and Records Administration, map, *Territory of Arizona*, Department of the Interior, 1879, Marked File 911.

64 **Half of the entire Navajo Tribe:** National Archives and Records Administration, Bureau of Indian Affairs, New Mexico Superintendency, Record Group 75,

File Mark S-581/1865, Navajo series IV, no. 1187. Indian superintendent Steck was completely opposed to the campaign by the War Department and General James Carleton's plan to create a new reservation on the Pecos River for all the Navajo. Some eight thousand were moved to the reservation at Bosque Redondo by Kit Carson, and some seven thousand escaped and moved farther west. On January 11, 1865, Steck, Indian superintendent for New Mexico Territory, responded to an inquiry from Judge T. W. Woolson of New Mexico regarding the Navajo campaign: "The seven thousand left in their own country have large herds and are able to support themselves. . . . [T]he 8,000 at Bosque Redondo have no timber for shelter. . . . Justice demands they be located elsewhere. . . . [T]he location is almost destitute of wood, a scanty supply of water, no building timber and no shelter for stock against the storms of winter, and can only be kept up at an enormous expense to the government. . . . [T]here is not enough water to irrigate and the Pecos is frequently dry . . . and is impractical as a locality for a reservation for the Navajos. . . . It is my firm conviction that more can be accomplished upon a suitable reservation in their own country with an appropriation of $250,000 than at the Pecos with $2,000,000."

65 **The agent was powerless to do anything:** National Archives and Records Administration, Bureau of Indian Affairs, Arizona Superintendency, Record Group 75, File Mark E-285/1880. On March 20, 1880, US Indian agent Galen Eastman wrote to the commissioner of Indian affairs about the urgency of setting a Hopi reservation boundary: "Believing that the Mormons are about to settle on land that ought to be embraced in a Moquis Pueblo Indian Reservation, I cannot await the tardy appearance of the expected new agent for these Indians but feel impelled to press their necessity upon your attention and request that you do immediately call the Executive notice to their wants, to wit, that a tract of land be set off as a Reservation for the Moquis Pueblo Indians bounded as follows." The reservation he proposed was a rectangle forty-eight miles east-west and twenty-four miles north-south.

65 **A previous Indian agent:** National Archives and Records Administration, Bureau of Indian Affairs, Record Group 75, Special Case No. 147, File Mark M-509/1880. On February 23, 1880, E. S. Merritt wrote to the commissioner of Indian affairs: "I have in my possession a long letter from the Hon. Comsr. Of Ind. Affairs regarding the segregation from the public domain of a Reservation for the Moquis Pueblo Indians, and also, as to whether they would consent to removal to the Little Colorado River. . . . Having lived in the immediate vicinity of Pueblo Indians and Mexicans for near twenty (20) years, I most emphatically state that they could not be induced to change their location and cannot be removed, except by force. . . . They, the Moquis, absolutely require Reservation and action should not be delayed. A piece of land 6 or 8 miles long and 3 or 4 miles wide in the form of a parallelogram, with the mesa and each village on or near the centre is all which is required." See also Agent J. H. Fleming to the

Commissioner of Indian Affairs, December 4, 1882, File Mark 22383/1882: "The lands most desirable for the Moquis and which were cultivated by them 8 or 10 years ago, have been take up by the Mormons and others."

65 **the 1879 map *Navajo Country***: National Archives and Records Administration, report by Inspector Howard, Map No. 630.

66 **"the coal deposit lies between Oraibi and Moenkopi"**: Fleming to Inspector Howard, 1882, National Archives and Records Administration.

66 **The Executive Order is dated December 16, 1882:** National Archives and Records Administration, Bureau of Indian Affairs, Record Group 75, Executive Order File, File Mark 23017/1882. The order concludes: "The tract of country in the territory of Arizona [lying between described boundaries] . . . is hereby withdrawn from settlement and sale, and set apart for the use and occupancy of the Moqui and such other Indians as the Secretary of the Interior may see fit to settle thereon." It is signed by Chester A. Arthur. Beneath the signature the Department of the Interior notes that the area described is 3,920 square miles and 2,508,800 acres.

CHAPTER 6. THE INDIAN LAWYER AND A BRIEF HISTORY OF COAL

69 **"Coal is a portable climate":** Ralph Waldo Emerson, *The Conduct of Life*, 86–87, quoted in Barbara Freese, *Coal: A Human History*, 10.

70 **"the biggest increase in global energy output has come from coal":** Daniel Yergin, *The Quest*, 403.

70 **In 2012 the US Geological Survey published a graph:** US Geological Survey, 2012, *Energy Resource Reports*, http://pubs.usgs.gov/of/2012/1205/pdf/ Coal_Fields_Map.pdf. See also J. A. East, 2013, "Coal Fields of the Conterminous United States—National Coal Resource Assessment," updated version, US Geological Survey Open-File Report 2012-1205, one sheet, scale 1:5,000,000, http://pubs.usgs.gov/of/2012/1205/. See also "BP's Annual Review Paints a Grim Picture of Global Energy Use"; and *BP Statistical Review of World Energy Use*, 2012, www.bp.com/en/global/corporate/about-bp/statistical-review-of-world -energy-2013.html.

71 **"Coal was no mere fuel":** Freese, *Coal: A Human History*, 10.

75 **The desire to conquer nature:** Ibid., 100–101.

78 **did the Ute work pro bono:** Boyden's daughter states, "John's friendship with the Indians and his empathy for their grievances motivated him to work for many years without pay simply because it was a cause he believed in." Orpha Boyden, *John S. Boyden: Three Score and Ten in Retrospect*, 164. Boyden worked on a contingency basis for a while, but it was clear he expected to be paid. Abbott Sekaquaptewa said that in 1951, "Boyden was really representing the people who were trying to get the Council back together. He was not paid." As soon as the tribal council was sworn in, however, and the BIA approved him as claims attorney for the Hopi, he knew

he would be paid. All Indian Claims Commission contracts confirmed that attorneys could receive up to 10 percent of the settlement amount the tribe received. The Hopi received a $5 million settlement. For reasons not clear, the Hopi council voted to give him a $900,000 fee, later raised to $1 million. A year later when Boyden was confirmed as tribal attorney, the tribe knew they had to pay him. In describing the exploration leases that the tribe signed for oil and coal, Sekaquaptewa said. "We were a poor tribe. . . . We were in a great need of money. For tribal operations . . . and to continue to have legal counsel." Anita Parlow, *Cry, Sacred Ground*, 203, 205. Legal suit by the Native American Rights Fund confirmed that Boyden was paid a total of $2.7 million in fees by the Hopi.

78 **shared a fee of $2,794,606:** Ernest L. Wilkinson and W. Cleon Skousen, *Brigham Young University: A School of Destiny*, 434n.

79 **"Bought, shot and left to rot":** Peter MacDonald with Ted Schwarz, *The Last Warrior: Peter MacDonald and the Navajo Nation*, 37.

79 **"It is well to remember":** Harold S. Colton, director, Museum of Northern Arizona, "Report on the Hopi Boundry [sic]," 12, John Boyden Papers, Special Collections, Brigham Young University, *Healing v. Jones*, Navajo Exhibit, no. 15A, December 1939. Although the Hopi villages are frequently described as independent entities, similar to the separate pueblos of New Mexico, they were never given Spanish land grant and therefore never recognized as separate pueblos. After 1848 and the US victory in the war with Mexico, they were treated as a single political entity by the US government.

81 **"My father was a driving force":** Abbott Sekaquaptewa quoted in Parlow, *Cry, Sacred Ground*, 203.

81 **"Boyden went through the villages":** Ibid., 204.

81 **"We have explained plainly":** Carl Hayden Papers; "Hopi Elders Seek to Avoid Court Test," *Christian Science Monitor*, Jan. 16, 1957, including "Draft Copy of Letter to Barry Goldwater" opposing S. 692, the three-judge-court legislation. Additional text of the letter reads: "Attorney John S. Boyden claimed he represents the majority of the Hopi people. That is a pure lie and he knows it. The fact is, the majority of the Hopis are against him as a lawyer. All the traditional villages rejected him when he first came on the Hopiland. Today the people in Lower Moencopi, including some of the Upper Village are against him. Hotevilla, Oraibi, Shungopavy, and Mushongnovi Villages are all against John S. Boyden, the so-called Hopi Tribal Council, and are strongly opposed to the Bill S. 692. . . . Boyden claimed he represented seven Hopi villages. This is not true. He represented only those who were pressured into signing his contract, or contracts, without knowing what was in those contracts. If the people in the 'Tribal Council' villages were given a chance to express their views on this matter it would be found that the majority of them are against Boyden, the so-called Hopi Tribal Council, and this Bill S. 692."

81 **"On top of all this":** Caleb Johnson letter, Hayden Papers, Feb 27, 1957.

82 **"Several recent efforts"**: Colton, "Report on the Hopi Boundry [*sic*]," 7.

83 **"We were a poor tribe"**: Parlow, *Cry, Sacred Ground*, 205.

84 **The extent of Black Mesa coal reserves**: Pierce and Wilt, 1911, quoted in the 1984 *Keystone Coal Industry Manual*, 480. "Black Mesa is an erosional remnant of Upper Cretaceous strata surrounded on all sides by older Mesozoic sedimentary rocks. Within Black Mesa, the Cretaceous strata have been warped into long and broad synclines and anticlines. The principal coal reserves within the northern half of Black Mesa are preserved within two of these downwarps, the Maloney and Black Mesa synclines. It is the former that contains the reserves being mined by the Peabody Coal Company. The Upper Cretaceous section is thickest to the north and thins southerly by erosion until the basal formation, the Dakota Sandstone, forms the surface on the south." See also the map titled *Geologic Cross-Section of Navajo Reservation—Black Mesa*, US Park Service and Zion Natural History Association, 1975.

85 **"When it comes to AMBITION"**: *Summit County Bee*, June 1924, quoted in O. Boyden, *John S. Boyden*, 13.

86 **Coalville and Grass Creek Mining Coal Company**: *WPA Guide to Utah*, 366. See also David Hampshire, Martha Sonntag Bradley, and Allen Roberts, *A History of Summit County*, 36, 46; and www.coalville.utah.gov/history.

86 **"I therefore hold"**: Opinion of Felix Cohen, acting solicitor, Department of the Interior, "Re: Ownership of the Mineral Estate in the Hopi Executive Order Reservation," Departmental Recognition of Indian Tribal Representatives, US Department of the Interior, *Decisions of the Dept. of Interior* 59 (January 1945–June 1947): 248–254. Also copy in Hayden papers, Arizona State University Libraries, 1946.

88 **Wilkinson's Washington, DC, firm and the Claims Commission**: The impetus to settle Indian claims came about during World War II, when a survey by the Interior Department determined that more than 30 percent of America's untapped energy reserves—coal, oil, uranium, natural gas—lay beneath Indian reservation lands in the West, lands previously considered useless for ranching or farming, but perfect for Indian reservations. Many mining companies, railroads, and ranchers occupied lands with ambiguous title because many Indian tribes still had treaty rights to the same lands. The government had granted the land twice, sometimes three times.

The settlement paid to the Ute Indians of Utah and Colorado was the single largest settlement ever paid by the US government to Indian people. Wilkinson was a Utah Mormon with a Harvard Law degree. Originally hired by a New York law firm (which included Charles Evans Hughes, future chief justice of the Supreme Court) to work on a complex tax case involving the merger of Utah Copper with Kennecott Copper, he was also given the Ute case. When he moved to Washington to open his own practice, he took the Ute case with him. Wilkinson knew of Boyden because he was tribal attorney for two bands of Ute in Utah. The claim of various Ute bands dated back to 1868 when a number of Ute Indian bands had given up vast tracts of Utah Territory in exchange for a treaty with the US government that guaranteed them payment for the ceded lands to Mormon settlers. Although the Mormon settlers continued to occupy more than 1 million acres, the promised payments never arrived.

Wilkinson's firm was well known because it was one of two firms that handled more cases than any other before the Indian Claims Commission. He was also well known within Indian law circles because he had actually helped to write the Indian Claims Law along with Felix Cohen, the brilliant solicitor of the Department of the Interior and the author of the definitive *Handbook of Federal Indian Law.* (In the Interior Department the Claims Commission files were known as the "Wilkinson files" because the firm had represented so many Indian tribes.) The commission was conceived as a solution to ambivalent land titles and the exceptional length of time it took to have cases decided before the US Court of Claims. Robert Gottlieb and Peter Wiley, *America's Saints: The Rise of Mormon Power.* See also Charles F. Wilkinson, *Fire on the Plateau: Conflict and Endurance in the American Southwest*; Ernest L. Wilkinson and W. Cleon Skousen, *Brigham Young University: A University of Destiny*; and O. Boyden, *John S. Boyden.*

90 **"The amount of service":** E. Wilkinson and Skousen, *University of Destiny*, 434.

90 **Boyden and Wilkinson's partnership on Ute case:** Wiley and Gottlieb, *America's Saints*, 171–174. See also C. Wilkinson, *Fire on the Plateau*, 155–160; E. Wilkinson and Skousen, *University of Destiny*, 452–468; and O. Boyden, *John S. Boyden*, 164–172.

90 **"A number of us have wondered":** Thomas S. Shia to Congressman Stewart Udall, May 15, 1957, author copy.

91 **"Dear Tom":** Udall response to Thomas Shia of Valley National Bank, May 17, 1957, author copy provided by Black Mesa Trust.

91 **"We have two problems out here":** Johnson letter, Hayden Papers.

92 **"Being a true friend of the Lamanites":** O. Boyden, *John S. Boyden*, 245.

CHAPTER 7. THE MORMON WEST

96 **Alta California was known mainly for the cattle ranches:** Mike Davis, *City of Quartz: Excavating the Future in Los Angeles*, 106.

96 **the US Army under President Andrew Jackson:** The Five Civilized Tribes were the Cherokee of Georgia; the Choctaw, Chickasaw, and Creeks of Mississippi and Alabama; and the Seminoles of Florida. The Cherokee had a written language, a newspaper, their own schools, public roads, agriculture, mills, and a well-organized political system. Their people were more literate than many of the white settlers who wanted their lands. (Individual Indians were not allowed to buy and hold title land.) In a suit against the government, they sued and won the right to hold their lands. Andrew Jackson was supposed to have said, "Justice John Marshall has made his decision, now let him enforce it." As president, Andrew Jackson enforced the Indian Removal Law and sent federal troops to force

sixteen thousand Cherokee to walk from Georgia to Oklahoma in December, during which an estimated one out of four Cherokee died.

The Choctaw, who had fought on the American side during the War of 1812 and had helped Andrew Jackson's weak Tennessee militia successfully defend New Orleans from the British, were not rewarded. Of the thirteen thousand Choctaw who were forced to give up all their lands in Mississippi and move to western Arkansas, four thousand died of hunger, exposure, or disease.

The Seminoles fought two wars against ten thousand US Army troops over a ten-year period in resistance to the effort of removing them from their lands in Florida and Georgia. The war against the Seminoles was the most costly and least successful of all the American wars until Vietnam. Some Seminoles retreated into the Everglades and others eventually did move to Oklahoma, but they never ceded defeat.

After the five tribes were moved, it opened up millions of acres for the expanding cotton kingdom of the South. A lottery was held for the newly cleared Cherokee lands in Georgia, and many of the new cotton plantation owners in Georgia, Alabama, and Mississippi were friends of Andrew Jackson. In 1837 Congress passed a Jackson-sponsored law that ended direct payments to Indian tribes for lands they had ceded or sold to the United States. Instead, the funds were to be held "in trust" and used for the benefit of the Indians. Irregularities were rampant: Indian trust funds showed no interest over decades and declining revenues despite deposits, and tribes were refused the right to audit their own funds. In a 1996 audit the BIA couldn't account for more than $2.4 billion in trust account transactions. In 2008 the Indian trust funds were still under negotiation.

Although historians have described Andrew Jackson as an icon of frontier democracy, he was a land speculator, a slave trader, and a merchant, and as a young lawyer he stood with creditors against debtors with property. As a politician and as president, he was the most aggressive enemy of the Indians in early American history.

99 **"The death of the modern Mahomet":** Quoted in Fawn M. Brodie, *No Man Knows My History: The Life of Joseph Smith*, 397.

99 **"I have been commanded of God":** Ibid., 478.

100 **the two men spoke in tongues:** John G. Turner, *Brigham Young: Pioneer Prophet*, 32.

100 **"He was a mythmaker of prodigious talent":** Brodie, *No Man Knows My History*, ix.

101 **"all of these vestiges":** Henry M. Brackenridge, *Views of Louisiana, Together with a Journal of a Voyage Up the Missouri River in 1811*, 182–283. Brackenridge also said that some attributed the vestige ruins to "a colony of Welsh or Danes."

102 **As treasury secretary Gallatin sponsored:** George Squier and Edwin Davis, *Ancient Monuments of the Mississippi Valley: Comprising the Results of Extensive Original Surveys and Explorations*.

102 **he made the correct connection between the similarities:** Francis Jennings, *The Founders of America: From the Earliest Migrations to the Present*, 62–66.

104 **"Their hatred was fixed":** *Book of Mormon*, Book of Enos, 1:20, 137.

104 **They "did till the land":** Ibid.

108 **"one of the foremost intelligences of the time":** DeVoto quoted in Robert Gottlieb and Peter Wiley, *America's Saints: The Rise of Mormon Power*, 43.

110 **A map in the Library of Congress:** The Map Division of the Library of Congress has a map of Deseret, 1850–1868, attributed to the Historians Office, Church of Jesus Christ of Latter-day Saints, showing successive reductions to the territory over those years.

CHAPTER 8. LEGAL THEFT

111 **"The first full-time missionaries":** Helen Sekaquaptewa with Louise Udall, *Me and Mine: The Life Story of Helen Sekaquaptewa*, 240.

112 **"The Book of Mormon," Wilkinson wrote:** Ernest L. Wilkinson and W. Cleon Skousen, *Brigham Young University: A School of Destiny*, 735.

112 **"teaching Emory [Sr.], Abbott, and me the Gospel":** Sekaquaptewa with Udall, *Me and Mine*, 241.

112 **"Here is a religion":** Ibid, 243.

113 **"the lands most desirable for the Moquis":** J. H. Fleming, December 4, 1882, copy in John Boyden Papers, Special Collections, Brigham Young University.

113 **"Believing that the Mormons are about to settle":** Galen Eastman to Commissioner of Indian Affairs, March 20, 1880, copy in ibid.

113 **when Toova and her great-aunt returned:** Sekaquaptewa with Udall, *Me and Mine*.

114 **"Coal mining on Black Mesa happened":** Brian Jackson Morton, "Coal Leasing in the Fourth World: Hopi and Navajo Coal Leasing, 1954–1977," 13.

115 **"New jobs, large tax benefits":** Kammer, 87.

115 **"a textbook example":** Alvin Josephy, "The Murder of the Southwest." Also quoted in Gottlieb and Wiley, *Empires in the Sun*, 45. Also author interview.

115 **"I was always involved . . . on behalf of minority groups":** Stewart Udall, oral history interview, John F. Kennedy Presidential Library, Boston. In 1964 when Secretary Stewart Udall was trying to build a new dam on the Colorado River to power the Central Arizona Project, one of the old-timers from St. Johns, Arizona, sent the following letter around to many Arizona and New Mexico politicians. Mo Udall, who was known for his wit and sense of humor, reproduced it in his political autobiography, *Too Funny to Be President*.

> Dear Sirs:
>
> I am an old man and I know a lot about . . . this Udall outfit. My father had a ranch on the *Little Colorado River* when I was a boy. We had cattle, sheep and goats and horses. In the bottom land we raised our corn and beans and chile

and we were contented and happy. Then *David K. Udall* moved down to Saint Johns . . . and he and some other men like him put in a dam across the Little Colorado. We objected because it was a dangerous place to put in a dirt dam but they went right ahead and put it in anyway.

When it broke, it ruined our land and drowned our cattle and goats and . . . I have been poor ever since. They never paid us a cent for the damages. I confess I do not like the Udalls and this is one reason.

Another reason is that you cannot trust any of them. The whole tribe were Republicans and David K. Udall and his brother Joe Udall tried for years to get the Mexicans, who were then all Republicans to give them a public office. But *Don Lorenzo Hubbell*, who was a great leader, saw through this scheme and never would let them get on the Republican ticket. And the Mormons, who were nearly all Democrats, would have none of them. But when *Franklin Roosevelt* came in, some of the Mexicans switched to him and the Udalls went along, or most of them did.

However David K. Udall, the big shot, had a second wife hid out down the river at a place called Hunt and this wife had some boys who stayed Republican and one of them got to be mayor of Phoenix. In this way the Udall family can now work both sides of the street. I want you to check up on this because I am an old man and want to be sure of my facts. But my granddaughter tells me this Stewart Udall is trying to steal the water from the Colorado and I can believe it. Because this is the way it happened fifty and sixty years ago. The Udalls have been at this business a long time.

Respectfully yours, Jose (Joe) Chavez

116 **"I came out of a political family":** Oral history, JFK Library.

121 **"It was ironic, indeed, that a society":** Rayna Greene, foreword to *To Lead and to Serve: American Indian Education at Hampton Institute, 1878–1923,* by MaryLou Hultgren, 12.

122 **"The posts that sent out men to kill their fathers":** Ibid, 12.

122 **"We marched to the dining room three times a day":** Sekaquaptewa with Udall, *Me and Mine,* 136.

123 **"Corporal punishment was given":** Ibid., 137.

125 **"Dear Mr. Phelps":** John Boyden Papers, University of Utah Library, Peabody Coal Company File, No. 823, Box 56, Folders 1–4, quoted in C. Wilkinson, *Fire on the Plateau,* 300.

126 **"The Navajo tribe has systematically":** US Congress, House Committee on Interior and Insular Affairs, Subcommittee on Indian Affairs, *Partition of Navajo and Hopi 1882 Reservation,* May 14, 1973, 26.

127 **"The locus of Hopi policy":** Mark Panitch, *Washington Post,* July 21, 1974. Because it was happening on Indian reservations, the extent of the ecological damage and the interrelatedness of burning coal, pumping water, and air pollution

were not well understood or publicized. Instead, what reached the public through newspapers, Sunday magazines, and the occasional television piece was a fabricated story about a range war between the sheepherding Navajo and the ranching Hopi.

128 **"I need not remind this committee":** US Congress, House Committee on Interior and Insular Affairs, Subcommittee on Indian Affairs, *Partition of Navajo and Hopi 1882 Reservation*, 25.

129 **"There is evidence":** Locke, 352.

130 **"Three hundred miles at fifteen miles day!":** Ruth Roessel, *Navajo Stories of the Long Walk*, 103–104.

132 **Carleton insisted that Steck clean up:** In 1865, Steck wrote to a New Mexico politician describing the failure of Navajo internment. See top paragraph on p. 256 for his letter.

133 **shipments of supplies disappeared without a trace:** The reputation of the Indian agency was one of the worst in Washington. Corrupt, with low morale, and inefficient, the Indian agents were drawn from a pool of former soldiers with discipline problems, deteriorating drinkers, and others of little education or prospects. The pay for an Indian agent was about fifteen hundred a year, the same as a clerk in a dry goods store. But unlike the clerk, the Indian agent handled thousands of dollars in Indian annuities and supplies. The Indian agents gave a cut to the politicians who helped them get the job and to suppliers who sent substandard goods. From the beginning, as one historian observed, "a more perfect recipe for corruption could not be found." Navajo who came to Fort Wingate with ration tickets were turned away.

CHAPTER 9. LEARNING FROM LAS VEGAS

138 **Helen Stewart was the unlikely owner:** www.reviewjournal.com/news/helen-stewart, February 7, 1999.

140 **His unsavory reputation:** www.senate.gov/artandhistory/history/common/contested_elections/089William_Clark.htm.

141 **"He is as rotten a human being":** Mark Twain, quoted in *Mark Twain in Eruption: Hitherto Unpublished Pages About Men and Events*, edited by Bernard DeVoto, 45.

142 **Photographs of the town from the 1920s:** Special Collections, Lied Library.

146 **"Now this dam is just a dam":** Joseph E. Stevens, *Hoover Dam: An American Adventure*, 46.

148 **Called a "natural engineer":** Robert L. Ingram, *A Builder and His Family, 1898–1948, Being the Historical Account of the Contracting, Engineering, and Construction Career of W. A. Bechtel*, 4.

150 **Tony Cornero arrived in Las Vegas:** James Roman, "The Original Wise Guy," *Chronicles of Old Las Vegas*, 51.

151 **"It set the stage":** Andrew J. Dunar and Dennis McBride, *Building Hoover Dam: An Oral History of the Great Depression*, 232.

152 **"They sent me an invitation":** Ibid., 233.

152 **"Potent in its charm":** *Las Vegas Age*, May 3, 1931.

152 **"He saw a Las Vegas of classy, carpeted casinos":** *Las Vegas Review-Journal*, February 7, 1999, www.reviewjournal.com/news/tony-cornero.

154 **"They will work under our conditions":** Quoted in Stevens, *Hoover Dam*, 72.

155 **at least fifty cases of carbon monoxide poisoning:** Dunar and McBride, *Building Hoover Dam*, 317–320.

158 **"Twelve hundred men with modern equipment":** Frank Crowe quoted in the PBS *American Experience* documentary on the Hoover Dam, www.pbs.org/wgbh/americanexperience/films/hoover/.

158 **"This morning I came, I saw and I was conquered":** Roosevelt quoted in Michael Hiltzik, *Colossus: Hoover Dam and the Making of the American Century*, 372.

161 **"There's a lot of desert":** Innovation America, "Bechtel's Man at the Nevada Site," *America's Journal of Technology Commercialization*, www.innovation-America.org.

161 **104 nuclear reactors from thirty-one states:** Department of Energy Information, www.eia.gov/tools/faqs/faq.cfm?id=207&t=3.

CHAPTER 10. CHINATOWN 2

164 **"It was amazing to me":** Stephanie Tavares, "Q&A, Pat Mulroy," *Las Vegas Sun*, May 1, 2009, 16.

165 **"Everything the city did was legal":** Marc Reisner, *Cadillac Desert: The American West and Its Disappearing Water*, 65.

166 **"Wicked dust storms":** Alissa Walker, "The Los Angeles Aqueduct Turns 100," Nov. 7, 2013. Also, NPR, Nov. 3, 2013, "How an Aqueduct Turned Los Angeles into a Garden of Eden."

167 **Thirty years earlier:** Infrared satellite map, US Geological Survey Map, 1981, NASA-LandSat-3 No. 36114-As-SI-2050, author copy.

170 **"prior appropriation" doctrine:** deBuys, 165. See Ambler, 214, for Indian priority dates.

170 **Pop Squires of Las Vegas represented Nevada:** Correspondence to Nevada governor, 1922, Special Collections, Lied Library.

172 **The numbers are posted every day:** www.usbr.gov/lc/region/g4000/hourly/mead-elv.html.

172 **scheduled for completion in 2014 but delayed until 2015:** *Las Vegas Review-Journal*, September 5, 2013.

173 **"DON'T WRECK YOUR BOAT":** Lake Mead National Park newspaper, February 2010.

174 **"Low water doesn't mean *no* water":** www.nps.gov/lake/naturescience/lowwater.htm.

177 **"They said Hoover Dam was going to silt up":** John McPhee, *The John McPhee Reader*, 323.

180 **security is central:** Climate change has changed the meaning of security.

180 **"We are on the verge of a new form of desertification":** William DeBuys, *A Great Aridness: Climate Change and the Future of the American Southwest*, 8.

181 **"I remember having Harry in high school":** Author notes from presentation to Gene Segerblom at the Nevada Women's History Celebration of 2010 in Las Vegas.

185 **"The thing I kept hearing":** Emily Green, "Not This Water," pt. 4 of "Quenching Las Vegas' Thirst."

186 **"[This] isn't a new idea":** Emily Green, "The Equation: No Water, No Growth," pt. 3 of "Quenching Las Vegas' Thirst."

186 **"An Owens Valley cannot... occur in Nevada":** Emily Green, pt. 4 of "Quenching Las Vegas' Thirst."

187 **Pat Mulroy assured a Senate Committee:** Pat Mulroy announced her decision to retire in September 2013. "Pat Mulroy to Retire," *Las Vegas Sun*, Sept. 23, 2013.

188 **"Pat Mulroy was in Washington this week":** Henry Brean, "Federal Officials Cut Water Delivery for Lake Mead, Speeding Reservoir's Decline."

CHAPTER 11. THE BECHTEL FAMILY BUSINESS

190 **"He had offers for $90 million":** Quoted in Tim O'Grady, "Children of Las Vegas."

190 **"This is a city of fifty-year old men":** Ibid.

191 **contractors "whose offices were in their hats":** "The Earth Movers," pt. 1, *Fortune*, Oct. 1943.

191 **"We will build anything":** *Fortune*, March 1951, quoted in Laton McCartney, *Friends in High Places: Bechtel, America's Most Secret Corporation and How It Engineered the World*, 55.

192 **America's energy resources lay beneath Indian reservations:** Marjane Ambler, *Breaking the Iron Bonds: Indian Control of Energy Development*.

195 **"A man with holy war views":** *I. F. Stone's Weekly*, November 7, 1960, quoted in McCartney, *Friends in High Places*, 97.

196 **Three-fourths of uranium:** Kate Tuttle, "The Feds, Uranium," *Boston Globe*, Oct. 5, 2010. See also Leslie Macmillan, "The Tainted Desert," *Tufts Magazine*, winter 2012.

196 **Stewart Udall was holding special hearings:** "Uranium Miners Suffering Described at Hearing." See also *Navajo-Hopi Observer*, March 14, 1990; and *Navajo Times*, March 15, 1990, 2.

196 **"The nuclear industry was so incestuous":** McCartney, *Friends in High Places*, 104.

197 **McCone became head of the CIA:** Although McCone was a Republican, a Catholic, and a supporter of America's intervention in Vietnam, he opposed the coup against President Diem and resigned from the CIA in 1965. He claimed no knowledge of the CIA's Operation Mongoose under the Kennedys, the secret plot to destabilize the Cuban government and assassinate Castro. John McCone, oral history interview, John F. Kennedy Presidential Library, Boston.

197 **One moonless night in northern Nevada:** John McPhee, *Annals of the Former World*, 111–112.

198 **"As we looked back":** Ibid.

200 **Brown and Root, a Texas construction firm:** Robert Caro, *The Years of Lyndon Johnson: The Path to Power*, 606, 618.

203 **It owned coal mines in ten states:** Arizona, Colorado, Illinois, Indiana, Kentucky, Missouri, Montana, Ohio, Oklahoma, and West Virginia. *Keystone Coal Industry Manual*, 1984, 896.

205 **"I believe the performance":** Peter MacDonald testimony, US Congress, "To Reauthorize Housing Relocation Under the Navajo Hopi Relocation Program and for Other Purposes," Senate Hearings on S. 1236, December 9, 1987, 23, 51.

205 **"There are many problems":** Dennis DeConcini testimony, US Congress, "To Reauthorize Housing Relocation Under the Navajo Hopi Relocation Program and for Other Purposes," Senate Hearings on S. 1236, May 19, 1987, 5; John McCain, 4; Ivan Sidney, 24.

207 **"Give us the money":** Wallace Stegner, *The American West as Living Space*, 9.

208 **"a raid on resources":** Robert Gottlieb and Peter Wiley, *Empires in the Sun*, 46.

208 **"The Bechtel organization wishes to operate":** Letter of C. J. Hallett, Caspar Weinberger Papers, Library of Congress.

209 **The Interior Department claimed the leases were confidential:** One Navajo Tribal Council member publicized a lease clause regarding the coal-slurry line and sale of Indian water rights that required separate approval by the tribal council: "The Southern California Edison Company, as a proposed purchaser of Black Mesa coal for operation of a new generating plant to be constructed by said company at Mohave, Nevada would not purchase the coal at the present high rates Sentry Royalty Company would have to charge on the basis of present high freight rates and the required cost of constructing a railroad from the vicinity of Flagstaff, Arizona. It is therefore in the best interest of the Navajo Tribe to grant to the Sentry Royalty Company the right to construct a slurry pipeline in lieu and instead of a railroad, and to authorize the use of water (which has already been discovered in deep drilling by said company in the said leased area of the Navajo reservation) and sale thereof the Sentry Royalty Company in an estimated amount of 2,500 to 3,000 acre-feet annually."

209 **"Our Mother Earth":** Excerpt from Proclamation of the Big Mountain Diné Nation, Declaration of Independence, Oct. 28, 1979. Author copy with signatures, courtesy of J. R. Lancaster.

CHAPTER 12. ROBERTA BLACKGOAT'S WORLD

211 **"Those are to catch rainwater for the sheep":** Author visit, February 16–19, 1991.

213 **"rude shelters known as hogans":** Cited in *Healing v. Jones* case summary LexisNexis, 6 of 50. "The Navajos were originally of an aggressive nature, although not as warlike as the Apaches. It was because they had become embroiled in a series of fights with white men that they were banished to Fort Sumner in 1863. By 1882, however, they had curbed their hostility to the Government and to white men

and, in general, were peaceably disposed, except for their proclivity to commit depredations against the Hopis, as described below. Desert life made the Navajos sturdy, virile people, industrious and optimistic. They were also intelligent and thrifty. . . . In the main, however, they were semi-nomadic or migratory, moving into new areas at times, and then moving seasonally from mountain to valley and back again with their livestock. *This required them to live in rude shelters known as 'hogans' usually built of poles, sticks, bark and moist earth"* (emphasis added).

214 **"Those are places like us":** In "Geopolitics Comes Home," Gottlieb and Wiley described the Grand Plan "as another of those exciting geopolitical visions, like the Pacific Rim strategy, spun out of the fertile relationship developed between Washington and the largest private corporations." Robert Gottlieb and Peter Wiley, *Empires in the Sun: The Rise of the New American West,* 46–47. Anita Parlow in an author interview described Black Mesa energy development and the Indian removal as "a domestic example of a global paradigm."

215 **Proclamation of the Big Mountain Diné:** Author copy, dated October 28, 1979.

216 **"Let's go look for some concrete":** Author notes, Feb. 21, 1991.

217 **"From our first meeting":** E-mails, telephone calls, and personal interview with Martha Blue, 2002–2010. See also Roberta Blackgoat in Judith Nies, *Nine Women: Portraits from American Radical Tradition,* 293–297.

223 **"That's where I went to school":** Author interviews, February 1991 and March 1993.

224 **"The Hopi are a timid and inoffensive people":** Case summary, *Healing v. Jones,* LexisNexis, 6 of 50.

225 **CERT, the Council of Energy Resource Tribes:** Peter MacDonald with Ted Schwarz, *The Last Warrior: Peter MacDonald and the Navajo Nation,* 228–233; author interview with Lucille Echohawk, CERT, February 27, 1991; annual report, CERT.

227 **"I never met Peter MacDonald":** Senator George McGovern, telephone interview by the author, May 23, 1993.

228 **"an Oriental potentate":** John R. Emshwiller, "Chief Under Fire," *Wall Street Journal,* Jan. 5, 1989, 1.

231 **"Are we going to have to listen to you all day?":** Accounts of the Hanson's stockholders meeting. Zoe Brennan, "Furious Hanson on the Warpath," *Daily Express,* Feb. 1, 1996. Tom Sevenson, "Insults Fly," *The Independent,* Feb. 1, 1996.

235 **"She was a hero":** Daniel Peaches, letter to the editor, *Navajo Hopi Observer,* May 1, 2002.

SELECTED BIBLIOGRAPHY

MANUSCRIPT COLLECTIONS

Boyden, John S. Papers. Special Collections, Brigham Young University, Provo, UT.
———. Papers. University of Utah Library, Salt Lake City.
Hayden, Carl. Papers. Arizona State University, Tempe.
John F. Kennedy Presidential Library, Boston.
Lyndon B. Johnson Presidential Library. Austin, TX.
National Archives and Records Administration. College Park, MD.
Special Collections, Lied Library. University of Nevada, Las Vegas.
Squires, Charles P., and Delphine Squires. Papers. Lied Library, University of Nevada, Las Vegas.
Weinberger, Caspar. Personal papers. Manuscript Collection, Library of Congress, Washington, DC.

GOVERNMENT DOCUMENTS

Congressional Quarterly Almanac. 93rd Cong., 2nd sess., 1974.
Constitution of the State of Nevada, Article 10, Section 5. "Tax on Proceeds of Minerals; Appropriation to Counties; Apportionment; Assessment and Taxation of Mines." Reno: State of Nevada, 2003.
US Congress. *Hearings Before the Special Senate Committee to Investigate Organized Crime in Interstate Commerce.* Pt. 10, Nevada-California. November–December 1950; February–March 1951. Washington, DC: US Government Printing Office, 1952.
———. *Report of the Committee on Interior to Accompany S. 692, a Bill to Set Up a Special Three-Judge Court.* 85th Cong., 2nd sess. Report No. 1942. June 23, 1958.
———. "To Reauthorize Housing Relocation Under the Navajo Hopi Relocation Program and for Other Purposes." Senate Hearings on S. 1236, May 19, 1987. Washington, DC: US Government Printing Office, 1987.

———. "To Reauthorize Housing Relocation Under the Navajo Hopi Relocation Program and for Other Purposes." Senate Hearings on S. 1236, December 9, 1987. Washington, DC: US Government Printing Office, 1987.

US Congress, Hearings Before Senate Committee on Indian Affairs. *To Authorize Partition of Surface Rights of Navajo Hopi Indian Lands. And to Provide for Allotments to Certain Paiute Indians and for Other Purposes*, September 14–15, 1972. Washington, DC: US Government Printing Office, 1973.

US Congress, House Committee on Interior and Insular Affairs, Subcommittee on Indian Affairs. *Partition of Navajo and Hopi 1882 Reservation*. 93rd Cong., May 14–15, 1973. Washington, DC: US Government Printing Office, 1974.

US Department of the Interior, Office of Surface Mining Reclamation and Enforcement. *Environmental Impacts and Proposed Permit Application for the Black Mesa–Kayenta Mine, Navajo and Hopi Indian Reservations, Arizona*. May 1990. In vol. 2 of *Comments and Responses*. Washington, DC: US Government Printing Office, 1991.

US District Court for the District of Arizona. *Case Summary and Decision in "Healing v. Jones."* 210 F. Supp. 125 (1962).

US Supreme Court, *Jones v. Healing et al.*, 373US758, June 3, 1963.

OTHER SOURCES

Akeman, Tom. "US Driving Off 10,000 Indians; 2 Tribes Struggling over Coal-Rich Land." *Sacramento Bee*, October 20, 1985, A1.

Allen, Paul Gunn. *The Sacred Hoop: Recovering the Feminine in American Indian Traditions*. Boston: Beacon Press, 1986.

Ambler, Marjane. *Breaking the Iron Bonds: Indian Control of Energy Development*. Lawrence: University Press of Kansas, 1990.

Anderson, Susanne. *Song of the Earth Spirit*. Introduction by David Brower. San Francisco: Friends of the Earth Books, 1973.

Arrington, Leonard, and Davis Bitton. *The Mormon Experience: A History of the Latter-day Saints*. New York: Alfred A. Knopf, 1979.

Associated Press. "Arizona Power Plant Ranks Among Nation's Dirtiest." *Arizona Republic*, April 14, 2000.

August, Jack L., Jr. "Carl Hayden, Arizona, and the Politics of Water Development in the Southwest, 1923–1928." *Pacific Historical Review* (1989).

"AuH2O." *New Yorker*, April 25, 1988, 43–73.

Austin, Mary. *The Land of Little Rain*. Introduction by Terry Tempest Williams. 1903. Reprint, New York: Penguin Books, 1997.

Balkenk, Eric. "A World Beneath Lake Powell Is Being Resurrected." *High Country News*, October 3, 2013.

Barboza, David. "Macao Surpasses Las Vegas as Gambling Center." *New York Times*, January 23, 2007.

Beam, Alex. *American Crucifixion*. New York: PublicAffairs, 2014.

Bender, Bryan. "Chief of US Pacific Forces Calls Climate Biggest Worry." *Boston Globe*, May 9, 2013.

Bergman, Charles. *Red Delta: Fighting for Life at the End of the Colorado River*. Golden, CO: Fulcrum.

"Blackgoat Wins National Award." *Navajo-Hopi Observer*, June 8, 1994.

Bleizeffer, Dustin. "Power River Basin Coal Model Goes Global." *Casper (WY) Star Tribune*, June 25, 2010.

Blue, Martha. *Indian Trader: The Life and Times of J. L. Hubbell*. Walnut, CA: Kiva, 2000.

Bolton, Eugene H., ed. *Spanish Exploration in the Southwest, 1542–1706: Original Narratives of Early American History*. New York: Charles Scribner's Sons, 1916.

The Book of Mormon: Another Testament of Jesus Christ. 1830. Reprint, Salt Lake City: Church of Jesus Christ of Latter-day Saints, 2009.

Boston Globe Editorial Board. "Breakfasting with Adelson." *Boston Globe*, July 31, 2012.

Boyden, Orpha. *John S. Boyden: Three Score and Ten in Retrospect*. Cedar City: Southern Utah State College Press, 1986.

"BP's Annual Review Paints a Grim Picture of Global Energy Use." *High Country News*, July 11, 2013.

Brackenridge, Henry M. *Views of Louisiana, Together with a Journal of a Voyage Up the Missouri River in 1811*. First edition, Pittsburgh, 1814. Reprint, Chicago: Quadrangle Books, 1962.

Brean, Henry. "Federal Officials Cut Water Delivery for Lake Mead, Speeding Reservoir's Decline." *Las Vegas Review-Journal*, August 16, 2013.

———. "Las Vegas Water Chief Seeks Disaster Aid for Colorado River Drought." *Las Vegas Review-Journal*, August 7, 2013.

Brennan, Zoe. "Furious Hanson on the Warpath: Indians' Protest Wrecks Meeting." *Daily Express* (London), February 1, 1996, 61.

Brinkley-Rogers, Paul. "Permit Revoked for Peabody Mine: Pollution Harms Tribe, Judge Says." *Arizona Republic*, May 19, 1998, B1.

Brodie, Fawn M. *No Man Knows My History: The Life of Joseph Smith*. New York: Alfred A. Knopf, 1945.

Brown, Nick. "Peabody on Hook for Some Patriot Coal Retiree Benefits—U.S. Court." Reuters, August 21, 2013.

Cannelos, Peter S. "Tribes Stand Ground in Dispute: Hopi, Navajo Press Claims on Ariz. Land." *Boston Globe*, February 17, 1997, 1.

Caro, Robert. *The Years of Lyndon Johnson: The Path to Power*. New York: Alfred A. Knopf, 1982.

Carroll, Rory. "Downtown Las Vegas May Have Found What It's Looking For." *Guardian*, March 24, 2013.

Cherob, Sandra. "BLM Approves Las Vegas Water Pipeline Project." *Las Vegas Review-Journal*, December 27, 2013.

Christian, David. *Maps of Time: An Introduction to Big History.* Berkeley: University of California Press, 2004.

Clifford, Frank. "Mohave Power Plant's Future a Thorny Dilemma." *Los Angeles Times,* February 15, 1998, A1.

Conaway, James. *The Kingdom in the Country.* Boston: Houghton Mifflin, 1987.

D'Agata, John. *About a Mountain.* New York: W. W. Norton, 2010.

Davis, James Joe, Jr. "The Effects of Coalition Building on Public Law 93–531: The Navajo and Hopi Land Settlement Act of 1974." PhD, University of Arizona, 2005.

Davis, Mike. *City of Quartz: Excavating the Future in Los Angeles.* New York: Verso, 2006.

Dean, John W., and Barry Goldwater Jr. *Pure Goldwater.* New York: Palgrave Macmillan, 2008.

DeBuys, William. *A Great Aridness: Climate Change and the Future of the American Southwest.* New York: Oxford University Press, 2011.

———. "The Least Sustainable City: Phoenix as a Harbinger for Our Hot Future." *Grist,* March 17, 2013.

Deloria, Vine, Jr. *Custer Died for Your Sins: An Indian Manifesto.* New York: Macmillan, 1969.

———. *God Is Red: A Native View of Religion.* Reprint, Golden, CO: North American Press, 1992.

Denton, Sally, and Roger Morris. *The Money and the Power: The Making of Las Vegas and Its Hold on America, 1947–2000.* 2001. Reprint, London: Random House, Pimlico, 2002.

DeVoto, Bernard, ed. *Mark Twain in Eruption: Hitherto Unpublished Pages About Men and Events.* New York: Harper, 1940.

Didion, Joan. *Where I Was From.* New York: Vintage Books, 2003.

Dizikes, Peter. "Understanding Gambling Addiction." *MIT News,* September 3, 2012.

Doenecke, Justus D. *The Presidencies of James A. Garfield and Chester A. Arthur.* Lawrence: University Press of Kansas, 1981.

Dubose, Lou. "More Carbon than Keystone: Peabody Energy and Warren Buffett Ship Coal to China." *Washington Spectator,* November 1, 2013.

Dolan, J. D. "Anniversary of a Disaster." *Los Angeles Times,* June 9, 2010.

Dunar, Andrew J., and Dennis McBride. *Building Hoover Dam: An Oral History of the Great Depression.* New York: Twayne, 1993.

Early, Pete. *Super Casino: Inside the "New" Las Vegas.* New York: Bantam Books, 2000.

"The Earth Movers." *Fortune,* September 1943.

Edsall, Thomas B. "Embracing Sheldon Adelson." *New York Times,* August 6, 2012.

Emshwiller, John M. "Chief Under Fire." *Wall Street Journal,* January 5, 1989, 1.

English, T. J. *Havana Nocturne: How the Mob Owned Cuba . . . and Then Lost It to the Revolution.* 2007. Reprint, New York: HarperCollins, 2008.

Ewen, Alexander, ed., for Native American Council of New York City. *Voices of Indigenous Peoples: Native Peoples Address the United Nations.* Santa Fe, NM: Clear Light, 1994.

Fallows, James. "Dirty Coal, Clean Future." *Atlantic,* December 2010.

Farrell, John Aloysius, and Jim Richardson. "The New Indian Wars." *Denver Post,* eight-part series published November 20–27, 1983. Part 2, "Divided Opposition: Peabody Coal Capitalizes on a Dispute Between the Hopi and Navajo to Get Cheap Coal."

Fox, Steven. *Blood and Power: Organized Crime in Twentieth Century America.* New York: Penguin Books, 1990.

Freeland, Chrystia. *Plutocrats: The Rise of the New Global Super-Rich and Fall of Everyone Else.* New York: Penguin Press, 2012.

Freese, Barbara. *Coal: A Human History.* New York: Perseus Books, 2003.

Geddes, Donald, ed. *The Atomic Age Opens.* New York: Pocket Books, 1945.

Gertner, Jon. "The Future Is Drying Up." *New York Times Magazine,* October 21, 2007.

Gillmore, Frances, and Louisa W. Wetherill. *Traders to the Navajo.* Boston: Houghton Mifflin, 1934.

Goldberg, Robert Alan. *Barry Goldwater.* New Haven, CT: Yale University Press, 1979.

Goldberger, Paul. "What Happens in Vegas: Can You Bring Architectural Virtue to Sin City?" *New Yorker,* October 4, 2010.

Goldsmith, Edward, and Nicholas Hildyard. *The Social and Environmental Effects of Large Dams.* San Francisco: Sierra Club Books, 1984.

Goldwater, Barry, with Jack Casserly. *Goldwater.* New York: Doubleday, 1988.

Goodell, Jeff. *Big Coal: The Dirty Secret Behind America's Energy Future.* Boston: Houghton Mifflin, 2007.

Goodman, Amy. "Hopi and Navajo Bring Demands on Coal Mining to Lehman Bros. NY Headquarters." *Democracy Now!* April 3, 2001. www.democracynow.org /2001/4/3/hopi_and_navaho_bring_demands_on.

Gordon, Suzanne. *Black Mesa: The Angel of Death.* Photos by Alan Copeland. New York: John Day, 1973.

Gottlieb, Robert, and Peter Wiley. *America's Saints: The Rise of Mormon Power.* New York: Harcourt Brace Jovanovich, 1986.

———. *Empires in the Sun: The Rise of the New American West.* Tucson: University of Arizona Press, 1985.

Green, Emily. "Quenching Las Vegas' Thirst." Pt. 1, "Satiating a Booming City." *Las Vegas Sun,* June 1, 2008.

———. "Quenching Las Vegas' Thirst." Pt. 2, "The Chosen One." *Las Vegas Sun,* June 8, 2008.

———. "Quenching Las Vegas' Thirst." Pt. 3, "The Equation: No Water, No Growth." *Las Vegas Sun,* June 15, 2008.

———. "Quenching Las Vegas' Thirst." Pt. 4, "Not This Water." *Las Vegas Sun,* June 22, 2008.

———. "Quenching Las Vegas' Thirst." Pt. 5, "Owens Valley Is the Model of What to Expect." *Las Vegas Sun,* June 29, 2008.

Hampshire, David, Martha Sonntag Bradley, and Allen Roberts. *A History of Summit County.* Salt Lake City: Utah Historical Society, Summit County Commission, 1998.

Hardeen, George. "Sekaquaptewa Remembered for Leadership Role." *Navajo Times,* August 13, 1992, A5.

Hiltzik, Michael. *Colossus: Hoover Dam and the Making of the American Century.* New York: Free Press, 2010.

Hirst, Steven. *I Am the Grand Canyon: The Story of the Havasupai People.* Flagstaff, AZ: Grand Canyon Association, 2006.

Hochschild, Adam. *King Leopold's Ghost: A Story of Greed, Terror, and Heroism in Colonial Africa.* Boston: Houghton Mifflin, 1998.

"Hopi Elders Seek to Avoid Court Test." *Christian Science Monitor,* January 16, 1957.

Horwitz, Mel. "Coal." In *Energy Future,* edited by Daniel Yergin and Roger Stobaugh, 9–107. New York: Random House, 1979.

Hultgren, MaryLou. *To Lead and to Serve: American Indian Education at Hampton Institute, 1878–1923.* Foreword by Rayna Greene. Charlottesville, VA: Hampton University, 1989.

Ingram, Robert L. *A Builder and His Family, 1898–1948, Being the Historical Account of the Contracting, Engineering, and Construction Career of W. A. Bechtel.* San Francisco: privately published, 1949.

Issacs, Matt, Lowell Bergman, and Steven Engelberg. "Inside the Investigation of Leading Republican Money Man, Sheldon Adelson." *Huffington Post,* July 19, 2012. Copublished with *PBS Frontline.*

Jacobsen, Annie. *Area 51: An Uncensored History of America's Top Secret Military Base.* New York: Little, Brown, 2011.

Jaimes, M. Annette, ed. *The State of Native America: Genocide, Colonization, and Resistance.* Boston: South End Press, 1992.

James, Harry C. *Pages from Hopi History.* Tucson: University of Arizona Press, 1974.

Jennings, Francis. *The Founders of America: From the Earliest Migrations to the Present.* New York: W. W. Norton, 1994.

Josephson, Matthew. *The Robber Barons.* 1934. Reprint, New York: Harcourt Brace Jovanovich, 1962.

Josephy, Alvin. "The Murder of the Southwest." *Audubon,* July 1971.

Kammer, Jerry. *The Second Long Walk: The Navajo-Hopi Land Dispute.* Albuquerque: University of New Mexico Press, 1980.

Keene, Jarret, and Todd James Pierce, eds. *Las Vegas Noir.* New York: Akashic Books, 2008.

Kluckhorhn, Clyde, and Dorothea Leighton. *The Navajo.* 1946. Reprint, Cambridge, MA: Harvard University Press, 1974.

LaFarge, Oliver. *Laughing Boy.* 1929. Reprint, Boston: Houghton Mifflin, 1962.

"Lake Mead's Water Level Plunges as 11-Year Drought Lingers." *New York Times,* August 13, 2010.

Lame Deer, John, and Richard Erdoes. *Lame Deer: Seeker of Visions*. New York: Simon & Schuster, 1972.

Lemann, Nicholas. "Desert Storm: Harry Reid." *New Yorker*, October 25, 2010.

Lewis, Oscar. *Sagebrush Casinos: The Story of Legal Gambling in Nevada*. New York: Doubleday, 1953.

Limerick, Patricia Nelson. *Legacy of Conquest: The Unbroken Past of the American West*. New York: W. W. Norton, 1988.

———, ed. *Trails: Towards a New Western History*. Lawrence: University Press of Kansas, 1992.

Lippert, John, and Jim Efstathiou Jr. "Las Vegas Running Out of Water Means Dimming Los Angeles Lights." *Bloomberg News*, December 7, 2010.

Littlejohn, David, ed. *The Real Las Vegas: Life Beyond the Strip*. New York: Oxford University Press, 1999.

Locke, Raymond. *The Book of the Navajo*. Los Angeles: Mankind, 1989.

Lopez, Barry. *The Future of Nature: Writing on a Human Ecology from "Orion" Magazine*. Minneapolis: Milkweed, 2007.

Lopez, Barry, and Debra Gwartney. *Home Ground: Language for an American Landscape*. San Antonio, TX: Trinity University Press, 2006.

MacDonald, Peter, with Ted Schwarz. *The Last Warrior: Peter MacDonald and the Navajo Nation*. New York: Orion Books, 1993.

Malone, Michael, and Richard W. Etulain. *The American West: A 20th Century History*. Lincoln: University of Nebraska Press, 1989.

Martin, Russell. *A Story That Stands Like a Dam: Glen Canyon and the Struggle for the Soul of the West*. New York: Henry Holt, 1989.

Mavin, Duncan, and Kate O'Keefe. "Wynn Resorts CEO Doubles Down on China Casino Business." *Wall Street Journal*, May 23, 2011.

McAllester, David P. *Hogans: Navajo Houses and House Songs*. Middletown, CT: Wesleyan University Press, 1980.

McBride, Peter, and Jonathan Waterman. *The Colorado River: Flowing Through Conflict*. Boulder, Colo: Westcliffe, 2011.

McCartney, Laton. *Friends in High Places: Bechtel, America's Most Secret Corporation and How It Engineered the World*. New York: Simon & Schuster, 1988.

McKibben, Bill. "The End of Nature." *New Yorker*, September 11, 1989, 47–105.

McLuhan, T. C. *Dreamtracks: The Railroad and the American Indian, 1890–1930*. New York: Harry N. Abrams, 1985.

Mcmillan, Leslie. "The Tainted Desert." Interview with Doug Brugge on uranium mining and its health effects on the Navajo reservation. *Tufts Magazine*, Winter 2012.

McPhee, John. *Annals of the Former World*. New York: Farrar, Strauss & Giroux, 1998.

———. *The John McPhee Reader*. Introduction by William L. Howarth. New York: Vintage Books, 1977.

Miller, Stan. "A Southwest Power Plant Saga." *Environmental Science and Technology* 10, no. 6 (1976).

Moehring, Eugene. *Resort City in the Sunbelt: Las Vegas, 1930–1970*. Reno: University of Nevada Press, 1989.

Moehring, Eugene P., and Michael S. Green. *Las Vegas: A Centennial History*. Reno: University of Nevada Press, 2005.

Moench, Brian. "No End to Nevada's Quest for Water." *Salt Lake Tribune*, April 6, 2013.

Moore, Lucy. *Into the Canyon: Seven Years in Navajo Country*. Albuquerque: University of New Mexico Press, 2004.

Morton, Brian Jackson. "Coal Leasing in the Fourth World: Hopi and Navajo Coal Leasing, 1954–1977." PhD, University of California, Berkeley, 1985.

Nafzigar, Richard. *Transnational Energy Corporations and American Indian Development*. Institute for Native American Development, American Indian Energy Resources and Development. Albuquerque: University of New Mexico, 1980.

Nagourney, Adam. "Witnesses to Sunrise over the Strip." *New York Times*, June 21, 2011.

Nies, Judith. "The Black Mesa Syndrome, Indian Lands Black Gold." *Orion*, Summer 1998.

———. *Native American History: A Chronology of a Culture's Vast Achievements and Their Links to World Events*. New York: Ballantine, 1996.

———. *Nine Women: Portraits from American Radical Tradition*. Berkeley: University of California Press, 2002.

O'Grady, Tim. "Children of Las Vegas." Forthcoming.

Olsen, Ken. "Digging into a Dirty Deal." *National Wildlife*, December–January 2014.

Ortiz, Roxanne Dunbar, ed. *American Indian Energy Resources and Development*. Development Series, No. 1. Albuquerque: University of New Mexico, 1979.

———, ed. *American Indian Energy Resources and Development*. Development Series, No. 2. Albuquerque: University of New Mexico, 1980.

Page, Susanne, and Jake Page. *Hopi*. New York: Harry N. Abrams, 1982.

Parlow, Anita. *Cry, Sacred Ground*. Washington, DC: Christic Institute, 1988.

Peabody Holding Company. "Peabody to Be Independent Company Owned by Lehman." Press release, May 6, 1998.

Peabody Western Coal Company. Fact sheet. www.peabodygroup.com.

Perlstein, Rick. *Before the Storm: Barry Goldwater and the Unmaking of the American Consensus*. New York: Hill & Wang, 2001.

Pierre-Louis, Yves. "Le choléra—MINUSTAH rebondit." *Haïti Liberté*, January 29, 2013, 4.

Pileggi, Nicholas. *Casino*. New York: Simon & Schuster, 1995.

Polingaysi, Qoyawayma [Elizabeth Q. White], as told to Vada F. Carlson. *No Turning Back: A Hopi Indian Woman's Struggle to Live in the World of Her People and the World of the White Man*. Albuquerque: University of New Mexico Press, 1964.

Powell, John Wesley. *Exploration of the Colorado River of the West*. Washington, DC: US Government Printing Office, 1875.

Prucha, Francis Paul. *Documents of United States Indian Policy*. "President Jackson on Indian Removal," 71; "Regulation of Indian Agents," 31. Lincoln: University of Nebraska Press, 1990.

"Q&A, Pat Mulroy." *Las Vegas Sun*, May 1, 2009.

Reeves, Thomas C. *Gentleman Boss: The Life of Chester Alan Arthur*. New York: Alfred A. Knopf, 1975.

Reid, Betty. "Navajo Who Resisted Land Transfer Is Dead." *Arizona Republic*, April 27, 2002.

Reid, Ed, and Ovid Demaris. *The Green Felt Jungle*. New York: Trident Press, 1963.

Reisner, Marc. *Cadillac Desert: The American West and Its Disappearing Water*. New York: Viking Penguin, 1986.

Reno, Philip. *Navajo Resources and Economic Development*. Albuquerque: University of New Mexico Press, 1981.

Reyes Castenaneda, Pedro. *The Journey of Coronado, 1540–1542: From the City of Mexico to the Grand Canyon*. Translated by George Parker Winship. New York: A. S. Barnes, 1904.

Robison, Jennifer. "Las Vegas Unemployment Reaches Record 15 Percent." *Las Vegas Review-Journal*, October 22, 2010.

Roessel, Ruth. *Navajo Stories of the Long Walk*. Tsaile, AZ: Navajo Community College, 1973.

Roman, James. "The Original Wise Guy." In *Chronicles of Old Las Vegas: Exposing Sin City's High-Stakes History*. New York: Museyon, 2011.

Rothman, Hal, and Mike Davis. *The Grit Beneath the Glitter: Tales from the Real Las Vegas*. Berkeley: University of California Press, 2002.

Royce, Charles C., comp. *The First American Frontier: Indian Land Cessions in the United States*. 1900. Reprint, New York: Arno Press and New York Times, 1971.

Salt River Project. *The Taming of the Salt*. Phoenix: Communications and Public Affairs Department of Salt River Project, 1979.

Sayre, Robert F. *Thoreau and the American Indians*. Princeton, NJ: Princeton University Press, 1977.

Schlosser, Eric. *Command and Control: Nuclear Weapons, the Damascus Accident, and the Illusion of Safety*. New York: Penguin Press, 2013.

Schuessler, Jennifer. "The Mormon Lens of American History." *New York Times*, July 2, 2012.

Schüll, Natasha D. *Addiction by Design: Machine Gambling in Las Vegas*. Princeton, NJ: Princeton University Press, 2012.

Schwartz, David G. *Roll the Bones: The History of Gambling*. New York: Penguin Books, 2006.

Sekaquaptewa, Helen, with Louise Udall. *Me and Mine: The Life Story of Helen Sekaquaptewa*. Tucson: University of Arizona Press, 1969.

Sheridan, Thomas E. "Central Arizona Project." In *Water, Culture, and Power: Local*

Struggles in Global Context, edited by John M. Donahue and Barbara R. Johnson. Washington, DC: Island Press, 1998.

Slotkin, Richard. *Regeneration Through Violence: The Mythology of the American Frontier, 1600–1860.* Middletown, CT: Wesleyan University Press, 1973.

Smith, John L. *Running Scared: The Life and Treacherous Times of Las Vegas Casino King Steve Wynn.* New York: Barricade Books, 1995.

Smithsonian, National Museum of American Art. *The West as America: Reinterpreting Images of the Frontier, 1820–1920.* Exhibition catalog. Washington, DC: Smithsonian Press, 1991.

Snipp, C. Matthew. *American Indians: The First of This Land.* New York: Russell Sage Foundation, 1989.

Squier, George, and Edwin Davis. *Ancient Monuments of the Mississippi Valley: Comprising the Results of Extensive Original Surveys and Explorations.* 1848. Reprint, Washington, DC: Smithsonian Institution, 1998. Reprinted for the Peabody Museum of Archaeology and Ethnology, Harvard University, 1973.

Stegner, Wallace. *The American West as Living Space.* Ann Arbor: University of Michigan Press, 1993.

———. *Beyond the Hundredth Meridian: John Wesley Powell and the Second Opening of the West.* Introduction by Bernard DeVoto. Boston: Houghton Mifflin, 1953.

Stevens, Joseph E. *Hoover Dam: An American Adventure.* Norman: University of Oklahoma Press, 1988.

Stevenson, Tom. "Insults Fly at Hanson Meeting." *Independent* (London), February 1, 1996, Business, 16.

Summer, Anthony, and Robyn Swan. *Sinatra: The Life.* New York: Vintage Books, 2005.

Swearingen, Marshall. "BLM Okays Controversial Nevada Water Pipeline." *High Country News,* January 10, 2013.

Talayesva, Don C. *Sun Chief: Autobiography of a Hopi Indian.* Edited by Leo W. Simmons. New Haven, CT: Yale University Press, 1947.

Tarantino, Fred. "Bechtel's Man at the Nevada Site." *Innovation America,* June–July 2004. www.innovation-america.org/bechtels-man-nevada-site.

Tavares, Stephanie. "Pat Mulroy, General Manager of the Southern Nevada Water Authority." *Las Vegas Sun,* May 1, 2009.

Thomas, D. H. *Southwestern Indian Detours: Story of the Fred Harvey Santa Fe Railway Trips Through Indian Country.* Phoenix: Hunter, 1978.

Thompson, Hunter S. *Fear and Loathing in Las Vegas.* New York: Warner Books, 1971.

Thomson, David. *In Nevada: The Land, the People, God, and Chance.* New York: Vintage Books, 1999.

Tolan, Mary. "Hopi Elders Abandon Tribal Council." *Flagstaff Sun,* March 16, 1986.

Turner, John G. *Brigham Young: Pioneer Prophet.* Cambridge, MA: Harvard University Press, 2012.

Tuttle, Kate. "The Feds, Uranium, and the Deadly Toll on Navajos." *Boston Globe,* Oct. 5, 2010.

Udall, Morris, and Donald Jackson. *The Job of the Congressman: An Introduction to Service in the U.S. House of Representatives*. New York: Bobbs-Merrill, 1966.

Udall, Morris, with Bob Neuman and Randy Udall. *Too Funny to Be President*. New York: Henry Holt, 1988.

Udall, Stewart. *Agenda for Tomorrow*. New York: Harcourt Brace, 1968.

———. *The Quiet Crisis*. Introduction by John F. Kennedy. Photos by Alvin Josephy. New York: Holt, Rinehart, and Winston, 1963.

Udall, Stewart, with Charles Concord and David Osterhout. *The Energy Balloon*. New York: McGraw-Hill, 1974.

Underhill, Ruth M. *The Navajos*. 1956. Reprint, Norman: University of Oklahoma Press, 1989.

"Uranium Miners Suffering Described at Hearing." *Albuquerque Journal*, March 14, 1990, 1.

Utley, Robert M., and Wilcomb E. Washburn. *The Indian Wars*. New York: American Heritage, 1977.

Vaughan, Bernard. "Bankruptcy Court Approves Patriot Coal Labor Deal." Reuters, August 20, 2013.

Venturi, Robert, Denise Scott Brown, and Steven Izenour. *Learning from Las Vegas: The Forgotten Symbolism of Architectural Form*. Rev. ed. Cambridge: MIT Press, 1988.

Viser, Matt. "In Jerusalem, Romney Vows Strong Support." *Boston Globe*, July 30, 2012.

Wald, Matthew L. "Coal Project Hits Snag as a Partner Backs Off." *New York Times*, November 10, 2011.

———. "Court Won't Intervene in Fate of Nuclear Dump." *New York Times*, July 2, 2011.

Wangness, Lisa. "Mormons Image Campaign." *Boston Globe*, June 20, 2011.

Waters, Frank. *The Book of the Hopi*. New York: Viking Press, 1963.

———. *The Colorado*. New York: Rinehart, 1946.

———. *The Woman at Otowi Crossing*. 1966. Reprint, Athens: Ohio University Press, 1987.

Wendland, Michael F. *The Arizona Project*. 1977. Reprint, Mesa, AZ: Blue Sky Press, 1988.

White, Richard. *It's Your Misfortune and None of My Own: A History of the American West*. Norman: University of Oklahoma Press, 1992.

Wilkinson, Charles F. *The Eagle Bird: Mapping a New West*. New York: Pantheon Books, 1992.

———. *Fire on the Plateau: Conflict and Endurance in the American Southwest*. Washington, DC: Island Press, 1999.

Wilkinson, Ernest L., and W. Cleon Skousen. *Brigham Young University: A School of Destiny*. Provo, UT: Brigham Young University Press, 1976.

———. *Brigham Young University: A University of Destiny*. New York: Newcomen Society in North America, 1971.

Willenz, Amy. *Farewell, Fred Voodoo: A Letter from Haiti.* New York: Simon & Schuster, 2013.

Williams, Terry Tempest. *Refuge: An Unnatural History of Family and Place.* New York: Vintage Books, 2001.

Winship, George Parker, trans. *The Journey of Coronado, 1540–1542: From the City of Mexico to the Grand Canyon of the Colorado.* New York: Barnes, 1904. (Translation of the narrative of Pedro de Castaneda about the mission of Coronado who sent Don Pedro de Tovar, Juan de Padilla, a Franciscan friar, seventeen horsemen, and three or four foot soldiers to the Hopi villages and the Grand Canyon in 1540. First published by the Bureau of Ethnography, US government.)

Works Project Administration. *Arizona: A State Guide.* 1940. Reprint, Saint Clair Shores, MI: Scholarly Press, 1977.

———. *Death Valley: A Guide.* Federal Writers Project.

———. *Nevada: A Guide to the Silver State.* The WPA Guide to 1930s Nevada. Foreword to the new edition by Russell R. Elliott.

———. *Utah: A Guide to the State.* WPA Guide. New York: Hastings House, 1940.

Worster, Donald. *Rivers of Empire: Water Aridity and the Growth of the American West.* New York: Pantheon Books, 1987.

Yergin, Daniel. *The Quest.* New York: Penguin Books, 2012.

Zolbrod, Paul G. *Dine bahane: The Navajo Creation Story.* Albuquerque: University of New Mexico Press, 1984.

INDEX

KIM INDRESANO

JUDITH NIES is the award-winning author of three nonfiction books: *The Girl I Left Behind: A Personal History of the 1960s*, *Nine Women: Portraits from the American Radical Tradition*, and *Native American History: A Chronology*, which won the Phi Alpha Theta prize in international history. Nies's journalism, book reviews, and essays have appeared in the *New York Times*, *Boston Globe*, *Orion*, *Harvard Review*, *Women's Review of Books*, and *American Voice*. She lives in Cambridge, Massachusetts.

The Nation Institute

Nation.

Founded in 2000, **Nation Books** has become a leading voice in American independent publishing. The inspiration for the imprint came from the *Nation* magazine, the oldest independent and continuously published weekly magazine of politics and culture in the United States.

The imprint's mission is to produce authoritative books that break new ground and shed light on current social and political issues. We publish established authors who are leaders in their area of expertise, and endeavor to cultivate a new generation of emerging and talented writers. With each of our books we aim to positively affect cultural and political discourse.

Nation Books is a project of The Nation Institute, a nonprofit media center established to extend the reach of democratic ideals and strengthen the independent press. The Nation Institute is home to a dynamic range of programs: our award-winning Investigative Fund, which supports groundbreaking investigative journalism; the widely read and syndicated website TomDispatch; our internship program in conjunction with the *Nation* magazine; and Journalism Fellowships that fund up to 20 high-profile reporters every year.

For more information on Nation Books, the *Nation* magazine, and The Nation Institute, please visit:

www.nationbooks.org
www.nationinstitute.org
www.thenation.com
www.facebook.com/nationbooks.ny
Twitter: @nationbooks